Letters to the Editors

Letters to the Editors

A Journal by Anna M. Szaflarski
with contributions by Ayami Awazuhara,
Salvador Bautista, Aleksandra Bielas,
Ilaria Biotti, Maggie Boyd,
Mariana Castillo Deball, Santiago da Silva,
Michele Di Menna, Kasia Fudakowski,
Eva Funk, Florian Goldmann et al.,
Blanca Gomila, Anna Herms,
Rodrigo Hernández, Valentina Jager,
Tiziana La Melia, Maryse Larivière,
Steve Paul, Barbara Plater-Szaflarski,
Natalie Porter, Post Brothers, Ayumi Rahn,
Stephen Remus, Malte Roloff,
Gabriel Rosas Alemán, Manuel Saiz,
Max Stocklosa, Peter Szaflarski,
Stanisław Szaflarski, Peter Wächtler,
Till Wittwer and Jacob Wren

BOM
DIA
BOA
TARDE
BOA
NOITE

AKV Berlin

Contents

	Letters to the Editors: Introduction Anna M. Szaflarski	13
LTTE no. 1 *Wishful Thinking* October 9, 2014	*Nowhere Man, A Man with No Name* Anna M. Szaflarski	27
	Readymade and *Readymade 2* Anna Herms	32
LTTE no. 2 *Relax* October 27, 2014	*Discover the Champion in you!* Anna M. Szaflarski	35
LTTE no. 3 *The Bigger Picture*, November 10, 2014	*Where have you been hiding?* Anna M. Szaflarski	41
	Poetry Manuel Saiz	47
LTTE no. 4 *Family Business* November 23, 2014	*Don't worry, I know a guy* Anna M. Szaflarski	49
	The Great Onus Probandi Peter Szaflarski	54
LTTE no. 5 *Suspicious Minds* December 6, 2014	*The Boy Who Cried Wolf* *Over for dinner* Anna M. Szaflarski	59

| | The Mexican State Kills Students | 65 |
| | Anónimo | |

LTTE no. 6
Secret Heart
December 19, 2014

	Ain't no mountain high enough	67
	Anna M. Szaflarski	
	Body-builders	73
	Gabriel Rosas Alemán	
	Go, gentle scorpio	74
	Rodrigo Hernandez	

LTTE no. 7
Where No One
Thought of
Going Before
January 1, 2015

	Stick in the Mud	75
	Anna M. Szaflarski	
	Time-Trivials	82
	Steve Paul	

LTTE no. 8
Nyma Graphia Cifra
January 17, 2015

	Where Is My End?	99
	Where Is My Beginning?	
	Anna M. Szaflarski	
	The Invisible Red Man	104
	Ayami Awazuhara	
	Make Space, Find Time	110
	Valentina Jager	

LTTE no. 9
Correspondence
January 29, 2015

	With all earned and due respect, No.	115
	Anna M. Szaflarski	
	situatión.1	120
	Salvador Bautista	

	Anna might become a writer: *an introduction* Santiago da Silva	121
LTTE no. 10 *Question of Perspective* February 18, 2015	*Right smack in the middle of it* Anna M. Szaflarski	125
	More World Material: *Dumber Than A Rock But* *Smarter Than A Diamond* Max Stocklosa	131
LTTE no. 11 *Tell me Lies* March 2, 2015	*Fill it to the brim* Anna M. Szaflarski	135
	An Artist from The Future, *or Just Ahead of his Time?* Post Brothers	140
LTTE no. 12 *Eluding Wisdom* March 16, 2015	*Let them run* Anna M. Szaflarski	149
	I'm a Mother, After All Barbara Plater-Szaflarski	154
	MYth YOUth Anna Herms	156
LTTE no. 13 *Social Arena* March 28, 2015	*Not all doors swing both ways* Anna M. Szaflarski	157
	Forget yourself, forget the others... Aleksandra Bielas	162

LTTE no. 14 *Promised Land* April 12, 2015	*Sei mal nicht päpstlicher* *als der Papst* Anna M. Szaflarski	165
	Dear Editor Maggie Boyd	173
LTTE no. 15 *Natural Causes* April 27, 2015	*A Bag of Winds: a letter* *to the art-immigrant* Anna M. Szaflarski	177
	Cuando pase el temblor Mariana Castillo Deball	183
LTTE no. 16 *Beat around the Bush* May 9, 2015	*There's Bushes and Then* *There's Pheasants* Anna M. Szaflarski	187
	Text Ayumi Rahn	194
LTTE no. 17 *The Rationalizations* May 23, 2015	*The Smoking Kids* Anna M. Szaflarski	197
	The Truth Maryse Larivière	202
	Unterscheidung im Kopf Valentina Jager	204
LTTE no. 18 *Forgetting* June 8, 2015	*The weight of the world* *in knapsacks and briefcases* Anna M. Szaflarski	205

	Today's date adds up	213
	Ilaria Biotti	
LTTE no. 19	*I Stand Here Before You*	217
Doubt That This Is It	Anna M. Szaflarski	
June 17, 2015		
	Four Manifestos and/or	222
	Semi-Manifestos	
	Jacob Wren	
LTTE no. 20	*Guild of Thieves: The Writing Table*	229
You and Me	Anna M. Szaflarski	
July 8, 2015		
	Transcribed Conversations	236
	Blanca Gomila	
LTTE no. 21	*Review*	239
Merely Humans	Anna M. Szaflarski	
July 21, 2015		
	Hitler's Eyes	245
	Malte Roloff	
LTTE no. 22	*Late Notice Means Early Rise*	247
Metempsychosis	Anna M. Szaflarski	
August 3, 2015		
	A Swiss Night	252
	Eva Funk	
	Smoosh	254
	Michele Di Menna	

LTTE no. 23
Clairvoyance
August 17, 2015

Clarity is of no importance because 255
nobody listens and nobody knows
what you mean no matter what
you mean, nor how clearly you mean
what you mean...
Anna M. Szaflarski

Women in the wilderness: 261
the legacy of the desert mothers
Natalie Porter

LTTE no. 24
The Insider
September 2, 2015

Living with Subtitles 265
Anna M. Szaflarski

Discovery 271
Staniław Szaflarski

LTTE no. 25
Deluge of Grandeur
September 17, 2015

Gottfried the Snake 275
Anna M. Szaflarski

Johnny's Yodel 283
Till Wittwer

LTTE no. 26
Hard Day's Night
September 25, 2015

Black and Incongruous Headlines 289
Anna M. Szaflarski

You Got a Good Job Right Out 295
of High School, Or, How
St. Catharines Had Dumb Luck
Stephen Remus

LTTE no. 27 *Foreign Affairs* October 12, 2015	*A Language to be Destroyed* Anna M. Szaflarski	299
	Dynamic Statement Florian Goldmann et al.	307
LTTE no. 28 *Can't Help It* October 26, 2015	*Obtuse* Anna M. Szaflarski	315
	The Waiters Will Not Help You Peter Wächtler	316
LTTE no. 29 *Omit, Admit, Emit* November 11, 2015	■ Anna M. Szaflarski	331
	Would you rather have a peach *or a painting of a peach?* Tiziana La Melia	338
LTTE no. 30 *Moments* *of Solidarity* November 30, 2015	*The Race* Anna M. Szaflarski	341
	We pay for our food, *We don't pay for our food* Kasia Fudakowski	347
	Epilogue: *Emergent Property Game II*	[insert]

Letters to the Editors:
Introduction

My oldest brother, Peter, wrote to me after reviewing an unrelated application, "I think you're trying to show the existence of emergent properties of groups, you seem to imply it but never come right out and say it." I printed out a copy of his email, highlighted the statement and drew a big question mark next to it. I had no idea what he was talking about. The question mark led to a Google search that brought me to a post written on www.researchgate.net by Issam Sinjab from the University of Leicester & University of Sussex. He wrote that "an emergent property is a property which a collection or complex system has, but which the individual members do not have." That's exactly it, Peter.

This book is the compilation of all thirty issues of Letters to the Editors [LTTE], a Berlin-based bi-weekly printed journal, which I distributed personally over the course of one year (October 2014–November 2015). Simply put, the hum-

14   *Introduction*

bly printed DIN A5 b/w journal was dedicated to publishing my own writing alongside original writing from artists and art writers. I wasn't aware of the "emergent property of groups" when I started, but the project morphed over the course of the year, and again after it was compiled.

When starting, motivated by a need to write, I implemented a disciplined routine to publish at a regular interval. Writing was not enough however, I wanted people to read and give me feedback on what I wrote. The readers would become my editors and critics, hence the title, "Letters to the Editors" emerged. Many artists around me, either virtually or physically, use writing as part of their practice, so I wanted to involve them out of curiosity, to see what they would write about if I asked them to. But I didn't curate the journal, in that I never gave prospective contributors themes or directions to base their writing on and I didn't preselect texts[1]. I didn't specify in which language the texts should be written (although only on two occasions did I receive German texts and on another a Spanish text), nor did I request any specific genre or writing style. I encouraged non-conformity, but did not stipulate it. Most of the writing was submitted by either artists, writers or a hybrid of both, but I didn't want to limit this aspect either and when my brother and parents showed interest in getting involved I wasn't about to deny LTTE reader's that pleasure. Without intentionally excluding anyone, the writing demographic was naturally influenced by my reality: I am an artist, who lives in Berlin (one of the most commonly written sentences of the decade), I converse and correspond with other artists and writers in

1 An exception was made for Issue 7, for which Steve Paul and I travelled in time to write, so I asked him if he could consider time travel as a general topic for his text.

English and German (and on very rare occasions Polish), and have spent extended periods in parts of Southern Germany, Mexico, Poland and Canada during the course of the year. The only limitation I deliberately enforced was length. Each issue was either 8 or 12 (DIN A5) pages and needed to accommodate both my text and the contributors' (font sizes were scaled accordingly, giving this rule a bit of flexibility). The individual issues were printed out on plain copy paper, giving me something tangible to give away for free directly into people's hands when meeting them on the streets, at openings or while travelling. Depending on the week, between 20–50 people would regularly receive LTTE into their palms. This led directly into conversations about the project, subsequently stimulating the recruitment process of future contributors; thus the distribution activated its production. At first, contributions were hard to come by, so whatever came, I'd print[2]; regardless if it had anything to do with what I had written. Based on Peter's terminology, you could say this initiated the first emergent property game. The theme and title of each issue were extracted from nestling the texts together. Side by side, the contributors' texts next to my own, generated a different meaning, and somehow they never failed to resonate with one another. This meant that each issue had several titles: the title of my own text, the title of the contributors' texts, and a third title for the issue that emerged from the intermingling of the two, sometimes three, all of which is listed in the detailed table of contents.

And that, in a nutshell, was the initial premise of Letters to the Editors. I wanted to write, to talk to people, to see

---

2 I must mention that due to the eventual overflow, some contributions were not included in the final editions.

16   *Introduction*

what other people would write or were already writing about, and wanted the project and its contents to develop under the influence of these exchanges. As the project progressed, my writing and what I received from the expanding circle of friends and peers increasingly adapted thematically to each other. The readers and the journal began to meld into one, and themes would reappear and span across issues. The letters came together and the body of LTTE formed: It had arms and legs, perhaps a brain but above all, a heart and a stomach, often aching, rarely satisfied.

Each of the sixty-four texts included in this collection is fairly short, and take on the characteristics of a short story or poem: following one impression, character or thought, they have the advantage of being free from the burden of a plot or thesis. A voice calls out and is quickly overtaken by the next and then the next, each leaving a trace in the greater reverberation. Readers will notice that some of the texts in this collection are more polished than others, perhaps reflecting a fleeting moment in which they were written, a current event, or a parallel project that the author may have been working on. They have for the most part been left unedited, and if edited, then minimally, and are written predominantly in English by an international pool of authors that do not necessarily speak or write English as their first language. *Thus was it written, [sic]* or *sic erat scriptum* with their occasional typos, syntax errors, and foreign phrases thrown in, and thus will it remain. This does not, however, detract from their quality, entertainment factor, and/or provocativeness, I would argue just the opposite.

Each issue is prefaced with a text of my own, in which I explore many topics in a myriad of essayistic and narrative styles, sometimes more successfully than others. I was on a search for a language of sincerity through the gutters of the banal and petty, sometimes wearing an overcoat of humor, and desperately dodging traps of artspeak; something that I can only summarize now after reading the texts again. But each text, mine and those from contributors, has a different story to tell and should be considered independently in terms of style and content, as much as a part of the larger collection. Together they illuminate the emergent properties of the texts, and perhaps of the group that wrote them, but I won't rob you the opportunity to discover this on your own. If after you've browsed the themes in the table of contents, read the texts through or jumped forward and backward to sample a few pieces of the collection, and are still curious of my take on things, I have left you a note in the epilogue. One interpretation perhaps, one last emergent property game.

When putting together the first issue in October 2014, I was almost haphazard in my decisions about the physical attributes of the project; the font, the layout, etc. I worked intuitively and I questioned very little of my decision making process. One thing I was often asked was, why print? Aside from the fact that I've been making books for the greater part of the last decade with the artists' book publishing house AKV Berlin, I chose printing issues over making an online blog[3], because with all of the distractions that the internet brings, I wanted people to hold the writing in their hands, take it with them on the train or to the bathroom. Frankly, I didn't care where they took it, as long as it departed from the computer

3   Due to accessibility complaints from international readers, the last seven issues were made available as on-line downloadable/printable PDF files.

18 *Introduction*

screen (maybe I even dreamt of you taking me with you…
away from my computer screen) and that they actually read it.
This desire remained when we started producing the book.
When the last issue was completed, I invited my close friend
and graphic designer Santiago da Silva to come on board.
Together we began to consciously rethink how the collection
could be reformed to reflect its final metamorphosis into one
body made of individual cells, and neatly close one chapter
of time. Letters to the Editors, the bi-weekly magazine has
come to an end, but new forms are likely to come, and in the
spirit of its tradition if you would like to send me a letter,
a poem, a story, a response or criticism to the writing in this
book or to the premise of its creation then, by all means, become our editors, and send it to me at: akvbooks@gmail.com.
I look forward to hearing from you.

Without a doubt the production of the Letters to the Editors
journal project and book would not have been possible with-
out the brilliant work from each and all of its contributors:
Ayami Awazuhara, Salvador Bautista, Aleksandra Bielas,
Ilaria Biotti, Maggie Boyd, Mariana Castillo Deball, Santiago
da Silva, Michele Di Menna, Kasia Fudakowski, Eva Funk,
Florian Goldmann, Blanca Gomila, Anna Herms, Rodrigo
Hernández, Valentina Jager, Tiziana La Melia, Maryse
Larivière, Steve Paul, Barbara Plater-Szaflarski, Natalie
Porter, Post Brothers, Ayumi Rahn, Stephen Remus, Malte
Roloff, Gabriel Rosas Alemán, Manuel Saiz, Max Stocklosa,
Peter Szaflarski, Stanislaw Szaflarski, Peter Wächtler, Till
Wittwer, and Jacob Wren;

and without the additional physical, technical, intellectual
and/or emotional support of Ana Ara, Kate Brown & Lauryn

Anna M. Szaflarski

Youden of Ashley Berlin, Michael Beutler, Wolf Bielstein, Pamela Chlebek, Bart Gazzola, Vincent Grunwald, Natalie Harder-Szaflarski, Greta Hoheisel, Matthias Hübner, Zofia Janiszewska, Kevin Kemter, Norbert Lang, Ida Lennartsson, the Martinez family of Atzompa, Philipp Modersohn, Anna Plater-Zyberk, Róża & Jan Plater-Zyberk, Jo Preußler, Mary Grace Quigley, Manuel Raeder, Melanie Roumiguière, Adrian Schindler, Annette Schryen, Emma Siemens, Vanessa Stewart, Iris Ströbel, Adam Szaflarski, Tyra Tingleff, Laura Träger, Stefan Träger, David Upton and George Wolowski.

Thank you,

Anna M. Szaflarski

Letters to the Editors

No. 5: "The Bigger Picture" November 10, 2014
Journal by Anna M. Szaflarski
A Letter from an Editor: Manuel Saiz, "Poetry" pg 8.

Where have you been hiding?*

There was a bush that I use to hide in, it grew at the front of the house, next to the gravel driveway. It was the shape of a rounded mushroom, and in the spring it bloomed large white flowers that I later would call Hydrangea. The bush was only dense on the outside while the inside was spacious and the floor was packed from my frequent visits. We, my brothers and I, invented narratives for this little hiding spot. Entrances and exits were of utmost importance, like portals, into our own world, unregulated by the outside. But what I remember most is just sitting there alone, imagining myself disconnected from the world, a refuge of independence.

There were several such places at our house, which stood on an acre of old farm land in Niagara on the Lake. A five minute walk from the Welland Canal where huge cargo ships from all over the world trudged along to Detroit. Across the street was a peach orchard, which later turned into rows of glass greenhouses. Down the street

* all my life.

Letters to the Editors

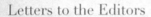

No. 12 "Eluding Wisdom" March 16, 2015
Journal by Anna M. Szaflarski
Letters from the Editors: Barbara Pfister-Szaflarski, "I'm a Mother, After All", pg. 6
Anna Hermn, "MYth YOUth", pg. 8

Let them run

I see a teenager walking down the street. His hair has been dyed green and his shoulders communicate slight apathy and disrespect, and I can't hold myself back from leaning towards him and whispering, "you know everything, don't doubt it for a second!" This, my sweaty forehead and the wide-eyed look I am most probably giving him, might be considered as creepy and a bit frightening, which is a great pity because in that moment I realize there is little chance that he might understand what I mean.

The true intention of my harassment of teenagers is to shorten, snip, compress something that I will audaciously call the loop of life. This ambitious term has no references to reincarnation nor any religion that I can think of. Because of its lack of creativity, I am sure its been used in several self-help books to describe everything from pregnancy to heart-burn, and I'm certain that its been enunciated like scripture by guests invited by Oprah, who strive to teach viewers about the true meaning

Letters to the Editors

No. 17: "The Rationalizations" May 23, 2015
Journal by Anna M. Szaflarski.
Letters from the Editors: Maryse Lariviere, "The Truth", pg 6
Valentina Jager, "Unterschreibung im Kopf", pg 8

The
Smoking
Kids

The paintings were so enormous that the walls fell down.
And so we were standing on top of the caved debris, looking down in between the cracks to see if we could catch a glimpse of a brush stroke, or decide if it resembled anything we had seen before. But we decided it must all be bricollage, because if it hadn't been so when it was painted, then at least now it was definitely all a mess.

Shoo, shoo!

We were actually being shoo-ed away from the site. They were serving wine and schörles on the edge of the premises so we scuttled off in that direction. One of the gallery assistants was trying to free a stack of exhibition texts that was wedged between a pile of bricks and a metal beam. She pulled so hard, and put all of her weight into it that she finally fell flat on her ass with only four sheets of paper to show for. Still down on the floor, she passed them out directly to the people who passed her by.

The fire department arrived and was giving free trials of the oxygen mask, and everyone was in a delightful mood.

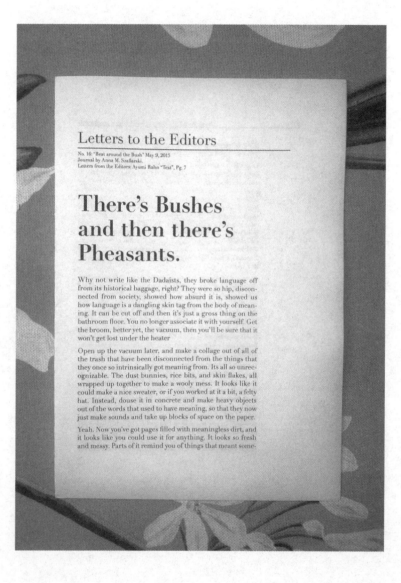

Letters to the Editors

No. 16: "Beat around the Bush" May 9, 2015
Journal by Anna M. Szaflarski.
Letters from the Editors: Ayumi Rahn "Text", Pg. 7

There's Bushes and then there's Pheasants.

Why not write like the Dadaists, they broke language off from its historical baggage, right? They were so hip, disconnected from society, showed how absurd it is, showed us how language is a dangling skin tag from the body of meaning. It can be cut off and then it's just a gross thing on the bathroom floor. You no longer associate it with yourself. Get the broom, better yet, the vacuum, then you'll be sure that it won't get lost under the heater

Open up the vacuum later, and make a collage out of all of the trash that have been disconnected from the things that they once so intrinsically got meaning from. Its all so unrecognizable. The dust bunnies, rice bits, and skin flakes, all wrapped up together to make a wooly mess. It looks like it could make a nice sweater, or if you worked at it a bit, a felty hat. Instead, douse it in concrete and make heavy objects out of the words that used to have meaning, so that they now just make sounds and take up blocks of space on the paper.

Yeah. Now you've got pages filled with meaningless dirt, and it looks like you could use it for anything. It looks so fresh and messy. Parts of it remind you of things that meant some-

Letters to the Editors

No. 20: "You and Me" July 8, 2015
Journal by Anna M. Szaflarski.
Letters from the Editors: Blanca Gusnila, "Transcribed conversations", Pg 7.

Guild of Theives:
The Writing
Table

I've been experiencing a reoccurring daydream. Basically, this dream
consists of compiling Letters to the Editors into a publication, which
then some head writer from an American television show reads, and
is subsequently determined... no, is obsessed... to get me to sit in on
one of their writing rooms for a half-year. Unfortunately, there are
two things that sour my dream in the end every time: 1. The general improbability of it happening. 2. The thought of the thousands
of hyper-elite 20 year-old writers and comics that are dreaming of
exactly the same thing. But unlike the army of ambitious teens, I only
want a taste of it, take a look and bring it back to show you what I have
learned.

I've been casually telling friends about this idea. It was initially
sparked three years ago when I read the writings of comedy writer
and tv-personality, Tina Fey. Her memoir is predominantly ridiculous, but insightful and something about the description of her group
writing methods fermented in my mind. She writes about how she
goes about hiring a writers' room; a mix between Ivy-league graduates, and street-smart comics. And how she adopts rules of improvisation from her theatre background into the dynamic of her team's
process. A similar collaborative process has been used by writers to
develop iconic television for decades. Today, refined ideas, plots, dialogues, comedy as well as drama is being pumped out of the United
States at an alarming rate, by individuals that I've been calling the

LTTE no. 1 — *Wishful Thinking*
October 9, 2014

Nowhere Man,
A Man with No Name.

Anna M. Szaflarski

Nowhere man, please listen
You don't know what you're missing
Nowhere man, the world is at your command.

After listening to the Beatles song, "Nowhere Man," Valentina and I thought, what a depressing prospect, the Nowhere Man was. I went away for two weeks to return to Berlin to find that Valentina had formed a new theory about the Nowhere Man: *he has no idea of his isolation*, she explained, *and therefore is content in his ignorance*. Two sides of the same coin, but a refreshing perspective.

The Nowhere Man is easy to imagine. He is a lone wanderer who has no lord, no master, is eccentric with a strong but unconventional sense of justice, and above all, has a extraordinary proficiency in some skill, like shooting a gun… or something.

28   LTTE NO. I — *Wishful Thinking*

The mere thought that the Nowhere Man exists, or even that one could somehow become him is the seductive fantasy that has nourished the creation of several fictional beings, including Batman, James Bond, Clint Eastwood's The Man with No Name, Mad Max, to name a few. There are some female counterparts, but they are rare, and evidently less interesting to the general public. No, they are more often lonesome men who have chosen moral drive, gadgets, and deep thought over human relationships. In fiction, and only in fiction can they really exist, living in vague places, that are often nondescript boundary-less voids, relentlessly going about things regardless of the fact it affects no one. Legend is his only witness.

Self-sufficient to the point that our admiration is of no importance to him, the Nowhere Man has no need for anyone's approval. He drinks and smokes not because he needs to, but rather because his body is immune to weakness. It gives him no pleasure, in fact, pleasure is not even a consideration. He is almost inhuman. And if he were to come somehow into contact with our reality, full of our petty needs and feelings, families, friends, co-workers, the Nowhere Man would cease to exist. He would be compared to those like him, might fall into a bout of insecurity, feel periodically pathetic, even embarrassed.

In moments when we feel most dependant on something we yearn to become the Nowhere Man most of all. Most people I know who live in Berlin depend on circumstances that are often precarious in terms of money, projects, location, relationships, friends. This is by choice, of course, but nevertheless at times of stress when we want everything to hold still, we realize that we are powerless to make it so. And even we were presented with the option of solidifying

Nowhere Man Skender

the ground beneath us, many of us reject it because it would mean the end to a privileged way of life. If we could only evoke the power of the Nowhere Man, then the world would swirl around us and we could be impervious to its rapid changes in values and trends. We could live as the artist *should* live, completely convinced by work, in need of no one, and desired by all.

No one, that is actually happy, has figured out how to do this. So instead, we gather up a group of people and agree on some sort of doctrine to live by, so that in our moments of insecurity, when everything just seems so damned senseless, we can go to one of our select members and get them to remind us why exactly we are doing what we are doing. It's a compromise. It's not exactly the isolated woodsman who whittles his sticks into a miniature universe for his own appreciation. Anyways, if you could be the Nowhere Man, you would on the one hand be viewed by the public as admirable, but at the same time as somewhat insane.

At the Venice Biennale last year (2013) there were some works made by individuals that were characterized as outsiders of society. They made objects produced in isolation. In trance states or insanity. Artworks produced outside the mainstream discourse. Outsider art. It was beautiful work, but by contextualizing them in that way as bi-products of human anomalies and then bringing them into the conventional exhibition space was at best like inviting James Bond to a high school prom, and at worst exotic specimens to the zoo. The objects were meant for a place where our values can't touch them, and the Biennale came off as being below their standards.

When you watch Clint Eastwood play the Man with No Name, you might wonder, what exactly is he thinking? Where does he find the motivation to get up every morning? Is it possible that his excellent appearance is a complete fluke or is he just as vain as the rest of us? I'll tell you a story to make you feel better. The Man with No Name, has a name, it's Bert. He wears a poncho because he once saw the guy who stole his first girlfriend wear one. In a desperate attempt to get her back he strutted around in his new outfit, and learned how to shoot a gun with precision. While he wasted his time shooting tin cans out back behind his grandma's house, this girl was making out with half the town. Ponchos were very popular at that time. Finally deciding that he should focus on intellectual self-improvement, he applied for several grants, but alas gets only negative replies. Frustrated, but motivated, he wanders the mountainous landscape working as a bounty hunter to fund a project he's been working on, that is hard to describe but could be loosely called "installation." After sweating over several versions of his pdf portfolio, he one day gets a positive response from the Desert Foundation of Art. Things are looking good. He goes back to town with his head high. Finds a good therapist. Buys a flat. Gets the girl. Lives happily and periodically sadly ever after.

He never could pull off being the strong silent type, it was all a misunderstanding, he's more like you than you think and it doesn't sound half bad.

Readymade

Anna Herms

Readymade

Von Fräulein Rose Desmond.

Hallo Liebe, Hoffe, dass diese E-Mail trifft man gut,
erlauben Sie mir bitte, mich selbst vorstellen zu können
bin ich Fräulein Rose Desmond die Tochter des verstorbenen
  Herrn
und Frau Michael Desmond von der Elfenbeinküste.

Wer war ein berühmter Kakao Händler hier in Abidjan
der Wirtschafts-Hauptstadt der Elfenbeinküste Cote d'Ivoire
  basiert. Ich suche für eure Hilfe, mir zu helfen
die Summe von $ 7500, 000.00 USD, die ich geerbt
von meinem verstorbenen Vater auf Ihr Bankkonto überweisen.

Ich bin bereit, Sie als eine Art der Entschädigung nach dem
  Transfer für Ihre Zeit
und Mühe, bieten 20% der Gesamtfonds. Alle notwendigen
  Dokumente zu diesem Fonds sind intakt.

Für weitere Informationen über diesen Fonds,
und ich werde gleich sende Ihnen meine Fotos
so dass Sie sehen und wissen, wer ich bin.
Warten auf Ihre Mitarbeit.

Ihre Getreu.
Rose Desmond.

Readymade 2

My Dear Friend.

Greetings to you my Dear Beloved
My name is Gina Hope Rinehart, a great citizen
of Australia, born in Perth, Western Australia.

I am sending you this email and I believe you must have been
getting some similar emails, but still seems
this is the only best way of communication
apart from telephone conversation.

So I advice you to settle down
and read this mail comprehensively
and you will know I am for real.

I have a mission for you worth
$200,000,000.00. Two Hundred Million Dollars
which I intend to use for CHARITY PROJECT, but
my present health condition wont permit me
to carry out this project myself.

I will need your assistance in carrying out
this Charity Project for the Less Privilege
and Godswill. Please reply if interested.

God Bless You.
Gina Hope Rinehart

LTTE no. 2 — *Relax*
October 27, 2014

Discover the champion in you!

Anna M. Szaflarski

Winter is coming. Today was the first dreary day of many to come. Its dark outside, and everything Sandy planned to do this morning has been delayed by each snooze button she hits on her alarm clock. She had intended to start the day with a series of self-initiated routines including self-improvement behaviours and menial domestic tasks. She had imagined that these two elements combined, would bring about a pyramid of mood stabilizing self-satisfaction; an convincing image that still shimmered in her memories from the night before.

Sandy woke up to find that the heavy pyramid had flipped upside down, and was now digging its golden point into her chest. The wide foundation that had offered small steps to victory was now far away from arm's reach, and the pressure of the previously promising point was paralyzing her.

When the alarm went off, she hit the snooze.

36   LTTE no. 2 — *Relax*

The snooze time on old Canadian alarm clocks, before mobile phones replaced them, was programmed at 9 minutes. It's genius. The one minute under 10 made it so much easier to except procrastination without any significant amount of guilt. It was contagious as it encouraged more snoozing as the last number in the 4-digit time would count down, each moving further away from a round number, always inspiring another push to snooze. 8:30 am, SNOOZE, 8:39 am, SNOOZE, 8:48 am, SNOOZE, 8:57 am...

At no time after 8:30, does it seem like a justifiable time to get up. 9 o'clock is skipped right over and you find yourself justifying how 9:06 is pretty much 9:15, which is a better than 9:30, and you deserve at least that much.

Sandy has a less forgiving clock that skips full ten minute segments and procrastination was slowly marching down a Victory Promenade of self-sabotage. Thankfully, these round numbers trigger a guilt mechanism that begins to accumulate into a parallel container. It resembles a pressure cooker and at 40 minutes after Sandy's intended time to get out of bed, the valve bursts, coinciding with the fourth snooze alarm.

If one were to attach a name to the her alarm's ringtone, one might call it, "transcendence", or "spring fields on Mars." Sandy smacks her phone. The snooze has been disengaged.

The first thing that Sandy has to do to come to terms with her morning is to bring her pyramid of aspiration into a realistic perspective. The night before it was a humungous thing of epic proportions, it was the type of pyramid that Pharaohs sought slaves for. In the morning it needed to be toppled over and rebuilt from the bottom up, while doing other things that required little thought. Showering, cutting toe-nails, scanning the news. In the micro-moments between these tasks Sandy begins to rebuild the pyramid with small manageable

This edition of LTTE was completed
by taking frequent breaks to watch 3 episodes
of Netflix's "House of Cards"

Lego-sized rectangles. It wouldn't stand in the center of the room but be hidden in the closet between the bed sheets and the towels.

Before the day can start, the news needs to be read and this morning reports the widespread outbreak of an out-of-control virus. Meanwhile, a tiny unfocused part of Sandy's brain has replaced the pyramid block for writing an entire application for a grant with the smaller job of consolidating her portfolio images, shifting the rest of the task to the following days.

After digging at every remaining discoloured fragment from underneath her nails, she sits down to start. The rest of the pyramid in ruins for now, as she figures that it will be simpler to visualize the rest of it when the base develops. Both the writing and the pyramid have been reduced into smaller subcategories. After she turns on the computer, she quietly

38   LTTE no. 2 — *Relax*

congratulates herself for starting, but this feeling of satisfaction is followed by a feeling of entitlement, and she's gone again; fooled into thinking that she has to pee, she heads into the other room, and on the way back out of the bathroom notices a new growth of imperfections on her face that needs attending to.

By the time she sits back down in front of her screen, two Canadian snoozes have passed. She looks through her folders, and recalls that there was some unsorted images sent to her by email. She opens the web browser and is transported to the greatest vehicle of distraction invented since the cigarette. Five Canadian snoozes pass.

There are a few effective ways of beating distraction and procrastination. I suggest jealousy. Albeit brutal, it is effective. To start, call up in your imagination the accomplishments of your friends. Next, isolate them, and rid them of any context whatsoever. Concentrate on the jobs they get, the projects they've achieved, the good looking friends they might have, the millions of hobbies they keep up. This fantasy, in its most out-of-control and delusional phase will describe individuals that are not only obsessive, disciplined, meticulous but also happy, and incredibly generous. You imagine that at 9:33, while you're dedicating your time to calculating how many hours you still deserve to sleep, they are out there changing bed pans for the elderly before heading off to a lecture on metaphysic catastrophes, followed by a casual visit to the library and two material experiment tests in the studio. This is all accomplished before you angle your clippers at the awkwardly shaped nail on your pinkie toe. As you start stuffing your laundry into the machine, your 'friend' has opened response letters from ten different institutions, which all read, "We are proud to inform you, Highly

Esteemed Doctor Professor Mr/s. X that you have been chosen from 1 million applicants, and we proudly invite you to our fully funded program!" While you pop pimples from your chin in front of the mirror, your imaginary Doctor Professor is baking a gluten-free cake for a Coeliac-suffering curator with absolutely no ulterior motive.

This method may bestow you with an increasing amount of grey hairs, anxiety issues, paranoiac behaviours, and a decreasing amount of friends but is successful in delivering short-term, explosive results. By the time you've cycled through a series of fantasies you'll be producing at a rate of a lab rat on Ritalin. This is followed by a drastic drop into self-hatred, but the good news is that you can start the cycle again anytime you want. Envy is a renewable resource, we just haven't found a way to make it move cars.

A similarly paranoiac tactic was recently introduced to me by my father, Stan Szaflarski. He had a professor at school that was a rich source of motivating idioms, a talent that my father would like to pass on to me, no less. In his story the professor replaces jealousy with revenge. In order to get his students to formulate their ideas on paper he would tell them to, "sharpen your pencils and write as if you were writing to your worst enemy." When my dad told me this, it took me some time to figure out what he meant. Because at first I imagined myself sharpening pencils into deadly spears for the purposes of writing hate mail. But then I put the pieces together. He meant that you should defend your ideas as if your worst enemy was trying to tear them down. So instead of inspiring a feeling of inadequacy to motivate you, you imagine the destruction or humiliation of your opponent. It's a pity that my dad had only told me this recently, because it would have explained a lot while I was growing up.

40   LTTE no. 2 — *Relax*

So, I tried this, but I find that you just end up lying in bed at 9:33 cycling through a very clever argument against your 'greatest opponent', which you first have to identify. Ten Canadian snoozes later you've crafted the wittiest comebacks and have got all the best explanations for what you're doing with your life, but you still haven't got your pants on.

By the time Sandy yanks herself away from checking before and after pictures of plastic surgery that has gone horribly wrong, and searching for the real reason the Franco-German war started (this is also a common procrastination technique to balance the guilty feelings: one celebrity gossip can be balanced by three Wikipedia pages about history and the Latin etymology of words you'll never use.), thirty-three Canadian snoozes have passed.

All the pressure cookers of jealousy and disappointment were about to blow, when Sandy receives a flattering email about her work from a friend; a real friend who believes in supporting her friends, not competing with them. Paranoid Tactic 1 and 2 have been disengaged, snoozes are forgotten, and at high noon, Sandy has recovered her self-respect and can finally work.

LTTE no. 3 — *The Bigger Picture*
November 10, 2014

Where have you been hiding? *

Anna M. Szaflarski

There was a bush that I used to hide in, it grew at the front of the house, next to the gravel driveway. It was the shape of a rounded mushroom, and in the spring it bloomed large white flowers that I would later call Hydrangea. The bush was dense on the outside while spacious on the inside and the floor was packed from our frequent visits. My brothers and I invented narratives for this little hiding spot. Entrances and exits were of utmost importance, like portals, into our own world. But what I remember most is just sitting there alone, imagining myself disconnected from the world in a refuge of independence.

There were several such places on our property, an acre of old farm land in Niagara-on-the-Lake. It was a five minute walk from the Welland Canal where huge cargo ships from

* ...all my life...

all over the world trudged along towards Detroit. Across the street was a peach orchard, which later was converted into rows of glass greenhouses. Down the street was a pig farm with angry owners and an even angrier dog who ran around a tree with such fury that his chain tightened leaving 3 inches between the tree trunk and his neck. In the other direction was another dog, a reddish pit-bull that stood next to an auto repair garage and patrolled far beyond his domain, chasing us periodically away from the bus stop, resulting in missed trips to the school and irritated parents.

You could hide between the towels in the linen closet. The back corner of the yard under the plum trees. In a tunnel through the pile of dry grass my Babka gathered. There was a spot in the attic in the garage where old encyclopaedias were collected and little worms made their homes. Behind the same garage and before crossing into the neighbour's chicken coop. There were hundreds of places where seemingly no one ever thought to look.

I dedicated a significant amount of time as a child looking for these places, realizing how unhidden you could be while being completely invisible. On a couch for instance, which was used only on holidays or when guests came over, could be used to take a deep uninterrupted sleep on without anyone finding you. I used these places to see if someone would come looking for me. I would invent stories of tragic self-pity and test if someone would sense my absence. Other times though, it was a way to remind myself of my individuality, separate from the prevailing family organism.

I watch nature documentaries obsessively. I particularly like the ones about insects. BBC's David Attenborough describes

St. Catharines, Ontario. 1989.

the behaviours of super-society insects like ants, bees and termites, with words like mutiny, war, care, ruthlessness, but surprisingly, attributes much of these being's activities to significantly less emotional motives. Like self-preservation, procreation or, the most vague of all explanations, to the release of an intoxicating hormone. Regardless of their motives, the super-society that is made up of sometimes hundreds, thousands or even millions of individual creatures seemingly can make decisions in fractions of seconds and never show any shred of doubt.

44   LTTE NO. 3 — *The Bigger Picture*

There are cameras these days that can zoom in on microscopic animals. You can search the eyes of an ant for some sort of recognition of individuality. Nothing. I've heard that the white part of our eyes is the most important in expressing emotion, and that's why dogs are so efficient in manipulating us. But, if there was any inner secret behind the facade of the ant's face, the two blood blister looking things on his head that we assume are its eyes, are not giving anything away.

I watched a particularly interesting segment about a migratory ant species, where millions of so-called worker, nursery with larvae and soldier ants moved across the jungle in search for a new feeding ground, destroying every creature in their path. Suddenly a dangerous hole in a leaf threatened the flow of the marching stampede, so an ant threw itself across it. Acting as a bridge, the rest of the swarm trampled over him safely. It might have been because some savvy film editing, but I was under the impression that the ant did not waste any time before martyring himself to the task. He didn't seem to ask as many human children would, "why me?, I did it last time, why can't ANT number one-million-so-and-so do it? She does nothing, and gets away with it *every time*." In the process of acting as a society, the ant never seems to call attention to its individuality by complaining, whining, or acting defiantly. Why not? A human child would stamp its feet and scream of injustice. How does the ant go on living its life without an occasional delusion of importance?

Some of the swarm videos however were more relatable. One showed how some bee colonies ended the summer season with a brutal mutiny against its queen. The daughters, who were otherwise submissive workers, sensed the season coming to an end and defied their queen by laying their own eggs. Sensing this, the queen would rampage through the hive devouring as many eggs as she could. The daughters, in turn, would murder their mother. After a long, peaceful and productive summer the colony ends with what seems to be chaos and tragedy. The larvae live on and the cycle begins again the following spring. Attenborough says hormones are to be blamed for this. The same thing we blame for monthly mood swings, teens zits, bad smell, machismo and several other anti-social behaviours. Hormonal behaviours are associated with feelings of glorified importance, insecurity, and as a constant distraction from our communal and shared existence.

As in the bee colony, we have this internal self-sabotage mechanism we blame hormones for, but unlike our reading of the bee colony we can't see what role hormones play in our bigger plan, if there even is one. The yearly chaos in the beehive allows for diversification of larvae, and prefaces the inevitable death of the adult bees. What exactly is the bigger picture of embarrassing adolescent acne?

It becomes a bit easier to compare ourselves to swarm animals with internet acting as our hive. Millions of things, often without a central authority, influencing our decisions. But unlike in our observations and assumptions about the tiny super-societies, we can't seem to take a step far back enough to make sense of what its all working towards. The grander scheme of things is all muddled up with our microscopic fixations on our complex subjective emotions and motivations.

I've met a behavioural sociologist that felt that he an his colleagues can read humans like insects. It made him feel smart, but made me awfully uncomfortable. He said that they've come up with a mathematical formula that can predict how many people would die on the planet from conflict per year, concluding that people are just reacting to some external pattern that can be empirically studied. This assumption replaces our ability for independant thought with a predetermined agenda, rationalizing that we have no control over what we do. Our constructions of self-importance, therefore, are only superficial constructions to sedate us while we obediently follow the masses.

In that movie where Werner Herzog interviews everyone at the base camp in Antarctica, and comments on the humongous size of the trucks, he films a single penguin who leaves his pack and heads for the mountains. They say it will definitely freeze to death by doing so. This seems ridiculous, so Herzog's team intervene and pick up the penguin to put him back with his group. Sure enough, the little guy turns on his heel and heads back towards the hills. Herzog just stands there watching the penguin who with puzzling determination walks to his death. Was it hormones or predetermined programming that sent him on his way? Or did the penguin just have enough of this life and was ready for what might come after?

Down deep in the burrows of the ant colony beyond the nursery where eggs are being tirelessly cleaned of fungus; past the soldier ants hauling carcasses of pill bugs, and the winged ants that march out towards the world where they will start their own colonies, is a small corridor. It doesn't have a designated purpose. It's empty, all for a single ant, and he's wondering if anyone's looking for him.

Poetry

Manuel Saiz

Philosophy is for those who cannot cope with poetry.
Essays are for those who cannot cope with philosophy.
Novels are for those who cannot cope with essays.
Films are for those who cannot cope with novels.
TV series are for those who cannot cope with films.
Facebook is for those who cannot cope with TV series.

LTTE no. 4 — *Family Business*
November 23, 2014

Don't worry
I know a guy.

Anna M. Szaflarski

I listened to an audiobook on creative writing, or creativity in general. The author says, that all you have to do to write a bestselling novel is write from 11 am until 4 pm without judgment or self-criticism. There was another author I heard talking on the radio. He recalled telling students his trick for success. He called it the GAIC tactic: Get Ass In Chair. The chair and sitting in it, while facing one direction for a significant amount of time seems to be important. This is not going to work, I thought. I'm the kind of person that has to move around a lot, otherwise I tend to invent unsolvable problems and go in search for someone to crack it (AKA. I am manic and I go bonkers).

There's a famous horror movie about a man who takes his family to a remote place in the mountains to look after a hotel during the winter. The hotel is completely empty but is undeniably haunted. The man thinks this is a great place to

50 LTTE NO. 4 — *Family Business*

write a novel, and tries his best to work daily without interruption. The man follows the advice of successful author one and two, and sits in his chair in one direction in front of his typewriter for hours on end. Well, he must be a restless kind of guy like me, because he ends up going crazy, tries to murder his wife and his son is tormented by dead people.

Another author wrote in his book that he's been keeping detailed notes every day about mentionable anomalies since 1980 and has meticulously processed those notes onto his computer. His note taking and processing is so obsessive to the point that his life sounds miserable. Nevertheless, I think: keep more notes! This is the key!

To no avail, I'm afraid. There are large gaps in my note book, and after a few days of not writing, I feel compelled to start my entry apologetically like a pathetic 16 year old, "Dear Diary, I'm sorry I haven't written in so long..." No, I won't stoop to apologizing to an overpriced Moleskin, there has to be another way!

There's this motivational speaker who will yell at you until you start pursuing your 'life-long dream'. I've never met him, I've only seen him on YouTube, but his face is so terrifying that you can imagine that he might exist somewhere not-so-far-away and might find you while you aimlessly meandering off course from your FULL potential, at which point he might proceed to force you to try one of his proven techniques for self-motivation. You can choose between, A. walking on hot coals and/or B. lying on a bed of nails. I believe that his mere presence might motivate people into doing a lot of things, but I'm arrogant enough to think that I already could walk on hot coals, which doesn't motivate me to do anything but walk on hot coals.

Cronyism Model #3 by Rodney Mockenberker.
Illustration from his study on "Leverage", published
in the Journal for Social Networking

All of these obviously well researched and academic references logically lead us to the conclusion that productivity followed by success, is not, and cannot be triggered solely by tactics of isolation, inner strength, pure determination, discipline, let alone ghosts, or self torment. I've heard that knowing people in high places is helpful.

When Europeans arrived to America, they brought with them a long tradition of hierarchy built on the foundations of family ties. The Ship Captain might have been the third cousin of Napoleon, the Mayor was the husband of some noble's niece who swore she had blood ties to Charles II. The

52   LTTE no. 4 — *Family Business*

Americans, who are famously the decedents of the rejected working class, felt that after a few generations the Europeans didn't need to bother sending over their royalty anymore; that they could do as good, if not, a better job. Well, that took some time to resolve and more than a few people died along the way, but eventually from the ashes dawned an independent America, and with it a new and slanderous understanding of nepotism. Before that, it had been a tolerated assumption that the world went round because of good connections. But in the new world, things were to be done differently.

I imagine that when the word nepotism became derogatory and the American dream prevailed, it caused a whole generation of confused youth to emerge. Shoemakers thought they could be hat-makers, carpenters thought they could be bee-keepers, writers thought they could cultivate probiotic yo-gurt, yogurt thought it could be tzatziki. Long kept traditions of "do like your daddy done" (B. Springsteen 1984) had been fractured, and eventually some time after that everybody was going to university and learning things that no person with hands and feet needed to know. People were told they could be anything if they only tried, and that not even the sky was the limit!

Then they graduated from those universities. Unfortunately the dismantling of nepotism was not so successful, just an illusion. While kids were learning that it's wrong, business continued as usual.

Now, I feel pretty ok with the fact that the higher echelon of the financial or political world is out of reach to me. Put those issues into my hands and we'd all be using wads of cash to balance out wobbly tables in restaurants. But I wouldn't mind having some Aunt in the west wing of some very important building who would attend Gala-this or Gala-that, and could drop my name at opportune moments; advertising my eligibility, versatility, talent, or simply great character. I am not saying that that each of her procured offers might interest me, but how will I ever know? She would be my glittery Wheel-of-Fortune, where behind each pizza-sliced section would be a glamorous options for my new life!

Never fear, another term that is just as criticized, can include you!

Cronyism, or favouritism based on friendship, is a lovely word because it has a mischievous ring to it. It alludes to shady looking guys hanging around dark street corners, making back-alley deals, distributing jobs between thieves and thugs. And both we and those who might criticize it, would possibly like to see it that way, but know its the most natural thing. Unfair but common. The fact is that we don't know how else it's supposed to work. We're not always willing to admit it, but we *want* our decision to be biased. *Of course*, we value your work and talent. But if you want someone to notice how many gruelling hours you spend in your chair facing one direction before you die, it might be to your advantage to act like a decent person, know good-looking people, have a car, make someone laugh, cook well, perhaps wear nice clothes, and know how to use a whoopie cushion properly. Because your greatest assets are your friends, who in your absence hopefully go to parties in a good mood, have just the right amount of red wine and are willing to tell stories about how great you really are.

The Great
Onus Probandi

Peter Szaflarski

Have you ever seen a magic show? Well you really should, it's great entertainment. The idea of a magic show is to entertain an audience with seemingly impossible acts. Of course the acts are not impossible, or they wouldn't be happening, so why do they seem like they are impossible, or at least inexplicable without very careful examination.

I heard a magician explain this seeming impossibility once, and it really opened up how I look at magic. He said that the reason that the acts seem impossible is not because of the act, but because of the implied intent. For example, if a magician were to pull a rabbit out of a hat, then it isn't really impressive since, without any context, we would naturally assume that the rabbit was in the hat just waiting to be pulled out.

But what if the magician somehow implied that the hat was empty? Maybe he could do this by putting it on, by showing us that it's empty, or by flipping it around a few times. Now a rabbit popping out is much more surprising. Of course, the magician didn't actually make a rabbit out of nothing. But, if he did his job well, then he would have made us believe that he did through the implied intent of his actions. Our minds have the remarkable ability to "fill in the blanks" for what we don't see, and many times the magician gestures an intent that causes us to believe something that did not actually happen.

There was an interesting experiment done on this some time ago. They divided an audience into two groups, and both groups watched a magic show. In the first group, the magician claimed to be able to bend a spoon with his mind, but left the spoon unbent. All he did was tell the audience that he was bending the spoon with only the power of his mind — in short, he lied. After the show the audience was surveyed to see if anyone saw the spoon bending. Surprisingly, about 20% (I don't recall the actual figure, but it was something like that) of the audience saw the spoon bend, despite the fact that the spoon remained unchanged. The magician's intent alone was enough to convince 20% of the audience that something was happening that was not happening at all.

Now let's visit the second group. Here the audience watched the same magic show performed by the same magician. Again the magician tried the same spoon bending trick with the same magically unbending spoon. The difference was that this time the magician had a conspirator in the audience. The conspirator's only job was to say "oh my god! That spoon is really bending!" during the spoon bending trick. After the show, the audience was polled again to determine how well the magician could bend the spoon. As it turned out, 100% of the audience claimed they could see the spoon bend.

It's not the fault of the audience, they weren't lying. They could, in fact, see the spoon bending. Their minds created a story about the spoon bending from the intention of the magician, who claimed to want to bend the spoon, and the exclamation of the conspirator, who seemed to just want to express his excitement for the amazing thing that was happening.

It's a frightening thought to realize that our perception is a fragile thing in this way, and it can easily be warped and

56 LTTE no. 4 — *Family Business*

twisted without our knowledge. But how far can this ability to twist go?

I was at a magic show recently. The magician asked for a volunteer from the audience, "Anyone that thinks that he or she is clever enough to determine how I do this next trick will win a genuine gold coin." An interesting reward to be sure. "You sir!" the magician pointed to me like a tonic salesman from the 1800s. Did I even volunteer? This part of a magician's routine is actually very much like a tonic salesman since the next question is something like "have we ever met before?"

"No," I answered honestly.

"You have to speak into the microphone." He was making fun of the fact that I was not as used to being on stage as he was. This is to show the audience that he is in control. The collective minds of the audience would hook onto this short exchange and acknowledge that they would defer to his authority over mine. The audience's decision to do this would be done unconsciously.

"No I have not met you before." I spoke into the microphone this time, smiling.

"Thank you." He got back to business, "now you said you wanted to win a gold coin, so here it is." He went on to show me, and the audience, a large gold coin. He placed it in my hand, "here check that it's real." He paused as I inspected the coin and then he followed with, "alright give it back now!" the intent was to joke that I was trying to steal the coin. Again this technique momentarily and unconsciously undermines my credibility. I hand the coin back to him and say "Seems real to me."

The reality of the coin has no bearing on the trick, but the fact that an impartial third party determined the coin to be real will now cause the audience's focus to be on the reality of the coin, instead of what the trick will be.

"Alright, a man I have never met before has confirmed that the coin is real, now keep an eye on it and watch!"

He waved his hands around a few times, then he made both hands into a fist concealing the coin. He blew into his hands and the coin vanished.

The audience applauded. The magician took a bow, then raised his hands as if to stop the applause and to be heard. He motioned to me to approach, rubbed my bald head with his hands and miraculously created the missing coin!

The audience applauded again, and the magician bowed again. When the audience was done clapping, he asked me, "So my friend... wait, are we friends?"

"Yes, I think so." This was the only answer I could muster.

"Good! So my friend, do you know how I made the coin disappear and reappear?"

I was nervous to give an answer. You aren't supposed to know how a magician does a trick, and if you do then chances are there is another trick behind it. But I knew this trick, I could even do this trick! Maybe not as well, maybe not with the same flair or banter, but I could do it!

"Yes. I think so." I answered cautiously. The audience murmured as if sceptical.

"Oh? Well then, please enlighten us."

I started to describe the trick to the best of my ability and my limited knowledge of the black arts. I said something like: *Well I can't be completely sure but I think that when you waved your hands around the coin you palmed it then ditched it, in your suit maybe. When you went over to me you used the fact that I couldn't see the top of my head and that the audience couldn't see that side of your suit to retrieve the coin and place it on top of my head.*

58   LTTE no. 4 — *Family Business*

The magician paused, "does this guy know magic or what?" The audience applauded for me. The magician handed me the coin as per our arrangement and, ever so briefly, I tasted victory.

"But wait!", before I touched the coin, he pulled it away, to the audience's amusement, and made the coin seemingly disappear again.

"Ordinarily you'd be right. But, I didn't ask how the trick COULD be done, I asked if you could determine how I did it, and that's not how I did it" he smirked, knowing that the audience felt slightly cheated.

"Who wants to know how it's actually done?" The audience cheered while I was still on stage feeling out of place.

"Well" he started again, slowly with his explanation, "the way I made the coin disappear is..." a long pause this time.

"MAGIC!"

With that he disappeared with a puff of smoke.

LTTE no. 5 — *Suspicious Minds*
December 6, 2014

The Boy who Cried Wolf Over for Dinner

Anna M. Szaflarski

A Freudian-sympathizing psychotherapist named Wolf, tried to convince me that my motives are not what they seem. He told me that no one forgets accidentally, things don't just slip your mind, there is always an agenda. It can be as simple as arriving late because you actually didn't feel like going to that particular party, or more complicated than that, like you arrived late because you felt that all the guests present should be aware of your 'omnipotence.' That's the word he used, 'omnipotence.' I thought, wow, my subconscious mind sure thinks a lot of itself, because my conscious self can barely pronounce the word.

The introduction of this type of thinking made me suspicious of myself. What else was I doing to prove my omnipotence? All social habits, which included some form of forgetfulness or apathy came under question. I'm bad at calling people back, I often order whatever someone else is getting

Advertisement

Ayami Awazuhara
evergreenyellow
3.12.2014 - 5.1.2015

Closed Circuit *

Things that never go yellow grow at the frontier of the cold
They keep their juices flowing deep in the pit of their heart

And in the cold they talk of winter withhold
To the odd southern fellow who's glare is uncontrolled

In the south, they're growing old and moldy
Breathing ever so slightly and moving ever so slowly;
Glowing from pores of tireless citrus

STUDIO LO
www.studioloonline.com
vorm Lützowplatz 9
10785 Berlin
open all day

* poem by Anna M. Szaflarski

at restaurants, I secretly try to keep clothes people lend me, when I cook for guests I make a variation of the same thing every time, I can't remember a name if my life depended on it. Is this all due to a covert operation titled, *Superiority Complex*, currently active in the deepest caverns of my mind? Perhaps. And if so, I blame the unrealistic role-model of my formative years, Stan Szaflarski, and I believe that Wolf the psychotherapist would encouraged it.

Stan Szaflarski can turn a piece of wood over and it will burst into flames. I kid you not. I have watched him sledge hammer beams into the ground by swinging a hammer way over his head in a manner that humans are definitely not supposed to do. Those kind of movements are reserved for exaggerated characters in video games who eat neon cherries. Stan will haggle the cost of bananas at a chain supermarket, he has absolutely no shame. I've watched him fall from a pine tree that was 7 meters tall. He broke something in his shoulder, he never went to the hospital, it still looks funny to this day.

When I was growing up, Stan still had a heavy accent in English, and used it to deliver a plethora of great phrases, like, "You can do whatever you want, but you have to be the best," "this country is the lowest common denominator," "mediocrity..." [mumbling while driving], "Why 95? What happened the to the 5%?", and when he came to one of my swimming competitions, "why didn't you move your arms faster?" Today, he defends himself saying that his abrupt parenting style was predominantly caused by loss in translation, and that the subtle intricacies of his messages are now martyrs of time. Without further assistance, I struggle to this day to imagine what kind of possible wisdom was hidden in his inquiries regarding my arm movement.

62   LTTE NO. 5 — *Suspicious Minds*

We children developed a definite resistance to Stan's influence. We preferred the gentler, more forgiving ways of the country we were born in. When Stan's solution was, "just punch him!", my brother Peter, the largest kid in his class, would slyly avoid the situation. Stan entertained us with stories of fighting in the streets, running through the mountains with a 200 pound athlete on his back, clever tricks that avoided jail-time or lawsuits; and we were very impressed, jaws wide open at the dinner table. But alas, even with all of his relentless indoctrination, instead of becoming the little Machiavellians he had hoped for, we strived more than ever to become what my dad perceived to be the worst possible thing: nice people.

My friend Armando sent me a text by Ricardo Piglia, in which he describes how writer Anton Chekhov was able to reduce the short story into its most condensed form: 'A man in Monte Carlo goes to the casino, wins a million, returns home, commits suicide.' Piglia explains that instead of logically ending the story with a description of a rich and happy man, the story splits into two, and questions arise limitlessly from beyond the tale. I read this yesterday, after having started this text about Stan Szaflarski and I realized something. Piglia points to the fact that every short story, regardless if it is revealed or implied, always tells two stories, but also, that like the short story, its predecessor *the human being*, regardless if it is revealed or implied, always tells two stories.

One story will encompass the other, will shroud and cradle it, and perhaps periodically in small rations or in moments of absolute stress or weakness, will the second show its face. In the form of the short story the dominant narrative is often a distraction, or simply a carrier of the more loaded yet fragmented second. The first is the jolly woman cooking in the kitchen, the second is the peculiar arrangement of her asparagus. She can't help it! She needs to express herself! Is it an accident that the vegetables fell onto your plate and spelled: [DIE]?

Wolf says no, there are no accidents.

There are no accidents, we are just living two lives, the one that we want to live and the other that is trying to squeeze through and is causing all of the mishaps, coincidences, mistakes, slips and oversights. All of these inconvenient behaviours are windows into our parallel universe. Forgot your keys again? You want to be a dancer! Missed a doctor's appointment? You are cheating on your husband.

We are often only vaguely interested in the first story. What did you do today? *Oh, I worked on a model, and emailed some people interested in showing something, and hey, you know, avocadoes are 1 Euro right now! Want some guacamole?* Oh shut up about pulverized fruit and tell me about your inner torment already!

On the other hand, we often can't handle the second story, and once revealed wished that it was a Chekov short story and that we could close the cover on the friend that has been crying on the phone for 3 hours straight. In its literary form the second story is so safe, it's hiding behind the first, arriving at the most clever moment and conveniently disappearing with the end of the story. Because otherwise it might get awkward. Everyone hates the part of the story where Clark Kent tells Lois Lane who he *really* is. The story just has to end there, the excitement was all hanging in the balance of this incredible tension between the mystery and the unveiling.

And in this story about the superhuman who flies, we are delighted to watch from our god-like position as his pro-

64   LTTE NO. 5 — *Suspicious Minds*

longed frustration plays out, wanting it to last forever. In our contradictory existence we want to perpetually bounce between 1. all secrets lasting forever, 2. impulsively revealing/ uncovering the secret, 3. the secret becoming secret again. REPEAT

The short story is an exercise that allows us to indulge in the second narrative, which is composed from possibly perverse, tragic, pathetic, embarrassing, sweet, romantic truths, without having to deal with the messy reality. It allows us fantasize that it only exists in fiction and grants us the ability to continue to deny that it reflects our everyday lives.

Stan consciously set-out to create super-humans in his family, but inevitably it was his second story that would influence us in the end. He thought, and on his bad days still thinks, that his kindness had delivered disappointing results throughout his lifetime and didn't want us to fall into what he believed would be the same trap. And when we watched him perform those great feats of superiority, we sensed that inside there was something telling him that he had to be even better, and that made us feel sometimes sorry for him. So instead of sprouting ambition in us, it cultivated empathy.

But he would be proud to know that I've left my EC card in a Fahrkarten Automat twice this year, I didn't make it to the blood test appointment I had made, and I continue to struggle to remember anybody's name, because I am a Szaflarski and that makes me OMNIPOTENT.

DER MEXIKANISCHE STAAT TÖTET STUDENTEN

EL ESTADO MEXICANO MATA ESTUDIANTES

THE MEXICAN STATE KILLS STUDENTS

LTTE no. 6 — *Secret Heart*
December 19, 2014

Ain't no mountain high enough

Anna M. Szaflarski

At the end of an hour-long guided tour through Anahuacalli, Diego Rivera's volcanic rock pyramid museum, the other visitors began to chatter. They spoke in Spanish and looked at each other with wide eyes and curiosity. I thought that maybe they had unanswered questions about the number of ethnographic pieces Rivera collected, about the inner architecture of the Teotihuacan-like structure, perhaps about the thematic levels ranging from the underworld to the gods or about if there was public access to the clay sauna at the perimeter of the grounds? I looked to Valentina who came with me and therefore was by default my interpreter, searchingly. No, she explained, they were trading notes about who else Rivera couldn't avoid having an affair with, and with whom his wife Frida took revenge. Ah.

68   LTTE no. 6 — *Secret Heart*

In México City there are lovers kissing at every corner. In exposed and often inconvenient places for passers-by, and it doesn't seem to bother them. On the way to visit the site of the Teotihuacan pyramids, there was a couple stealing kisses on the only stairs to the bus, in the tight corridors to the subway, leaning against passengers in the sardine packed wagon. They were constantly blocking our way to ancient sites, and they didn't seem to care. The pyramids will hopefully last forever, but a kiss is of the moment and is a resource that demands constant replenishing.

To keep the pyramids from melting away a shell of concrete and stones has been applied to the original adobe structure. Like armoured armadillos, two mountains stand patiently waiting for you. So why not buy something first? "For your mother-in-law!" a merchant suggests. You can buy a ceramic turtle flute, a bird flute, a terrifying ceramic jaguar that roars, a bow and arrow, a blanket with an Aztec "calendar" motif, a hat, actually there's an expansive variety sombreros. When we arrived in the morning, the calls of the turtle, the bird and the jaguar sang in unison; played by the merchants. Without noticing the exact moment of transformation, the men became children, their wrinkles vanished, and only their melodic voices remain. By the afternoon, their choir was replaced by every visiting child who had bought a flute. Remarkable! This place must be an ancient source of youth, "a symbolic geometry of petrified time; four points coming together, halting the perpetual rolling plains below."

Based on mathematical and astrological references, some people reckoned that the builders must have made one pyramid for the sun, and the other for the moon. Why not, that makes perfect sense. But someone else came along and said, no, no, it can't be. With all these lovers around, they must

Tlaloc accompanied by his wife

be lovers, too. The big one was made for Tlaloc the rain deity, and the smaller one for his wife who makes thunder and things fertile. And they quarrel happily with each other.

Water doesn't come from the sky but from the inside of a mountain. Like the ones behind the pyramids. Like the ones you see on the way to Oaxaca. There are deep crevasses cut into the mountains, making way for cars, pickup trucks and our bus with movies playing. They've covered the jagged cliffs with concrete keeping the source of water from escaping onto traffic, making them into armadillos too. Parts where the armour couldn't hold, the inside of the mountain was sliding out, but instead of water I only saw something like sweet halva, or packed cinnamon coming out. The water must be somewhere deeper.

In search for water in México, some have discovered remarkable things! Some time ago, on a another mountain a man met a young woman. And he thought, she must be the Virgin Mary. She told him to gather flowers in his oversized t-shirt and sent him home. When he reached his small village he told everybody about his hiking encounter, but no one believed him. He thought, well, at least take a look at these awesome flowers. And at that moment there was an amazing silk screen pattern of the virgin printed on his shirt. And then no one could deny that, his was a dope t-shirt. Today, one can view this t-shirt in a chapel at the cathedral in México city. They call the woman Guadalupe, and since then she must have re-enacted the same miracle an infinite amount of times because you can get her on key chains, bags, scarves, almost anything. But the boy's, Juan Diego's, oversized threads are unique, and I haven't found anything similar to it yet.

Mountains are not made in a day, and that goes for the pyramids too. It was explained to me that the pyramids were an accumulation of layers and that reminds me of a gigantic sand pile that we used to visit as children. It stood next to a large canal near Niagara. My dad would say, *grab your goggles and your sleds!* He'd park the van and we would burst out and climb anxiously to the top. Up there we would see the world as never before, we were big, and the world was small. Down below my dad was shovelling the city's sand into his van, for some construction project. He had a talent for finding slumbering materials lying about the city. Our sand pyramid was asleep but not unneeded, more like a resting giant. In the winter the sand came alive and was spread all over the city's icy streets, keeping cars and women with grocery bags on their chosen paths. No one made our sand pile into an armadillo and so it didn't stay in one place. It would disappear, until the following summer when it would appear again. I don't know where the sand came from but it arrived on a barge and would pour out of a long tube that reached high into the sky. It piled up like the lower half of an hour glass.

It's no wonder why someone would want to built a pyramid. It's no wonder that we want to climb all over it, to be in the middle and overtop. And it's no wonder that once we've built it, we never want to let it go. And when there isn't a barge around delivering new mountains every year, renewing it like fresh kisses in the subway, then the only way we have to keep it from melting is to armour it against the elements of time.

EXACTO! ES UNA TRANSFORMACIÓN, PUES AUNQUE SE QUERÍA UNA EXTINCIÓN DE EVIDENCIAS. EXTINCIÓN DE SERES, EXTINCIÓN DEL CAMBIO, EXTINCIÓN DE EXPECTATIVAS. LO QUE YO CREO QUE PROVOCARON. ES LA TRANSFORMACIÓN DE PENSAMIENTO, LA TRANSFORMACIÓN DEL MIEDO, DE LA INCONCIENCIA; PORQUÉ ESTOY INTERESADO EN ESE DE TEMA? BIEN, YA HABÍA EXPLICADO QUE COMO NUNCA ANTES EL CRIMEN, EL GOBIERNO, LA POLÍTICA EN MÉXICO Y SU VIOLENCIA. ME HABÍAN CONMOCIONADO, MI PENSAMIENTO ES OTRO RESPECTO A TEMAS POLÍTICOS, NUNCA MÁS SERÉ AJENO A ESTO, EN REALIDAD NUNCA LO FUI, SÓLO ERA IGNORANCIA VOLUNTARIA, AL MISMO TIEMPO QUE BAJO DECISIÓN PROPIA MIS ACCIONES BUSCABAN SER UNA NUEVA POLÍTICA.

NO SE DICE DESTRUCCIÓN ES LA CONSTANTE TRANSFORMACIÓN. LA CONSTANTE TRANSFORMACIÓN NO ES DESTRUCCIÓN. EXTINCIÓN DE EVIDENCIAS.
EXTINCIÓN DEL CAMBIO, TRANSFORMAR EL PENSAMIENTO, LA TRANSFORMACIÓN DEL MIEDO.
GENERAR MIEDO
EXTINGUIR EL RECLAMO
EXTINGUIR LA CONFRONTACIÓN.
LA CONFORMACIÓN DE UN CUERPO NUEVO, LA CONSTANTE TRANSFORMACIÓN; ES COMO UN MANUAL PARA PRODUCIR UN CUERPO NUEVO, UNO DE CONSISTENCIA Y PESO INDETERMINADO. UN CUERPO EN EL QUE CABEMOS TODOS O TODOS FORMAMOS PARTE DE.
LA TRANSFORMACIÓN NO OCURRE PARA UNOS CUANTOS SINO PARA TODOS LOS QUE SON AFECTADOS.

Body-builders

Gabriel Rosas Alemán

Manual para la conformación de un cuerpo nuevo o la transformación de cuerpos tangibles en intangibles. Cómo perder peso, extinguir evidencias y modificar el volumen del miedo. La transformación de cuerpos o sobre la transformación del cuerpo colectivo:

– reúna una cantidad considerable de cuerpos
– añada combustible diésel
– queme por más de quince horas
– recoja los restos en bolsas
– lance al río

Manual for the conformation of a new body or the transformation of tangible bodies to intangible ones. How to lose weight, extinguish the evidence and modify the volume of fear.

The Transformation of Bodies or About the Transformation of the Collective Body:

– Collect a considerable amount of bodies
– Pour Diesel fuel over them
– Burn for over fifteen hours
– Pick up the remains and put them into bags
– Throw into the river

Go, gentle scorpio

Yesterday I had dinner with two persons I didn't know. I came back home walking and slept sad and cold. I am sleeping so lightly lately, I told you, that I wake up remembering the most useless pieces of the last days: you holding a big spoon in the air, my bike in front of the museum, Silvia crossing the bridge that same morning when you were waiting for me in bed. I came back and was happy to find you. I have tried to think about something else, taking books and notes with me to bed. But when I turn off the lights, you appear again in the dark.

Rodrigo Hernández
written on the occasion of the exhibition
"Go gentle scorpio"
Parallel Oaxaca, 19 Dec – 16 Jan, 2014

LTTE no. 7 — *Where No One Thought of Going Before*
January 1, 2015 (Released on February 28, 2016)*

Stick in the Mud

Anna M. Szaflarski

Something changes when you travel through time. You can move freely like flipping through pages of a magazine, frontwards and backwards, scan from top to the bottom, and vice versa. The passage of time become incredibly light, you are not attached to any particular event, you hold no stakes in wars or victories, revolutions or evolutions. Each moment becomes as insignificant as the next, and curious patterns that did not seem obvious or interesting to scientists and historians alike begin to catch your attention.

Spaghetti is most popular when coinciding with an influx of fireflies. Words animated life when nose picking became an

---

* Disclaimer: "We stopped to produce this issue on January 1st, 2015, while travelling unconventionally through time. Before distributing it, however, we were on our way again. It's hard to explain, but just beware of confusing tense changes throughout. We had a hard time keeping track of which time we were living in and in which we were writing." (Anna S.)

76 LTTE no. 7 — *Where No One Thought...*

epidemic. Those are the kind of things that catch your attention. Another thing you notice is a strange accumulation of certain characters throughout history. Instead of living and dying, some beings reappear time and again. I observed this on many occasions and deduced that they weren't caught in some sort of cyclical reincarnation, —like some faiths offer as an explanation—but are more like running on a skipping record. I'm convinced that the reappearing characters are connected to each other somehow, but I couldn't figure out exactly how. I would describe them as often chasing some desire, some object, some person, maybe, that they believed to be just out of reach, and always managed to slip away. And they run like that through time losing their way, catching up, and losing it again. It's all very hard to explain, of course, but what I'm trying to say is that when you travel through time, you notice that other people are travelling through it as well, but strangely enough they don't seem to be aware of it. During my trip I was consumed with watching the world from an general perspective, studying the spaghetti boxes as they flew off the supermarket shelves and the dark woods as they filled with bioluminescence. The reappearing characters would instead show up repeatedly with a determination that could only be attributed to someone who has not felt the lightness of time.

When I returned to this, our shared time, I sat down immediately to try to find a way to explain what I had seen.

I visited the Niagara Falls many times on my travels, I watched the eroding ridge of the cascade, and then went backwards in time to see it grow back again like the finger nails of an infatuated teenager. Pretty much as soon as humans found the location of the waterfalls they started throwing themselves down it. That is a fact. At the same time when the first woman sent herself down the cliff there was a barely visible pink eye infection ravaging the rhinoceros beetle population, and thousands of villagers in the northern hemisphere were producing an artefact that looked a bit like a paperclip. I took very little notice of the people throwing themselves down the falls. Some did it accidently, others for faith, suicide or attention. All in all, there has been quite a few who have jumped down them or still will. Banal as it is, a particular incident finally did catch my attention.

A Dog in the Rapids Above the Falls.

From The Niagara Falls Cataract, May 6.
A dog on what is known as Avery's rock in the rapids, above the American falls, created considerable excitement early yesterday. The animal had apparently been thrown into the river, as he had a rope attached to a heavy article around his neck. John McCloy of the inclined railway attempted to shoot the animal and end his suffering, but the bullets went wide of the mark. The dog finally jumped into the rapids and went over the falls.

May 6, 1895

DOG MAROONED AT NIAGARA.

Army Sharpshooter Hits Animal on Islet and It Plunges Over Falls.

NIAGARA FALLS, N. Y., March 25.— Marooned on a tiny islet in the upper rapids of the Niagara River 200 feet above the brink of the American Falls, a mongrel dog was shot today by a sharpshooter from the army post at Fort Porter to keep the animal from starving to death.
Every effort of rivermen, city firemen and reservation employes to reach the dog failed. Then policemen tried to shoot the animal, but failed. The commandant at Fort Porter was asked to send his best rifle shot here to kill the dog. The soldier hit the dog with his first shot. The wounded animal leaped into the rapids and was carried over the falls.

March 25, 1926

78   LTTE no. 7 — *Where No One Thought...*

Between 1895 and 1925 the Niagara Falls eroded or moved backwards upstream by some 30 meters. It was barely noticeable to the thousands of tourists who visited it every day. I visited both time periods, and found the former profile of the cavern to be more to my liking.

Now, I wouldn't have believed it either unless I saw it with my own eyes, but would you believe me if I told you that it was the very same dog trapped on the rocks on both days thirty years apart? And that it was the very same man who tried to shoot it?

I was surprised to find the newspaper articles from those days report that the man tried to shoot the dog apparently in order to end its suffering. What a silly conclusion! It's an explanation written by reporters who feel the weight of each moment on their shoulders. If they had only known that a strange mutation evolved in two different insect species, each respectively one day after each of those mentioned incidents, they might have come to very different result.

While thinking about another matter completely, I caught myself watching a tightrope artist walk high above the Niagara Falls in 1886. The stunt held my attention for a moment before I lost interest and flipped a few pages in this or that direction, stopping immediately on spotting the man who tried to shoot the dog in 1895 and apparently succeeded in 1925. Indeed, a long way he came.

JUMPED FROM GOAT ISLAND BRIDGE.

BUFFALO, N. Y., June 10.—Niagara Falls can claim another victim. Between 9 and 10 o'clock this morning a man then unknown walked onto the bridge leading to Goat Island. When about half way across he threw his hat off, and with a run sprang over the railing and disappeared in the tumbling waters beneath, being immediately swept over the falls. That it was an act of deliberate suicide none can doubt. To several hackmen near the bridge, who solicited his patronage, he replied that he was tired and had come a long distance by rail. He also made inquiries about the depth of the water at the bridge, the swiftness of the current, whether a man who jumped into the river from the bridge could be saved, &c. Being apparently satisfied on this score, he walked onto the bridge and jumped over. There were several persons on the bridge when the man sprang over the railing, but so quickly did he do it that none realized what he was about until he was gone. From a card found under the sweat band of his hat, it is supposed that the man was Hiram B. Wadsworth, of Holley, N. Y.

June 11, 1886

I didn't give it much thought then. It was just a man caught on a skipping record, I thought, like so many other beings in this universe. Nevertheless, many times while happily watching bacteria bore through layers of limestone in fast-forward, I would catch the same man returning to the waterfalls. He did not always get his feet wet, so to say. He paced with a determined expression on his face, and often left without incident.

80   LTTE no. 7 — *Where No One Thought...*

He always looked the same, completely oblivious to his surroundings. In the company of both a pterodactyl and an android, his expression was constant, his disappointment unchanged. After taking note of his behaviours over a random period of perhaps millions of years, it became obvious to me that the man was fixated on retrieving something he had lost at the base of the falls, but didn't know at which stage of erosion it was lost.

I hadn't noticed the dog at first, but he must have always been close by. I assumed that the dog was even more oblivious to his surroundings than the man. Because it was in fact the man who tied the rocks to the dog, and who had MISSED the dog BOTH times with his gun. At some point or other, I assumed the man lost the nerve to dive into the waters himself and therefore trained the dog to retrieve whatever was down there for him. The dog must have been trained for just such a purpose, but still needed some "motivation" to take the plunge, hence the rocks and the shooting. It was all a poorly planned obsession, really.

The newspapers will always report whatever is myopically convenient. Whatever tells a good story. The facts, the names, the places are usually all wrong, all crafted to make something more meaningful then it really is. But one day in 1931, even I felt a bit sentimental.

OWNER GETS NIAGARA DOG.

Claims Animal When He Reads It Went Over Falls.

NIAGARA FALLS, N. Y., July 6 (P).—A police dog which climaxed a day afield with a successful jaunt over Niagara Falls was back home today.

The animal slipped out of his collar last week while tied in the rear of his home here. His wanderings led him to the falls where he jumped into the river and was carried over the cataract. He landed in a whirlpool beyond the rocks and was rescued by a concession owner. Today his master, Andrew Terogsz, called to claim his pet, saying he had read in the newspapers of his dog's bid for fame.

July 7, 1931

Whatever it was that the dog and man were after, they felt the satisfaction of finally retrieving it. Unfortunately, it only lasted until the comet shower later that evening, which brought an alien bacteria to our planet; a whole other story.

When I saw the dog and the man again, it was far into the future from now. The Niagara Falls had eroded as far back as where Detroit stands today. The dog was holding a gun, the man carried stones.

Time-Trivials

Steve Paul

Das Gefühl für den Augenblick

Ein Android im Dienste der Vereinigten Föderation der Planeten versucht die Begriffe der relativen Zeitwahrnehmung zu ergründen. Für ihn existiert die Zeit als gleichmäßige Konstante, geregelt durch seinen inneren Chronometer. Eine mehr entsprechende Form einer Inneren Uhr. So verläuft die Zeit für diesen Androiden immer gleich und unbeeinflusst von Stimmungen, Emotionen, Ablenkungen oder Aufmerksamkeiten. Ganz im Gegensatz zum Mensch, dessen Wahrnehmung durchaus durch solche Faktoren wie Gefühle, Stimmungen etc. beeinflusst wird und für den die Zeit auf Grund dieser Interferenzen relativ verläuft.

Man spricht zwar beim Menschen von einer Inneren Uhr, doch ist diese ein Produkt innerer Zyklen biologischer Prozesse. Im Vergleich zu einer technischen Variante ist sie somit viel anfälliger für Ungenauigkeiten.

In der gedanklichen Zeitreise dieses Androiden durch die Momente seines Lebens, an die er sich beindruckender Weise allesamt im Detail erinnern kann, ist es ihm verwehrt die Besonderheit dieser Momente durch das Gefühl und die relative Zeitwahrnehmung zu bewerten. Die Emotionslosigkeit verhindert die Differenzierung seiner Erlebnisse anhand des Gefühls wie: Diese Nacht der heißen Liebe ging viel zu schnell vorüber oder der Schmerz in meinen Beinen nahm kein Ende. Doch der Android hat mit der Zeit andere Algorithmen entwickelt, um die Wertigkeit von Erlebnissen zu bestimmen. Die Hierarchie der jeweiligen Perspektive wird auch hier bestimmt durch die Tiefe des Universums.

Kindliche Architekturen der Fantasie

Um in der Tradition zu bleiben Anna S. in den Texten beim Namen zu nennen, ein Auszug des Telefongesprächs:
Anna: Es muss auch nicht um Zeitreisen gehen.
Steve: Aber warum denn nicht?
Das Reisen durch die Zeit erscheint mir schon immer als eine der Sehnsuchtsunternehmungen der Träumer und Fantasten. Eine magische Idee, um in seinen idealen Vorstellungen zu existieren oder einfach nur Abenteuer zu erleben.

Die Fähigkeit vergessene Orte zu besuchen oder an Ereignissen der Vergangenheit mit dem Wissen aus der Zukunft teilzuhaben. Frühere Fehler wieder gut zu machen, Hitler direkt schon im Kindsbett zu erdrosseln oder sich in den niederen Gedanken den heimlichen Vorteil auszumalen. Wie in der Geschichte des Biff Tannen, Dem größten Glückspilz auf Erden, der seinem jüngeren Ich in der Vergangenheit eine Chronik aller sportlichen Wettergebnisse der, aus der Gegenwart gesehen, vergangen 50 Jahre übergibt und damit zum reichsten und mächtigsten Mann der Welt wird.

Der Besuch in der Zukunft wird wiederum von den Vorstellungen der Gegenwart beherrscht. Sind die Utopien oder prophezeiten Katastrophen wahr geworden?

84   LTTE NO. 7 — *Where No One Thought…*

Mein Favorit war eigentlich immer die Reise in die übertriebene Zukunft in 10, 20 oder 100.000 Jahren. Dieser abstrakte Ort, an dem selbst die Vorstellungen der Science Fiktion oft in mittelalterliche Konzepte zurückspringen. Oft in höchst degenerierte und verkommene Gesellschaften, eingebettet in Supertechnologien. Als ob sich die Menschheit nicht einmal in der fernsten Zukunft aus dem Morast ihrer eigenen Abgründe befreien kann. Ich versuche da lieber Gene Roddenberry's LSD Ideen einer humaneren, toleranteren und aus den Gräueln der Vergangenheit lernenden Zukunft meine Sympathie zu schenken. Auch wenn diese Geschichten nur oder erst in den nächsten 3–4 Jahrhunderten dümpeln und noch zu sehr als Spiegel der Gegenwart dienen. Um diese Spiegelung zu verlassen, erscheint mir die übertriebene Zukunftsreise durch ihre abstrakte Überspannung doch etwas interessanter. Gäbe es eine Möglichkeit in der die programmierbare Zeitspanne nach oben offen ist, würde ich definitiv auch mal einen Blick eine Millionen oder Milliarden Jahre usw. in die Zukunft werfen. Ganz in der Neugier nach einer kleinen Vorschau, weil ich es nicht abwarten kann. Leider hat das nichts mit Ungeduld zu tun. Da man gar nicht so lange abwarten könnte, selbst wenn man wollte.

Ein Lieblingsklischee der Vergangenheitsreise ist wohl die Vorstellung, dass man automatisch und direkt an besonderen, historischen Ereignissen teilhaben könnte. Nicht nur am genauen Zeitpunkt, sondern ebenfalls durch selbstverständlichen Zugang zu den exklusiven Zirkeln und Gruppen, welche die Auslöser dieser Ereignisse sind. Im filmischen Idealfall ist man selbst das Bindeglied der Geschichte.

Eine weitere Vorstellung, die sich inzwischen als ungültig erwiesen hat, könnte zumindest durch eine Zeitreise noch einmal vertröstet werden.

Früher dachte ich, wenn man gewisse Situationen besonders aufmerksam und bewusst lebt, sie in ihrem Realitätspotenzial regelrecht ausbeutet, ließen sich diese Momente besser und komplexer in der Erinnerung erhalten. Doch irgendwann hat man dann festgestellt, dass diese Erinnerungen mit der Zeit alle zu kleinen Haufen Scheiße zusammenschrumpfen. Mit so einer Zeitreise könnte man diese Momente dann wenigstens noch einmal mit all den späteren Reflexionen neu und intensiv erleben. Die Reflexion ist dabei eine tückische Angelegenheit, da sie wiederum zu einer anderen Utopie verleiten kann. Hätte man eine bestimmte Entscheidung anders getroffen, in einer Situation anders regiert, wäre das Leben bestimmt besser gelaufen oder was man sich so oft im Nachhinein zusammmen fantasiert hat.

Was dann zu einem letzten Gedankenspiel führt.

Dass diese anderen Entscheidungen durchaus getroffen wurden und das Leben auch besser gelaufen ist. Zumindest kurzfristig für diese bestimmte Situation.

Denn dieses bessere Leben wurde deswegen bestimmt nicht von anderen, neuen Problemen und Fehlentscheidungen verschont. Auch wenn diese dann ebenfalls wieder in einem weiteren Leben umgangen wurden usw. usw. Der Android vom Anfang hat das alles mal sehr präzise mittels einer Theorie (VWI/MWI) zusammengefasst. „Für jede Begebenheit existiert eine Vielzahl an möglichen Folgen. Durch unsere Entscheidungen bestimmen wir welche dieser Folgen real werden. Doch in einer Theorie der Quantenmechanik (*) werden alle möglichen Folgen einer Begebenheit real, in alternierenden Quantenrealitäten/Paralleluniversen/ Welten. Also all diese Leben mit allen Fehlentscheidungen, ausgewichenen Problemen (und umgekehrt) wurden und werden gerade ebenfalls gelebt.

Die Erinnerung überlebt als
vertrautes Gefühl bevor auch sie
im Nichts verschwindet.

Ein Mann scheint am Ende zu sein. Sie sagen, er sei wie durchgebrochen. Er habe Brüche im ganzen Körper. Sein Kind steht an seinem Bett und versucht zu weinen, doch es ist noch nicht die Zeit. Das letzte Mal, als sie sich sahen, war in der Höhle seiner Wohnung vor fast einem Jahr. Es war ein Streit über den verkommenen Zustand des Mannes. Doch der Mann winkte nur ab, nahm tiefe, sehr tiefe, starke Züge in kleinen, schnellen Abfolgen von seiner Zigarette. Im Stoß des Rauches aus allen Kopföffnungen krächzte er nur, dass sei seine Sache und dass es zur Zeit nun mal eben so ist.

Nun liegt der Mann zerbrochen und verkümmert wieder im Krankenhaus. Diesmal ist es endgültig die Intensivstation. Sein geschrumpfter Körper ist ganz verrenkt, als hätte man ihn falsch zusammen gesteckt. Er röchelt durch die Schläuche und windet sich zwischendurch wie ein Wurm.

Sein Kind wusste schon damals, dass das „es zur Zeit nun mal eben so ist" nichts als ein Witz war. Der Mann hatte sich schon vor Jahren aufgegeben und keines der sieben Paradise auf Erden könnte ihn wieder auf seine dünnen Beine heben. Sein Gehirn ist kaputt und das schleichende Vergessen hat längst angefangen.

Im klinischen Neonlicht der künstlich erstarrten Zeit erkennt sein Kind zum ersten Mal wieder das Gesicht, wie es es aus seiner Kindheit kannte. In den letzten Jahren hatte sich der Mann den Bart und die Haare aus Faulheit oder Desinteresse einfach wachsen lassen. Nun im wieder freigelegten Fleisch der Gesichtszüge des Mannes finden sich nach und nach die gemeinsamen Erinnerungen wieder. Das Kind geht ganz nah heran und steigt hinab in den Atem des Mannes, um das zu finden was einmal sein Vater war. Das geliebte Wesen, auf dessen warmer Brust es immer gelegen hat, so groß und sicher wie auf einem atmenden Berg. In dessen Blick all die nur mögliche Liebe eines Vaters strahlte und für das Kind einmal den Kosmos bedeutete. Wieder versucht das Kind zu weinen wegen der wenigen Zeit, die noch bleibt im Gesicht des Mannes auf Reisen zu gehen. Auch versucht es zu weinen, weil es auf diesen Reisen nun allein ist.

Der Mann windet sich. Versucht sich unter der Last seiner Decke heraus zu drehen. Doch man hat ihn zu seiner eigenen Sicherheit festgeschnallt. Nach kurzen Versuchen gibt er wieder auf und sinkt zurück in die Tiefe seines Bettes. Das was er war, das Ich seiner eigenen Vorstellung, ist hinter die mehligen Augen eines Fisches zurückgetreten. Wo ist die Kindheit geblieben? Die Gegenwart dämmert nur noch vor sich hin, als verdorbenes Stück Fleisch mit Schläuchen und Kabeln perforiert. Die Zukunft sieht dabei ähnlich verfault aus wie die Gegenwart.

Das Kind ist wütend, dass der Mann es um ihre Zukunft betrogen hat. Selbst die Gedanken, welche für gewöhnlich frei sind durch Raum und Zeit zu reisen, sind durch die Realität des sterilen Raumes mit am Krankenbett festgebunden.

Doch das Kind kann dem Mann nicht böse sein. Zu sehr kennt es die Hintergründe. Das Kind überlegt noch ein-

88   LTTE NO. 7 — *Where No One Thought...*

mal den Mann aus dem Bett hochzureißen, um ihn mit aller wahnsinnigen Kraft durchzuschütteln, dass der Mann vielleicht doch noch einmal zu sich kommt. Zurückkehrt in die Welt der Eigenständigen. Wie bei einem dieser angeblichen Wunder, wo Leute, die schon für tot erklärt wurden, durch irgendeine dieser wundersamen, nicht erklärlichen Begebenheiten, ins Bewusstsein zurückkehren.

Das Kind des Mannes fragt nach der Ärztin. Sie erklärt ihm, dass das Herz des Mannes einen Anfall hatte und der Körper voller Gift sei. Sie wisse noch nicht wie es ins Blut gekommen sei. Die Ärztin hat gute Haut. Man möchte dran riechen. Ihre Augen sind wie buntes Glas und sie hat etwas Sportliches. Man sieht eine gewisse Muskelstruktur bis ins Gesicht. Was diese Sorte von sportlichen Typen ausmacht. Sie hat trotzdem auch etwas Zartes, etwas Vorsichtiges. Sie versteht sich offenbar gut mit einem der jungen und ebenfalls sportlichen Pfleger. Ob sie sich von ihm ficken lässt? Das Kind ist im Grunde schon ein Mann und stellt sich vor wie die Muschi der Ärztin schmecken würde. Es konnte sich gegen diesen Gedanken nicht wehren. Es ist alles ein großer Mist. Als die Ärztin wieder weg ist, versucht das Kind nun wirklich mit aller Kraft zu weinen. Für einen kurzen Augenblick verzweifelt es über diese ganze Situation. Das Weinen klappt wieder nicht. Wenn niemand da ist, um seine Trauer zu sehen und Anteil zu nehmen, wozu dann überhaupt heulen? Alleine am Krankenbett weinen. Wenn man anfängt darüber nachzudenken kommt das einem auf einmal affektiert vor. Was für ein ekelhafter Gedanke. Die klinische Kühle des kargen Raumes scheint sich nach innen auszubreiten. Kalt, hohl und verkommen. Wie kann das sein? Dann die Rettung. Ein warmer Brei. Es ist die Scham. Du warme Scham holst mich wieder zurück ins Gefühl. Was für eine Erleichterung.

Das Schämen für sich ganz allein. Die Rückkehr der Empfindsamkeit hat über die schäbige Kälte der Realität gesiegt. Das Kind ist wieder ganz nah bei dem Mann. Seine Liebe aber auch seine Traurigkeit sind wieder zurück. Vielleicht gab es gar keinen Grund sich zu schämen. Es waren nur Gedanken. Es kannte diese Gedanken schon von Beerdigungen. Sie kamen aus ihm, aber waren nicht seine. Gegen ein Gefühl von Schuld kann es sich trotzdem nicht wehren. Denn für solche Gedanken möchte man nicht mal von sich selbst erwischt werden. Diese Gedanken entstehen oft nur aus der Vorstellung heraus diesen Gedanken zu denken. Was wäre wenn man so denken würde? Vielleicht muss man verstehen oder unterscheiden, dass diese Gedanken eher wie Einfälle sind, gefangen in solchen Situationen.

Wie wenn man sich vorstellt, was wäre wenn man bei diesem Festessen das fremde Kind dort am anderen Tischende einfach aus dem Fenster schmeißen würde. Was wäre dann los? Man ist manchmal vor der eigenen Fantasie nicht sicher. Aber in Gedanken ist man eh immer viel grausamer als in Realität. Wie oft hätte man sonst diesen oder jenen schon erschossen und erschlagen. Dazu noch aus den trivialsten Gründen. Dieses Austoben in der Imagination ist wohl eine der wichtigsten Sicherheitseinrichtungen der menschlichen Psyche.

Das Kind streichelt die Hand des Mannes und küsst ihn auf die Stirn. Dann küsst es ihn noch ein zweites Mal und flüstert, dass es morgen oder übermorgen wieder kommt. In Wirklichkeit dauert es 4 Tage.

Time-Trivials

Steve Paul

A Feeling for the Moment

An android serving the United Federation of Planets attempts to grasp the concept of the relative perception of time. For him, time exists as a uniform constant, regulated by his internal chronometer. A more competent form of an internal clock. So, time for an android always runs the same and is unaffected by moods, emotions, distractions or attention. Unlike the human whose perception is entirely influenced by factors such as their feelings, moods, etc.; interferences that cause time to run relatively.

One refers to a human having an internal clock, but it is a product of the cycles of an internal biological process. In comparison to the technical variant, it is much more prone to inaccuracies. In the mental time travel of the android through the moments of its life—which it can recall in impressive detail—is denied the ability to judge the extraordinariness of these moments by feeling and a specialized perception of time. Its lack of emotion prevents it from differentiating its experiences on the basis of feeling: That night of hot love ended much too quickly, or, the pain in my legs was endless. But the android has evolved over time to acquire new algorithms, which can determine the value of an experience. The

Childlike Architectures of Fantasy

To stay within the tradition, Anna S. is referred to by name in the texts, an excerpt of the conversation:

Anna: *It doesn't have to be about time travel.*

Steve: *But why not?*

Traveling through time always strikes me as being longings of dreamers and fantasists. A magical idea, to exist in your own ideal imagination or simply experience adventure. The ability to visit forgotten places or events of the past with knowledge of the future. To rectify earlier mistakes, strangle Hitler directly in his crib or to secretly envision base thoughts about taking advantage.

Like in the story about Biff Tannen, The luckiest Charm on Earth, who gives his younger self in the past a sports chronicle containing all of the betting results over the next 50 years, and becomes the richest and most powerful man in the world.

Visits to the future is on the other hand dominated by the ideas of the present. Have the utopias and prophesied catastrophes come true?

My favorite was always the journey into the exaggerated future, in 10, 20 or 100,000 years. This abstract place, where the image of science fiction often reverts back to medieval concepts. Often in the most degenerate and depraved societies, embedded in super-technologies. As if humanity in the distant future couldn't free themselves from the morass of their own abyss. I prefer to grant my sympathies with Gene Roddenberry's LSD idea of a more humane, tolerant and

92   LTTE NO. 7 — *Where No One Thought...*

'learning from the horrors of the past' kind of future. Even though these stories only bob up and down or start in the next 3-4 centuries, they serve too much as a mirror of the present. Leaving this reflection behind, the exaggerated journey into the future through its abstract overvoltage seems more interesting to me. Given the possibility that the programmable time period is unlimited, I would definitely throw a glance at a million or billion etc. years in the future. Completely out of curiosity, for a little preview, because I cannot wait. Unfortunately, it has nothing to do with impatience. Since you couldn't want so long, even if you wanted to.

A favored cliché of traveling into the past would probably be the idea of automatically and directly taking part in important historical events. Not only in an exact moment, but also in the self-evident access to the exclusive circles and groups, who trigger the events. In the cinematic ideal, one becomes the essential component of history.

Through a journey through time, an idea that has since proved to be invalid, but could be at least derailed.

I used to think that if you live with attentiveness and awareness during certain life situations, to try to downright exploit the potential of reality, these moments would be kept better and in more complex ways in memory. But at some point you realize that with time these memories shrivel up into small pieces of shit. Then at least by time travel you could experience these moments again, differently and intensively, with all of the reflections that came later. Reflection is a tricky matter, in that they can lead to another utopia. If you had decided on certain things differently, reacted in certain situations differently, life would have gone certainly better or so we often fantasize in hindsight.

Which then leads to a final thought experiment.

That the other decisions were decided on well and that life has run better. At least in the short term in this particular situation. Then this better life is certainly not spared by other, new problems and mistakes. Even when they had been also bypassed again in another life, etc., etc. From the start, the android has summarized everything much more precisely my means of a theory (VWI/MWI), "For every event there is a wide range of possible consequences. Through our choices we decide which of these consequences become real. But in a theory of quantum mechanics(*) all potential consequences of an event become real in alternating quantum realities/parallel universes/worlds. So all of these lives along with their mistakes, and evaded problems (and vice versa) have been and are currently being lived.

Memory Survives as a Familiar Feeling
Before She/It Disappears into Nothingness

A man appears to be at his end. They say he is as if broken through. He has fractures throughout his whole body.

His child stands at his bedside and tries to cry, but it is not yet time. The last time they saw each other, it had been in the cave he called home almost a year ago. They had argued over the degenerate state of the man. But the man just waved him away, took deep, very deep, strong drags in small quick intervals from his cigarette. In a blast of smoke exiting every orifice he cawed, that it was his thing and that for now, it is the way it is.

Now the man lies broken and atrophied again in the hospital. This time it's the final intensive station. His shrunken body is all contorted, as if someone had put him together wrong. He gasps through hoses and writhes in between them like a worm.

His child knew back then already, that the "for now, it is the way it is" was nothing but a joke. The man had given up years ago and none of the seven paradises on earth could lift him on to his thin legs. His brain is broken and creeping forgetfulness had started long ago.

In the clinical neon light of artificially frozen time, his child recognizes the face that he had known as a child once more. In the past years the man had let his beard and hair grow out of indifference. In the re-exposed meat of the man's face, common memories revealed themselves. The child comes very close and descends into the breath of the man to find what his father had once been.

The beloved creature, on whose warm breast the child always laid upon, so large and safe like on top of a breathing mountain. In whose gaze beamed with all the love possible, which to the child had once meant the universe.

Again the child tries to cry because there remains little time in the man's face to travel. Also because the child is now alone on the journey.

The man twists. Tries to wrench himself from the weight of his blanket. But for his own safety he's been strapped down. After brief attempt he gives up again and sinks back into the depths of his bed. What he was, that I of his own imagination, stepped back behind the mealy eyes of a fish. Where has childhood gone? The present dawns only to himself, like a rotten piece of meat perforated with tubes and cables. The future looks as rotten as the present.

The child is livid that the man swindled their future. Even thoughts that are normally free to travel space and time are tied to the hospital bed by the sterile room. But the child cannot be angry at the man. The child knows the reason for things too well. Thinks again about tearing the man from his bed, to shake him with frenzied force, so that maybe the man would return to himself. Return to the world of the autonomous. Like in one of those alleged miracles, where people who've been declared dead, by some wonder, inexplicable incident, regain consciousness.

The man's child asks for the doctor. She explains to him that the man's heart had an attack and that his body was full of poison. They didn't know yet how the poison had gotten into the blood. The doctor had good skin. You want to smell it. Her eyes are like colorful glass and there's something sporty about her. You can see a bit of musculature in her face, which constitutes these sporty types. But she has something tender, something careful. She evidently gets along with the younger and equally sporty nurse. Does she let him fuck her? The child is basically already a man. He imagines what the doctor's pussy would taste like. He can't avoid thinking about it. Everything is a big shit. When the doctor leaves again, the child tries with all of his strength to cry. Crying doesn't work. When no one is there to see and share your sadness, then what's the point in wailing? Crying alone in a hospital bed. When you start thinking about it, it becomes affected. What a disgusting thought. The clinical coolness of the barren room seems to move inwards. Cold, hollow and depraved. How can this be? Then the rescue. A warm porridge. It's shame. You warm shame, bring me back into feeling. What a relief. Ashamed for oneself alone. The restoration of sensitivity has triumphed over shabby cold reality. The child is again close to the man. Love and sadness have returned. Maybe there hadn't been a reason to be ashamed. They were just thoughts. The child already knew those kinds of thoughts from funerals. They came from the child, but were not of the child, and nevertheless, was defenseless against the feeling of guilt. After all, you don't want to be caught with these kind of thoughts, not even by yourself. Often those kind of thoughts arise solely by the idea of thinking them. What if someone thought that? Maybe you need to understand or differentiate that those kind of thoughts are more like incidences trapped in certain situations.

Like when imagining, what would happen if at a banquet dinner you threw some kid sitting at the other end of the table out the window. What would happen? Sometimes you're not safe from your own fantasies. But in your mind you're much crueler than in reality. Otherwise, how many times would you have already shot or punched this or that person. For the most trivial reasons, no doubt. This release in the imagination is probably one of the most important safety features of the human psyche.

The child caresses the man's hand and kisses him on the forehead. Then kisses him a second time and whispers that the child will be back the next day or the day after that. In reality, it takes 4 days.

Advertisement

Join us in the not so distant future for the launch of the
Letters to the Editors book
March 30, 2016, 6-10PM | *Ashley* Berlin*, Oranienstrasse 37, 10999
with select readings from contributing authors!

Contributing authors: Ayami Awazuhara, Salvador Bautista, Aleksandra Bielas, Ilaria Biotti, Maggie Boyd, Mariana Castillo Deball, Santiago da Silva, Michele Di Menna, Kasia Fudakowski, Eva Funk, Florian Goldmann et al., Blanca Gomila, Anna Herms, Rodrigo Hernández, Valentina Jager, Tiziana La Melia, Maryse Larivière, Steve Paul, Barbara Plater-Szaflarski, Natalie Porter, Post Brothers, Ayumi Rahn, Stephen Remus, Malte Roloff, Gabriel Rosas Alemán, Manuel Saiz, Max Stocklosa, Peter Szaflarski, Stanislaw Szaflarski, Peter Wächtler, Till Wittwer, and Jacob Wren.

* Part of "Intercalating the Drift", an exhibition series curated by Kate Brown and Lauryn Youden, including overlapping exhibitions from Mirak Jamal, George Rippon and Michele Di Menna. [other-projects.com]

LTTE no. 8 — *Nyma Graphia Cifra*
January 17, 2015

Where Is My Beginning?
Where Is My End?

Anna M. Szaflarski

The universe was a ball of tightly bound knots, and reality was made up of the continual expansion of that mass; an untangling and re-tangling mess. Just a complete mess. When the knots came tumbling out of that tightly wound ball, some strands looked for ways to attach themselves to others, not yet ready for life outside of the comfortable cuddle. They made patterns and surfaces, covered things and made themselves, some would say, even useful. Other strands got tangled in themselves, without being asked or pressed just wrapped themselves around. Each knot became a word, an idea, and soon made sounds and even had voices. Two or more strands together in a knot was considered a consensus, a dialogue, or an intervention. And they never wanted to come undone, they got tighter and tighter as they pulled in opposite directions by distant relative strands.

The original ball of knots was the navel of the earth. Inside of it was all the slack in the world and all of the tension that made bowline, slip, true lover's and noose knots. All the meaning of the universe, life, death, love, was wrapped up tightly together like a can of worms. The outside of ball was kept together by a series of tight square knots. The square knot is also known as the strong Hercules' Knot. It's when two strands meet, twist around each other once, turn around twist around each other again, and go on their way in the direction they had come. The first pass is an encounter, the second is an assessment: where did the other come from, what is it made of, what's that tension inside of it? And without a complete answer and partially perplexed, they go on, but the bind remains, always rubbing the encounter gently, informing the next knot they make.

These encounters and questions are what initially kept the ball together. But the outside strands of the square knot were of the impatient type. Each unanswered questions sent them looking for the next to intertwine with, making the ball tighter and tighter. You wonder, might it all only be one very long strand? Perhaps so blinded by their own impatience, they didn't recognize that the mysterious other might be a distant part of themselves.

Meanwhile, inside there were all sorts of combinations of knots that preferred to stay intertwined for longer periods. They weaved large carpets, going back and forth along each other, asking the same unanswered questions again and again thousands of times over. Their questions were answers enough. The outside became tighter and tighter, while the consensus inside became denser and denser and eventually, somewhere, a strand snapped, and the ball came apart.

Do you know what happens when you put a rope loosely into a bag, and let it sit for a time on the top of your shelf? Behind the curtain of privacy, the rope will twist and turn restlessly until it has entangled itself. Even when alone the string goes on asking questions. And when you pull it out, it's done nothing to answered them. It too is perplexed. And lets say you introduce another string to accompany the first and place the bag back onto the same shelf. They will twist and turn, and be a whole mess when you retrieve them and try to pull them apart.

Well when the ball exploded and the consensus came apart and all of the encounters came loose, there was something, nevertheless, imprinted on the suddenly speechless and silent string. The feeling of the writhing mass didn't disappear, and when given the chance the string began to writhe even though there wasn't anyone to writhe against.

If the navel of the earth, was in fact only one string, an endless loop, its explosion left it with two loose ends. Most parts of the string are glad enough with any other part, they enjoy spiralling or braiding conversations with any other string segment that comes along, but the ends are particularly aware that they are part of a greater whole; that it has lost something greater. The end is searching for its beginning. It doesn't spend much time intertwining with other parts, instead crisscrosses the universe in search for its continuation. The snapped string always asks the same questions, over and over again. *Where is my beginning?* And its beginning is searching just as emphatically, asking, *Where is my end?*

This is the painful love story, that keeps the universe from collapsing completely. If the string was satisfied to be a straight line, to leave its hands out in the cold instead of tucking them back inside, the end and beginning would pull tightly away from each other. Eventually no knots would exist, and the universe would become a straight line making no sounds. The end and the beginning are being constantly thrown off

102   LTTE NO. 8 — *Nyma Graphia Cifra*

course while other parts are fighting for more slack to make meaning through complex webs, hammocks, angler's knots and cowboy's lassoes. But eventually, I imagine, they will find each other again. Such determination can't be doubted.

The Invisible Red Man

Ayami Awazuhara

As the title says, he is invisible, we can't see him. So I didn't know how old he was, how tall he was, and what he was looking at exactly. If he stood with crossed arms or sat on a dusty red stone in front of me. But in the direction from where I heard his voice, I saw an orange small soft feather floating and rotating without wind.

"I have travelled throughout the world and made maps," The invisible red man said.

"Was it your work, to make maps?"

"It was more of a hobby than a job, I would say. I was a busy man, but I tried to make maps when I had time."

The air was dry and there were only quiet plants with heavy leaves around. He didn't speak loudly but we were the only ones that made any noise. So his voice reached my ears without losing any sense. Based on his voice, I imagined what he could look like.

"I learned how to see things by making maps. When you make maps, you have to see your surroundings very carefully. You have to walk on your feet, you can't cheat yourself, because the paths you take will become the lines on your maps," he explained. "Now, I'm making a map of the world scale one-to-one. This is my newest project. For example, look at this…" And with that he took out a small box from his bag

LTTE no. 8 — *Nyma Graphia Cifra* 105

and opened it onto a table. "Look here, this is a map of this table."

It was a traced line of the table.

"It is not called a map, and also a one-to-one map does not fit just anywhere. It is unnecessary and impossible," I noted. I heard him laughing.

"Have you heard of the story about Columbus's problem with his crew? As some say that the crew nearly mutinied because they regarded the Earth to be a flat disc, and feared they might sail off its edge. But it was actually the reverse," he seemed rather excited about telling this particular adventure story. "They believed that the Earth was a ball, and knew that if they were to go over the edge they would slip and would not be able to get back. Columbus had to put them in irons and beat them until he convinced them that they weren't going over any curve, and that they would be able to return to their families soon."

I felt somehow that the invisible red man was staring at me.

"So, do you still believe that the Earth is round?" he questioned me. "It's a nice story from yesterday."

"Anyways," he interrupted me before I could answer. "May I continue?"

"Yes, sure."

He began with, "It was the age of white. I used to be white."

"Were you also an invisible white man?" I wondered.

"No, well maybe for some people, yes, but I was much more white than invisible. The emptiness of color is not same as the absence of color, if you follow my drift.

"At that time, I was in a city where the word 'color' doesn't mean only things like red, blue, green, yellow or whatever we use to describe a spectrum that is sent from the surface of an object to the brain as a signal, but also means 'love'. If you get

106 LTTE NO. 8 — *Nyma Graphia Cifra*

attentions and affections, you are a colorful man. If you are meeting someone particular, you are living a colorful life! It all makes perfect sense, doesn't it?"

"Yes, it makes sense," I agreed.

"The streets in that city are very tight and geometrical, like a chessboard. The houses are made of wood, which at first do not seem large, but after entering you can see that they are long. And colorful people live in them. That was very practical for me. Colorful people wanted to be with me. I was like the sun-bleached-brown-wood of their architecture, and would make them even more colorful in contrast. The emptiness of color has much potential. I could fit anywhere. As a white man, I fit in everywhere and it was perfect for me to do business there," he sighed. He seemed to be dreaming of the good times of the past.

"Well, before I started making maps, I had never travelled. I was in my hometown my whole life up 'till then. I had never thought of leaving there, but I was also very young, ambitious and brazen. That was my age of green. I was in the city that was covered with water. The city consisted of islands floating like boats. There were many bridges of black volcanic stone and blue birds flying overhead…

"An infinite number of raindrops makes a river. One will be two and two will be three. And rivers gather together and will become an ocean. So, three will be four and four will be five. Can you think in reverse? Where five can be four and two can be one? How many raindrops can you imagine in your head? The concept of number is such a fragile thing. Why is not possible to count water? Because there is no beginning nor end. It's a closed circuit."

Before the night rolled in, the amber colors of twilight warmed the sky. We (or so I thought we were doing so together) were looking at the setting sun that was lowering gradually behind the mountain. The sun moved faster than had I remembered and it made me think of the Earth's rotation. When the sun disappeared, it got suddenly cold. I felt the wind blowing from the north.

"Can you see me in green? What do you think about that color?" The invisible red man broke the silence.

"I like green. I like to be surrounded by green."

"Green needs a lot of water like us. Green is exactly like us. It wants to go up further and further until it touches the sky. But don't forget, when there are too many greens, we are already dead. There will be only ruins.

"The city has changed," his voice was not directed to me. He seemed to be still looking at the mountain where the sun had set. "Now there is no water left in my hometown. It means that there is less green than before. The black bridges look like thirsty lizards. Old maps lost their meaning and we could not use them to orientate ourselves anymore. So we had to make a new map using new techniques. I needed to learn, they told me. So I had to go."

Image on next page: "The Invisible Red Man", Ayami Awazuhara, 2015

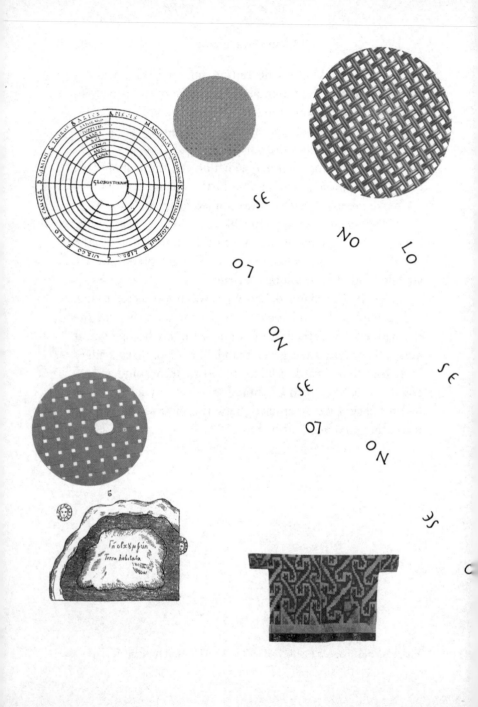

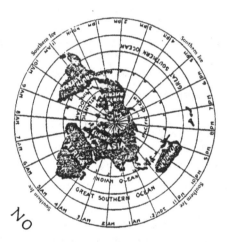

Make Space, Find Time

Valentina Jager

I.

The world of U is quite a singular one.

The State in the world of U is administered, organized and ruled by a sort of assembly chosen by *the* man. This assembly, chosen by *the* man at the beginning of the 18th century, consisted in those early times of 11 human members—just like a football team, excluding its substitutes—and had the purpose of preserving the integrity of its letter citizens with the most "propriety, elegance and purity," as stated by law.

After well-known conquests, the State spread to a considerable part of the South, Middle and North Americas, and the world of U found fertile ground for flourishing. It adapted itself and transformed slightly throughout each region. Although the geographical features are diverse enough, this hasn't encouraged a free development of U's society. The government of *the* man, carried out by its assembly, constrained the entire society of U to an established structure, which condemned it to a fixed situation that would be changed occasionally by the assembly.

Although the use and the organization between individuals and between groups has been assumed to have no hierarchy at all, and the arrangement between them is supposed

LTTE no. 8 — *Nyma Graphia Cifra*

to be left to the free will. Yet, this apparatus is far from being one without casts. Knowledge is dependent either on heredity or the learning and teaching of the norms. This system is, as one can immediately see, far from anarchy. Even when in some cases it is the man itself who disrupts the structure and alters it, it is of common knowledge that he has conceived this frame previous to the arrival of its inhabitants.

Despite the fact that in recent years all panegyric discourses of the assembly have been transformed in order to serve the needs of its citizens—without breaking the essential unity of the kingdom—any disruption to the established regulations is still seen as bad manners, or even worse, as lack of education. It is important to note here, that even with the arrival of democracy to U's world, the assembly continues to bear the title of *Royal Academy*. Popular opinion suggests a name change to *Democratic Academy of the Spanish Language*, which should also transform simultaneously its structure. This suggestion still remains in passive status.

Given these conditions, it is surprising that some comrades have decided to be stubborn throughout the history of the Spanish language and defend their place at all costs during the arrival and establishment of the pan-Hispanic linguistic politics. This is the case with X, who has served as a bridge between worlds and is a perfect example of a letter in resistance. But the history of X deserves a text of its own.

In the world of U just a few fellows manage to have a meaning of their own. 27 letters constitute the entire world of U. U being one of these. Most of them need to be accompanied by others to make sense or to have meaning. They need a partner, or a crew, or a family to accompany them. Hermits are rarely found and are also not so well seen. This most likely depends on where these characters reside, but as this U lives in a Spanish speaking country, we will focus mostly on the inhabitants of this land; the 27 as before mentioned. A, E, O, X and Y, are some community members that are often seen hanging around on their own; in the park, on the street corner, trying to fix or split up some couples... U is also one of these rebels.

Apart from being a rebel, U is relatively shy. His introverted character has developed a special sense of imagination and a great sensitivity for himself and other beings — or as U likes to call them, other worlds. Unfortunately, introversion has also brought some disadvantages. Whenever a Q or G accompanies U, U feels oppressed. The roundness of them and their closed—or almost closed—lines, makes him feel incomplete; as if the open end would be a constant sign of his incompletion. Next to them, U falls mute. Experts cannot tell exactly when it was that U decided to take action concerning this situation, but most probably it was during one of U's mind wanderings that opened a hole between his world and another one. What happened though, was that on his way back to consciousness, U left another hole in the paper. This happens every time, when sawing for example, the needle needs two holes for its journey, one backward and one forward. Can we tell that the thread went in and out if a needle comes and goes through the same gap?

In none of the former annals has it been mentioned that a member of the world of U would carry two holes with itself. It is indeed a matter of concern how anybody, either from the world U—or any other world of the Newtonian Space-Time Continuum, for that matter—could carry holes at all, as holes are not commonly conceived as a three dimensional *objects*. This brought up to the table the possibility that U could actually be carrying two black holes above its head! In his introversion, U hasn't even yet noticed the great scientific discovery that surrounds him. For U, these small dots on top are simply to be used as crutches to stand next to his colleagues, Q and G.

The discovery of this passageway and its further research is of interest to both scholars and amateurs, as it might show the threshold to another — yet unknown — dimension...

II.

About love, intrigue and something more...
Containers, wrapping, ribbons and something more...
Latin dance and something more...
Particles, bodies, gravity and something more...
(...)

III.

A short reflection on the usage
of two punctuation marks

We are told that in written language, the opening interrogation and exclamation marks are characteristic to the Spanish language and are not to be omitted or imitate other languages that use only the closing mark. Quite inconvenient it is! You might realize after a couple of times of using them, that this rule leaves a very short space for doubt and second-guessing. One must already know beforehand when it is that a question will begin — much before the first letter is to be expressed! That also goes for exclamations and any such sign of excitement. The writer — not specifically a professional one, but any person who writes in Spanish — shall formulate a sen-

114   LTTE no. 8 — *Nyma Graphia Cifra*

tence or group of words in his or her head, then proceed to think about the emotional content it might have, be cautious of its alternative connotations, choose the appropriate mark, and then write it down. After this procedure, the rest of the letters and words may follow, without forgetting to give them some closure.

When the words and letters in between are omitted, the interrogation or exclamation might look something like this: ¿? ¡! There is a space between the two characters that suggests that something is missing. Is it possible to make space for existential hesitation when everything is supposed to have a beginning and an end? How is uncertainty supposed to fit in such a tight space?

LTTE no. 9 — *Correspondence*
January 29, 2015

With all earned
and due respect, No.

Anna M. Szaflarski

Dear Applicant,

First off, we would like to thank YOU for realizing how amazing our program is, which has been appropriately reflected by the amount of applicants who have sent their work for review this year. It exceeded even our wildest dreams. And thank you for supporting it through your generous yet mandatory application fee, that so many others have also paid. For pure entertainment our accountant sat in front of his screen watching the amount of money rise minutes before the application deadline. As stated in our mandate, our organization is horizontally structured, everyone's happiness is important, even the accountant's, and YOUR happiness is also a very important.

The quality of the work submitted for review this season was of the highest kind, which has made the selection process for our committee very, very, very difficult.

116   LTTE NO. 9 — *Correspondence*

Before announcing the result, we would like to inform you that we have reached our multicultural quota. Yes, there have been applicants from all over the world, including remote islands such as Guadaloupe, Mingingo, and Liouciou. And the diversity of educational backgrounds of applicants is so vast that the process has even opened our eyes to new degrees, for example, one that combined a dance doctorate with kindergarten, and chakra sensing. The assortment of documented portfolio items has been also very interesting, not to mention the few animal carcasses that we have received from previous applicants.Very interesting indeed, but please note, we do not except hard copies, only portfolios in cd-rom format (max. 700 MB).

The poorly paid individual we hire to load your portfolio images onto the projector, and arrange the cookies for each of our several coffee breaks has been well compensated instead by the rapid growth of his arm muscles that he has accumulated from bringing photocopied versions of your online application forms to our round table. If you are one of those unfortunate applicants, which has filled out the form incorrectly, we cannot notify you of it, but need to be clear that your application was automatically and without hesitation tossed into the paper shredder. But fret not! In this case, you have also contributed to the expansion of an amazing project. The paper from the shredder is being used by a current resident to build a remarkable sculpture, titled, "eternal disappointment" and will be, without a doubt, a hit. It is projects like this one that gets us very excited, as they are conceptual, sensual, cynical, intellectual and above all indescribably *real*. We feel that you can feel it too!

Let us take this opportunity to share with you a bit of our selection process that was carefully comprised from a hodgepodge of techniques, including séances, dice throwing, tea cup readings as well as referring to our grandmothers' tastes and opinions. Some mornings we selected applicants based on the number of vowels in their names, other afternoons we would throw sand in our eyes and choose those images that were most bearable to look at. We discussed discourse, relevance, Simpson's episodes and jokes regarding involuntary bodily functions. We tried several different mood and perception inducing substances. The whole selection process took an extended and unexpected period of three months, and could have been described as something between a rave and prenatal class. Yes, that's how we the jury would like to describe it.

The expertise of the members of the jury ranged like the aromas of a Skittle bag. Different colours but basically the same taste! Oh, but when you dump them all in your mouth at the same time, *what an intoxicating flavour*!

We took turns getting grumpy and embodying the Prima Donna. We would refer to our own accomplishments and expectations, fluctuating between elevated feelings of self-importance, sincere enthusiasm and utter apathy. It was a cleansing opportunity for us all. Psychoanalytically we found our mothers in the finer lines of your drawings, and our bodily insecurities in your video art. Upon leaving, we felt that we knew each other and ourselves much better, and even found a few clever solutions for our own work.

I regret to inform you however that we have selected other applicants than yourself. Don't write us asking why, because it would be too difficult to trace what exactly we were on when we made the decision, so just accept it, and we recommend that you move on. We hope that you didn't plan your life too much around the hypothetical chance that you might

118 LTTE no. 9 — *Correspondence*

get this, or tell too many of your friends about the fact that you applied.

We highly encourage you to apply next year. There will be a whole new bag of experts to throw a glance at your portfolio, and you might just catch them in a good moment. Please do not interpret this the wrong way, that we felt that your work was not worthwhile or of unsatisfying quality, it could have been the case, but we honestly can't remember.

Dear Applicant, let me talk to you now tenderly and let us pretend that I know of the name that your mother calls you. I have some advice for you.

Instead of wallowing in shame and disappointment, I suggest that you adopt a sense of accomplishment. I am sure you are working really very hard. It's easy for me to write this, as I do not know you at all, but I like you, you are a very nice person and in the off chance we might meet somewhere, I'd like to have a beer with you and share laughs with you.

You're right in thinking that I genuinely have no problem writing these rejection letters, as I only have to write it once (written mostly by my assistant) and if you haven't already suspected, send the same letter to thousands of sorry applicants. But contrary to popular belief I do not enjoy doing so, and I hope that you will blindly take faith and like me too.

I'm a bit misty now.
Take care of yourself dearest Applicant,

Hogart Gerald Brufnofsky
Committee Head
Institution of Complex Studies of the Ambiguous Arts

Still from the *Simpsons* Season 4, Episode 15 "I Love Lisa" found on www.buzzfeed.com under the title
20 "Simpsons" Moments That Made You Cry

situación.1

Salvador Bautista

Voy caminando desnudo en la calle…
con las manos atadas a un punto ciego,
apretando los dientes para no dejar salir el viento.

I am going walking…
naked in the street with hands tied to a blind spot,
grinding my teeth to keep out the wind.

Anna might become a writer: an introduction

Santiago da Silva

Maybe four months ago
a poem appeared in my notebook
"Anna might become a writer"
and it's been laying there ever since.
So I thought to write these
introductory lines
to make up
or make something up.
Smart or arrogant or insecure or shy?
I won't even transcribe the poem anymore,
but only its introduction,
and the poem will probably never exist.
Truth is, Anna,
the poem wasn't that good
or good
at all.
But there is a poem Anna promise
it's true because
this is an introduction to it
the introduction to a poem.

114 LTTE no. 9 — *Correspondence*

. . .

The other day someone told me
my English was "flawless"
As a writer, what do you think of this word, Anna?
flawless
It sounds very good I think,
like pronouncing it
soothes an itch
on your palate.

Maybe you thought about this
because you do enjoy talking, the act of it.
We've shared some joyful times doing so,
talking beyond communicative purposes.
I mean making funny accents
and inventing annoyed characters
who talk and talk
not saying something.

. . .

Well, I guess I spoiled it.
I already told you
you are a writer, and I meant to keep that
for the end of my introduction.
Just one interruption,
I wanted to say:
Remember to weave
and sculpt and to draw!

Santiago da Silva

. . .

Anna, you are in Mexico!
Did you know that there is only
four edible species of chilli
in the whole world?
Every known variation of chilli in this world
depends on the place where it grows.
This means the earth in Oaxaca and Guntur
make things grow and taste differently.
I hope your airplane on the way back home
leaves during the night time
then you will see
how beautiful!

. . .

To come to a conclusion Anna
What do you think, as a writer, of all this?
How full of accidents it is to be a writer.
Do you agree?

LTTE no. 10 — *Question of Perspective*
February 18, 2015

Right smack in the middle of it.

Anna M. Szaflarski

You've done something wrong. It was a mistake. You knew it was a mistake when you did it. You did it anyways. And it pains you to think about it.

It was bigger than not dividing your trash, it was smaller than murder. It was worse than not putting the toilet seat down, it was not as bad as shoplifting. It was more lousy than lying about liking something you didn't like, but significantly better than lying to the law. It was like bending the truth for the sake of an innocent child about something it wouldn't understand anyways. But not really, not exactly.

Somewhere between swiftly kicking a dog and insider trading you did something that you know you shouldn't have. But now it's done. A timid and uncertain inner advocate offers his assistance: maybe there was no other option. Maybe your sin saved someone else from having to make hard decisions. Maybe you are a martyr. *Maybe you are even a hero?*

That's not helping much. Regardless of how you spin it, somewhere above your belly button things are contracting at a slow and steady rate. The intestinal witch-hunt is on, and someplace below your forehead and above your toes there are pancakes flipping frantically above an uncontrollable fire.

You are hungry. That is confusing. The morally injected emotions are being seasoned with competing corporeal reflexes of survival. They are so similar, and difficult to divide! I suggest before you get all worked up, eat something hearty, rich and full of soul, before returning to the moral examination of your dark innards.

While chewing down a ham sandwich you consider your situation carefully. If no one knew, then maybe it wouldn't be so bad. If it were possible to stow it away aboard a sea bound boat, and send it into uncharted and unobserved oceans where moral codes haven't yet been written, and local ones couldn't be easily decoded by westerners, the heavy clouds of blame could be out-sailed.

As you all too quickly try to swallow a half chewed lump of meat and mustard, you realize that a spot that lies somewhere between the collar bone and the diaphragm is being tugged on and must be intrinsically linked to the nose of your most holiest of grandmothers, who no longer walks on this earth but instead sits on top of your head, which makes her very difficult to shake. And at this very moment that nose, along with its head is rattling in severe disapproval. The hardness of your ribs are her hardened lips, as she says nothing but projects a massacre of chagrin.

Somebody amongst the breathing knows about it, and they're not all too happy either. They left you letters that could blind, and chatter atrociously about you to those, who might not be all that invested, but are still enthusiastic witnesses to the impressive display of words that wear hideous monster masks, dance and whisper your name in damning fashions to heeding angels.

You are doomed.

Perhaps for the time being, sometime between now and your eventual death it would be better to accept yourself as despicable. Not as penance, but as rest. To apologize now and try to right your wrongs would only bring on exhausting demand for explanation. Let the pig sty mud envelope you completely, and know that when you are this bad, no one expects anything good from you. So relax.

Take a note from the confusing moral allegory of Jonah, who they say tried to escape the wrath of god and was, in turn, gobbled down by a gigantic whale. Even then he did not repent! He stayed in the bellows of the beast and used his punishment as some sort of rehab clinic or sanctuary found in the admittance of his evil.

So, now that you're resting comfortably and your appetite is satisfied, you can start thinking about your new evil persona. What kind of sick hobbies will you commence? I suggest instead of torturing small animals, choose something less obvious like building houses out of playing cards, or cultivating bonsai trees. Something that could be easily misinterpreted as both an innocent past time and a maniacal need to control something.

There are plenty of role models, so bring to mind a selection of your most favorite hero counterparts; the arch-enemies and nemeses. You notice how they are always better dressed, their houses seem like luxurious places and they have fantastic ambitions of world domination that include not altogether rational but extensively stylish and elaborate multi-step

execution plans. On the other hand, however, they don't seem to have better sense than to surround themselves with anybody but incompetent henchmen, they don't care much about getting fresh air or sunlight into their lairs of damnation, and although they do seem to live with clear purpose, at some point, especially in more modern renditions of old stories, their simple persona is sabotaged by the revealing of a scarring childhood occurrence, which we are led to believe is the true source of their evil. Well, you'll need to reform that part.

The villain as unloved child quickly transforms into a victim, and your eyes begin to water a bit with empathy while imagining Dr. Claw, The Predator, Khan, Magneto, Cat Woman, Hannibal Lecter, HAL 9000 and yourself at group therapy all manoeuvring a group hug. You are having difficulty navigating around the individual bodily eccentricities ranging from metal arms, metal heads, claws, no body at all, to a uncontrollable desire to kill. After the hug you sit and each begins a long explanation of how good intentions just got away from them. How they've truly come to know the meaning of misunderstanding. They talk shop about their outfit decisions, stylistic choices, and how it is not OK to stop caring about how you look even after you've become evil, and sometimes that looking good is enough to get through the day.

After a long day of compassionate sharing, the group turns to you. Predator has returned from the bathroom, where he felt more comfortable to sob his green heart out, settled back into his seat and nods to you encouragingly that you should begin. You look down at your blue jeans, and two regular hands, and struggle to find an impressive story about early disappointment. You stutter, and think that maybe it's best

130   LTTE no. 10 — *Question of Perspective*

to start with the results of your evilness than its impetus. Anecdotes aren't coming naturally however, and Cat Woman begins to anxiously tear the upholstery off her arm chair. This in turn irritates Hannibal's schizophrenic sensibilities, who is quickly sedated by HAL 9000's voice. Magneto finds this irritatingly patronizing and starts warping the computer's wiring with his mind. Before you know it, chaos explodes and everybody is at each other's throats. Predator is still holding a handful of tissues when he starts laser-ing the heck out of the place, and even though you try your best to get out of the way, its no use. Wrong place, wrong time. You're dead.

You didn't make it to heaven. Somewhere better than 6 feet under and worse than the kingdom hereafter, you are exactly where you deserve to be.

More World Material:
Dumber Than A Rock
But Smarter Than A Diamond

Max Stocklosa

Like in a cartoon; everything behaves on the same ontological field. A rock, a drawn rock and a rendered rock sit next to each other.

> What can we do with this ever growing screened world? How can its quality be measured? Where can we collect evidence of its materiality? The natural resources, which quietly dive into a green screened tablet the size of the equator.

> We will never touch the material in front of us. We slip right through it, as if we had already breached the limit of bodies.

> If we can force the texture of our real world on to the screen, won't we then finally understand its material behavior? A smart wall might still hurt us the same way a brick wall would, should we bump into it… navigate yourself until you hit the rendered curtain, this is the place where we might be able to meet the entanglement, the slit of equality.

> What are contour lines… it's nothing specific. Believe it or not, it is not true that every object has a line around it! There is no such line. The access is blocked. We live among the

132   LTTE NO. 10 — *Question of Perspective*

already inaccessible (real)! This is why physics are seemingly forced to explain one marvel with another, and that one with yet a third. And we wonder why every footage looks alike, why it is so hard to compare. The images don't know either. We try to find images that are less deceptive. They...should act like as what they are.

> Look, again, you stand at the Hudson River, you automatically focus your lens on the simulation. You recalibrate backwards. You get dizzy from the feeling that this body of water and the scenery in the background are not what they seem. We've already been here and done that. This is the city where everyone exists at the same time. We learned your breath, odor and sound long before we encountered your limitless body. Your images have produced and warped you more into reality then the feel of touch of some landmark-brick-bridge ever could.

> The trouble is that something physical is present but never appears. We only know of their presence, because they affect our (measuring) instruments in certain ways. Ask the Membrane: the Membrane is the master, it is the illuminated screen. It is the only selfie that a digital entity can possess. If you smash it, you will be blind and lose your senses—the Membrane is your sensual tool, it enables you to see—it is also, of course, the gate and the gate keeper between the physical and non physical entities. All objects in this room can exist only because of her.

> How can I cope with the material vagueness of rendered stones, ghostly digital particles or supercomputer simulations of astrophysical behaviors? And what is happening

when these seemingly absent but profoundly real simulations refuse any ontological pattern, once you have pulled the electricity cord out of its socket? What does this mean for the composite conditions and relations of material elements and bodies; particles and molecules, light rays and grainy bits? If the simulative gesture of the digital will merge fully into the concept of the physical world, it might ultimately be on the verge to offer a new space for a material reality. Deep time-media-minerals, eventually.

> A simulation machinery, that is based on algorithms, protocols, data, infrastructures, technologies and concepts of calculus, which process a parallel universe of the sensual world. Just like the never ending hunt for the smallest particle in physics — which has long escaped the world of the human senses — so is the effort to construct the perfect simulation of the natural world, (re)creating a world of its own that is seemingly outside the boundaries of the sensual. A projection of data structures onto our material reality, one that is produced under the conditions of technical performativity.

> Humans are home to the odorous, the flavorsome or the tactile, nevertheless, they have established a world without any of these sensualities; a world of artificial deaths via blackouts and severe info-pollution. Paradoxically, these digital versions are supposed to bring the material world closer to the human and subsequently make sense of the world and untangle it. Contrary to the intention of these simulations, they are even more fey then what we usually encounter on the other side of the telescope, even more unreachable and stalled within the illuminated screen.

> All attempts to contrast the virtual with the real have been rejected, stating that the former must be one of the latter's dimensions.

> They become. After all, this is the destiny of pixelated entities. Their data based trees ought to move by chance in the calculated wind. Just like the molecule filled branch will fall whenever it pleases.

LTTE no. 11 — *Tell me Lies*
March 2, 2015

Fill it to the brim
(A dialogue consisting of
words with one syllable only)

Anna M. Szaflarski

Tell me more of why you do what you do.

I'm young. I don't know so much nor have I felt much yet.

Ah then, for now, use words that you've heard or seen. Don't fear that you might not know them. Just put some words next to each other, in this way and that. And one day you can fill them up.

But the words are so long, and come from men whom I do not know. They talk of things I do not feel or see, and talk of those whom I have not heard of.

Look, just make nice strings of words. It's not a point for me, what it means. But make it sound smart.

Oh dear. I can bring thoughts and signs in strings and lines.

I can make it sound good but it runs off. It's not a part of me like a hand or a foot, but more like a thing from space. Then I try to say, that this is where my art comes from. This is why it is the way it is. This is what I want from it. And you look at me and do not know what I speak of, but it sounds good. You're glad that it is done. It fills a gap of some sort, but you still don't trust it, or me. It's not what I know or feel, it's just found stuff from other spots.

I see that when you write with robbed thoughts, you make a twin, a clown who holds all of the smart words and dances with them, and makes a real nice show. But it's a cheap show, and no one seems to know what it should mean! Yes, the clown sends smoke and lights to the crowd. She can make all things seem big and great. She can blow hot air into in a flat blob and make it grow and grow. But there are those who know her tricks. They are old tricks, and some will get bored. Clowns seem to like the show, but no one else.

It could be that you just need to read more. You need more things in your head, so you can put them in your smart texts. Things 'they' think are smart. You can talk of those who make math, mix test tubes, and take from the fields and crafts that you didn't learn. Show them that you are as great as the greats who use great words. They will not be sour that you lied a bit, and you should not be blue!

But I am a bit blue, and feel like a fool. I have to write to those who have give cash. They asked me why do you do what you do? I want to say, I do it as I have no other thing that I could do. It makes me feel fine, just grand. I tried to tell them this but they said that its not the right start. So I thought, I need to be smart and fold words side by side, and bring them in like warm pals for my work. In the end, I was not sure if what I wrote was good. The things line by line on my screen were odd to me, not like old friends at all. But I still asked them to stand there and sing a nice song for me. I told them, when asked of me, to not look strange but act cool. But they must have not known what I meant, because no one thought they were in tune. They knew that they were sly souls with false tales. And no one wants to give me cash.

Ah well. And If you could speak the truth, what would you then say?

I like to tell a tale or two. I like to sit in a chair and make lines and hues. I like to bring the real world in with the fake, and say 'Hey! There it is! It is not grand?'

That is nice. From this I know how you live like the sole gnat in a big fruit bowl; blind and a bit spoiled.

But could it not be that I am just blind and a bit spoiled!?

Hmm. Yes, but you need more of a myth to tell. Perhaps a tale from your youth. Were you not a sad child?

No! I was put into my dad's boots and told that I should be like him. He builds huts and homes, and lives a full life. I felt and thought lots of things as a child. They are still with me when I make things now but most things were great and not bad at all!

This will not work. They want to know if and how they can put you next to the tales of pain from the greats of old. How they can put you in a book, or in a show next to the works from those who say the same things. If you felt great pain or lived a bit of strife that could help. But a gay youth is of no help.

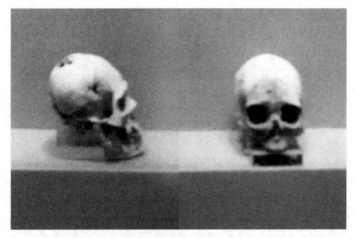

A thing that once held a brain.

Well I had not so much pain, but I do like to read the news. I feel a lot when I think about bad things in the world. I don't know what to do for it. I want to make things that spring tears, and do things that are big, and make people think. I want to tell you why the things I make can do that, but they can't.

No, no, calm down. You take the wrong path. You will not change the world. Not now, and not like this. But, in a way that should not be too clear, you could say a thing or two about the world.

What can I say!? There are times when I read and I am moved. I can feel them like ghosts, which pass through my skin and shake the cords that hang down from my heart. So I ask them to help me say what I make, but they are just guests and don't feel at home. There are times when I see things that chime with how I feel. Or shock things in me that I thought were so sure. Change how I look at things. So, I ask them to chime in with me. But I don't have all of the keys, and not all I do has a clear sense. But I just keep on. I have to keep on.

No no, don't turn off your brain! Tell me, do you seek the keys of shapes and tones, or have the breath of old tales on your tongue? Can you be more wise than you are? Are you rare? Who are you like, than just you? Can you tell me when you first thought this way?

You see, I'm tired of this quiz. You rouse me from my calm self, and I see no sense in it all. I am young and don't know so much nor have I felt much yet. Leave me in peace, and it could be that time will tell more.

An Artist From The Future,
Or Just Ahead Of His Time?

Post Brothers

New York City, NY—Morniel Mathaway's paintings have quickly gained tremendous notoriety since first appearing earlier this year. The Greenwich Village artist has recently skyrocketed to art world fame, but claims that he is an imposter. The man believes that he is not Morniel Mathaway, but rather an art historian from five centuries in the future.

The man claims that he was sent back to meet and study the artist Mathaway but became entangled in an insidious scheme and was stranded in present day. He insists that Mathaway's work will be singularly responsible for the entire aesthetic and cultural sensibility in the future. Displaced in this time, the man has apparently appropriated Mathaway's identity and taken up painting. He denies, however, that his ground-breaking style is his own, arguing that he is actually copying from memory the works he had studied in the future.

Until recently, Mathaway was virtually unknown to the art establishment, save a limited number of friends and acquaintances. The few that do scarcely remember Mathaway's work from earlier days each recount the paintings as poorly executed abstract experiments in material and surface effects. They remember the artist as a narcissistic and self-aggrandizing man who would speak relentlessly about his self-professed "aesthetic innovations" such as his "Intestinal period" and the technique "smudge-on-smudge."

A local dealer who recalls viewing the work from that period testifies that he saw "nothing" in Mathaway's previous neo-abstractionist paintings. "It didn't even have the interest of those paintings that a chimpanzee did a couple of years ago," the dealer asserts. The dealer, speaking on condition of anonymity, continues that he believed Mathaway to be "just another of those loudmouth, frowzy, frustrated dilettantes that infest the Village," yet now he hopes to represent Mathaway's work in the future. The dealer is not alone in completely reversing his opinions regarding Mathaway's work, and now is in total consensus with his fellow critics, dealers and artists that Mathaway is currently the finest artist alive, and perhaps of all time.

Many art experts argue that the reason Mathaway's stylistic relevance has been ignored for so long is due either to Mathaway's seemingly fruitless gestational period never reaching the proper public, or that his style was employing a language and aesthetic regime that was so forward thinking that the public was unable to understand it until the proper time.

Despite his wild success, Mathaway derides his adoring fans and critics. When asked about his rising career and critical acclaim, the artist said, "What's the matter with all these people, praising me like that? I don't have an ounce of real talent in me. All my work is completely derivative," the artist maintains. Furthermore, the artist has advanced the claim that not only does he feel his works are uninventive, but that he is not Morniel Mathaway at all, but rather an art historian from the distant future who has taken on the persona of the artist Mathaway.

The man alleges that his true name is Glescu and that

142   LTTE NO. II — *Tell me Lies*

he was born in the year 2449. Growing up in the area formerly known as Manhattan (current place names have been discarded), the man says that he originally had wanted to be an artist but transitioned into art history after discovering the work of an artist from present time who is purported to be responsible for the aesthetic sensibility of the future: the painting, architecture, arrangement of cities, texture of clothing, and shape of artifacts, of times to come. The man claims that in his time he was the foremost expert on the life and works of this artist, named Morniel Mathaway.

When asked how he arrived to present time, the man professes that in his era, the ability to travel through time has been reached. Due to the enormous expenditure of energy required, a trip is reserved for outstanding scholars only once every fifty years, in a manner of prestige akin to the present day Nobel Prize. Normally, the man added, the privilege is given to historians who want to observe key moments in world history such as the Siege of Troy or the first atomic explosion. The man avows that he was the first scholar of art to be granted this award, and was chosen due to the tremendous influence Mathaway has in his time.

A well-regarded figure traveling from the year 2487, the art historian was sent back to study in vivo the artist whose designs and special manipulations of color, the man asserts, will dominate architecture and fashion for the next five centuries and with whom modern painting, in its full glory, is said to have definitely begun.

Using a transmitting device called a "skindrom" (created, as Mathaway asserts, by the yet unborn and unsubstantiated inventor Antoinette Ingebord), the man says that he appeared in the original Mathaway's Greenwich Village apartment so that he could meet the artist he had studied for so long and

Post Brothers

to gain new insights regarding the work. This studio visit was intended to be very brief, as the transmitter can only work for half an hour before sending the holder back to the future.

"Glescu" purports that when he saw the works in the studio, he was both unimpressed and disgusted by the original Mathaway's amateurish and abject paint handling and "smudge on smudge" technique. He recalls that he pulled out a pocket catalogue raisonné from the future (a sourcebook to the artist's oeuvre) that bore no resemblance to the talentless paintings in the studio.

The artist who claimed he was Mathaway looked at the book and asserted that he, in fact, had painted one of the works, but had given it to a neighbor because he was unsatisfied with the results. Directing the art historian to the neighbor's door in an elaborate ruse, the conceited artist then allegedly stole the historian's time machine and sourcebook in order to claim his fortune in the future, leaving the art historian stuck in this era when the time traveling period expired.

When asked why no one from the future had come to his rescue, the man replied that he signed a required waiver of responsibility in case he was lost. With no birth certificate, social security number, or other documents, the man had no choice but to assume the identity of the painter and remain tied to our time.

Authorities challenge Mathaway's story and have officially asserted that not only is Mathaway exactly the same person as his documents suggest, but time travel is simply not possible. Experts and laymen agree that although Mathaway may be at the vanguard of fine art, without evidence to prove otherwise, he certainly is not from the future.

The only corroborating witness to Mathaway's fantastical account is the writer David Danzinger, who attests that he was in the room with the original Mathaway when the art historian from the future appeared. "Everyone is astonished at the change in Morniel Mathaway since he was discovered," the writer attests. "Everyone, that is, but me." Danzinger was apparently the only friend to the original Mathaway, and remembered him as a megalomaniacal, dishonest, and untalented Greenwich Village painter "who began almost every second sentence with 'I' and ended every third one with 'me'." Danzinger has confirmed all of the details of Mathaway's story, adding that it was a consistent habit of the original artist to steal and cheat anyone he encountered. Danzinger also has admitted that it was his idea that the time traveler assume Mathaway's identity and has helped him adjust to life in present society.

Having always wanted to paint, the art historian has been working vigilantly in the studio on his craft and has quickly gained high regard in the art world. He doesn't believe he has any natural talent but attests that "there are all kinds of artistic novelties I know about, all kinds of graphic innovations that don't exist in your time." But after studying the work of Morniel Mathaway for decades, the man believes that the works he has presented and continues to produce are only poor counterfeits of the reproductions of paintings published in his missing sourcebook.

When asked about this claim and its bearing on his celebrated style, the artist reportedly said, "I've tried to do something, anything, that was completely my own, but I'm so steeped in Mathaway that I can't seem to make my own personality come through. And those idiotic critics go on raving about me—and the work isn't even my own, it's Mathaway's of course." The artist believes that he is copying paintings from the absent sourcebook by memory.

Post Brothers

A number of physicists, time specialists, and art historians contest Mathaway's allegations, arguing that it isn't possible for a painting to be copied from a future reproduction and so have no original artist. Mathaway's testimony presents a time paradox that leads to further questions.

How can he remember that which he is yet to produce? How can the expert have studied quondam images that he himself had produced in his future, but in the past? Can a representation precede the original presentation? How can his paintings be copies of copies from the future? Where is the original? Who is the author? Who is the "real" Mathaway? When is the "work" brought into being, what cultural procedures allow and constrain this ordination? What kind of profound parallax can be discerned between the original and the copy? Is there a missing, real masterpiece?

When interrogated about his memory of the alleged sourcebook, Mathaway was unable to recall any sufficient detail. He has long refused to think about or discuss the book in a deliberate attempt at not copying the images. "In my heart, I know," he says, adding, "I'm copying from that book by memory." What is the relationship between forgetting and creativity? Is a poor copy an original?

Regardless of whether or not any of his story is true, by forgetting the painting reproductions, Mathaway has effectively become the real author of the celebrated works. This means that he, and not the original artist, created the paintings in the missing catalogue. But he could not have done so without having seen the catalogue in the first place, which presents a causal loop.

Thus, Mathaway's story is an elaborate example of retro-causality, where the past is a product of the future's interest in the past. The man is caught in a personality crisis of transtemporal proportions. The expert had become the producer, the analyst had become the analysand. In Mathaway's story, the original Morniel Mathaway was only imitating the nature of an artist, standing-in until "Glescu" arrived to imitate him, therefore eventually inventing and becoming the "real" Morniel Mathaway.

In this story, the historian precedes the history, calls it into being, and the criticism retroactively constructs the work itself. Is Mathaway's testimony an appeal for a more productive form of criticism, one where the art historian and the artist's influence on the work is in constant re-negotiation? In what ways are the traces of the past constituted retroactively, determined by future configurations of knowledge?

If one accepts Mathaway's propositions, then it is not that the man has thrown history out of its intended course by becoming an actor in the past, but rather that it is by his intervention into the past that the future he knows exists. The style from the future actually influences the future, making one question the very nature of claims of being forward thinking or futuristic.

Much to his discredit, critics disagree with Mathaway's account and have pointed to numerous examples of artists declaring themselves to be aiming at, channeling, or speaking to a distant future. While some argue that Mathaway's announcement is merely the self-promoting performance of an eccentric artist, others believe that his statements are the ravings of a mad genius overcome by the anxiety that accompanies fame and recognition.

Though still enamored with his works, many in the public admonish the artist's story as a lie. But, as Picasso said, "Art is a lie that makes us realize truth." Regardless, all parties agree that Mathaway's radical works are avant garde, each pushing aesthetic boundaries and defining the language of the future, whose effects will be elucidated only in times to come. Mathaway has been recorded saying jokingly, "I can't wait until you see what I do next, you thought it was excellent."

One critic cites that "Aristotle, in the Poetics, provides the most direct analysis, describing artists who imitate the past, artists who imitate the present, and artists who imitate the future."

LTTE no. 12 — *Eluding Wisdom*
March 16, 2015

Let them run

Anna M. Szaflarski

I see a teenager walking down the street. He's dyed his hair green and his shoulders communicate slight apathy and disrespect, and I can't hold myself back from whispering to him, "you know everything, don't doubt it for a second!" This, my sweaty forehead and my wide-eyed look, might be considered creepy and a bit frightening, which is a pity because I realize there is no hope that he might understand what I mean.

The true intention of my harassment of teenagers is to shorten, snip, compress something that I will call the loop of life. This ambitious term has no references to reincarnation nor any religion that I can think of. Because of its lack of creativity, I am sure it's been used in several self-help books to describe everything from pregnancy to heart-burn, and I'm certain that it's been enunciated like scripture by guests on Oprah, who strive to teach viewers about the true meaning of life. Yes, ok, you've got me. I want to talk about the

150   LTTE NO. 12 — *Eluding Wisdom*

meaning of life. And you think, who does she think she is? And I will respond with, you're right, I am not an authority on life, not anymore, but I was one at 16!

These loops in life can include monumental occurrences but are also prevalent in our daily lives. A simple example of just such a loop begins when messing up the bed at night while sleeping, then making the bed the following morning, followed by getting back into bed later that same day just to mess it up again. As children, this particular loop often provokes one of our first intellectual debates. This simple ritual makes no sense to us whatsoever! *Why make the bed NOW, if I know, and YOU know full well that it will be messed up again in a few hours* (for children it is an exaggerated case since they really are awake for significantly fewer hours than adults). We rationalize further with: *It's my bed, no one else's,* and might even go so far to say, *I like it that way, when its all messed up and expressive!*

At the time of our juvenile revolution, our resistance to the ridiculous circus of loopism is not due to our inability to see the point of participating, our disobedience stems from the fact that someone is commanding us to do it. Loopism gains absurdist momentum when dictated from a third person. When someone tells us to trust them, throw away our own logic into the wind, and just go through the motions.

I am sure that that teenager on the street has watched at some point a film, in which an old person is about to die. Or better yet, one of those hospital programs where one or two people are about to die every episode. You don't really have to watch it to know that the people, shortly before they take their last breath, have a message for us: *life is not what they originally told me it was going to be about.* It has been repeatedly reinforced that dying people have access to a treasure

A teenager knows something

box of wisdom that is not out of our reach, per se, but we are too stupid to reach for it. Ask the investment-banker-man who has enjoyed a comfortable life driving Porsches and getting tans on golf courses but also has a deadly bacterial infection. Or the ambitious actress lady who aside from a brain tumor also has a creative legacy that will outlast not only her neglected children but generations of neglected children to come. The rich, tanned and also dying man holds his son's hand for the first time in years and drops the truth like an unsuspected bomb. Hold your breath. Wait for it. Oh, wait… that? It's not a bomb at all, because we've heard it so many times. It's about family, right? It's about love or something. It's about that burning feeling in your chest when you get excited about seeing someone again, and is distracting you from anything productive. It's about miniature hands that are connected to a corresponding and equally miniature

152 LTTE NO. 12 — *Eluding Wisdom*

body that your wife produced with nothing but her belly and some spice you might have added. Well, that's what successful multi-billionaire albeit dying man in the movie is telling you.

But doesn't this wisdom sound familiar, green-haired boy? Didn't you lie in bed at one point and think about sweet Sandy or clever Johnny all night, wondering if she/he liked you? Did it not consume 99% of your already limited 3% brain capacity? The multi-billionaire from General Hospital was talking your language, HE UNDERSTOOD YOU. Meanwhile there's some unsympathetic yet perfectly healthy adult knocking on your door everyday asking if you've applied for college, gotten a job, or finally gotten a hair cut. *No, look dad, that's not important, ask the guy with the Porsche.* 'Dad' hears nothing, but sees you pointing to a television, which does not inspire him to listen further, and leaves.

The funny thing is that tanned dying man seemed to have been the only one who *did* understand. While television mortality is teaching us about how 'all you need is love', the rest of the world is trying to tell you that rich dying man can only say that stuff because he first drove Porsches every other day in his life.

And that just might be true. Maybe we can only say that love, and all that, is the most important when we spend our whole lives chasing other things, in the way that our parents, teachers, and presidents told us too. Maybe we can only appreciate love when we get stuff first, and when groups people clap for us on more than one occasion. Maybe it's only ok to return back to teenage mentality, shortly before signing off completely. Maybe they—the people telling us to work hard and make our bed's every morning—are right, and tanned man is out of his mind, or at least short-sighted.

But there's a reason why we want to watch tanned-man say the same thing as the previous actor who pretended to die and wait for tanned-man to be replaced by ambitious actress lady in the next episode, who basically says the same thing. And even when we're not willing to comply with his blessed words, we yearn for him to tell us again and again to do exactly those things that we tell teens to snap out of. Tanned-man's dialogue may have been crafted by highly ambitious, over-worked and successful writers, who don't follow their own advice, but maybe it's high time that someone takes their word for it, snips all that adult stuff out of the loop of life, and sticks to teenage business full-time. And that brave individual who dares to do so, instead of calling him/her a slacker or immature, let's consider actually rewarding him/her for it. Because if the tanned-man is right about something, then let us at least admit that the teenager might be also. Either way, wise or naïve, I think they're on to something.

I'm a Mother, After All

Barbara Plater-Szaflarski

Have you ever wanted to be a fly on the wall or wear a magic hat that renders you invisible? Is it even possible?

At some point, everyone experiences being so preoccupied with whatever they're doing, that eventually they become entirely oblivious to their surroundings. Such instances can be immediately exploited by mothers, who desperately want to learn something about their teenagers' lives. When she poses a simple question like—*How was school today?*—she can, at best, expect a short, unrevealing and yet reassuring answer—*Fine.*

However, opportunities to learn more about your teens will arise when, for example, driving your offspring and their friends (friends are almost essential, but in some cases siblings will do) to after-school activities. The parent-driver becomes one with her car, part of the same machinery that will take her chatty youth from point A to point B. None of the passengers will pay any attention to the driver, just as much as they don't notice the wheels of the minivan, in which they are sitting. Instead, they talk freely about their teachers and friends, exchange their views on a just-completed test, or... life in general.

This parent can consider herself very lucky, as her commuters do not choose to discuss shopping sprees or Britney

Spears* (unless they turn brief attention to their chauffeur and decide to intentionally annoy her), they prefer to talk about upcoming training practice, holiday plans or current events. Sometimes a computer game will be a subject of conversation, however this is always discussed in a foreign language unknown to this parent parent and therefore cannot be evaluated herein.

The answer, therefore, must be yes, you can disappear in broad daylight like a tree in the forest. The trick is to seize that moment and bask in its glory for as long as it lasts.

* Pop culture idol of the 90-ties, comparable in style to today's Kardashians.

MYth YOUth, Anna Herms, 2013

LTTE no. 13 — *Social Arena*
March 28, 2015

Not all doors swing both ways.

Anna M. Szaflarski

Monkeys have discovered capitalism. With the help of scientists, whose source of cash flow and general motivation has remained unspecified, the primates were taught to learn the value of currency, and to the surprise of their keepers some proved to be very thrifty, even cheap, while others careless and lush. One particular monkey stacked all of his bananas obsessively in a corner. He showed obvious interest in having one of those soft synthetic mats, which was available for purchase, but was clearly worried that if he started spending bananas, they might all disappear. He became an insomniac as he feared that any lack of consciousness might compromise his ability to protect his bananas effectively. In the middle of the test grounds stood his counterpart primate, who took advantage of every novelty item that one could buy at the Simulation Deposit Shop. To compensate his out-of-control spending habits, he had taken to stealing bananas from other,

158   LTTE NO. 13 — *Social Arena*

including the former, more conservative monkeys. This became a problem because not only were the bananas now considered currency, but because they remained as the primary food source.

The scientific discovery of capitalist behaviour in our evolutionary relatives was hugely popular among the people of this earth. The scientists from the monkey lab were so busy doing interviews with every paper and news syndicate of international importance to realize that a gangster society had formed in the enclosed habitat. Wild cries went unheard beyond the sound-proofed walls, as big spenders started bullying timid savers. Violence ensued, commodities were stolen and destroyed and soon bananas were being neither saved nor spent but smashed into the ground until a fine paste of purée covered every inch of the floor.

The principal researcher Dr. Patranowisch had left the complex to dedicate himself entirely to lecturing in every important city in the western world, and the monkeys, without food or currency, were left predominantly to their own devices. Bananas were being divvied out in a regular fashion from a mechanical dispensing machine; a careful economical design that intended to prevent inflation. However, the regularity of its dispensing became too infrequent for the monkeys. They gathered around the heartless machine as their hunger began to grow. One monkey collected stones to mark the passage of each day. It had been five weeks since the first signs of capitalist comprehension had appeared in the group.

Dr. Patranowisch had just finished his lecture in a dramatically lit conference centre in Paris. As in each of the 30 previous lectures it was followed by astounding cries and jeers. His audience was not impressed per se, nor intellectually

stimulated, but rather relieved! The failure of the economic system was no longer their own faults, the scientists had proved that they were instead inherently incapable of managing money. They enjoyed watching footage of the monkeys behaving foolishly in their fiscal situation. Each lecture on the doctor's tour became increasingly more casual and boisterous. In Budapest, popcorn and beer was sold at the entrance. In Vienna, attendees began a trend of whistling and clapping when a monkey would choose credit over paying up front, and imitate the rude sounds of a fart with their mouths when a monkey who gathered too many bananas for too long would find himself on top of a rotting and worthless heap; *he got what he deserved, with interest* they yelled. In Berlin, musicians were invited to perform a live sound track for the footage. The trombone and bass would rumble menacingly when the most conniving monkey of all would enter the scene. A dipping slide whistle accompanied every slip on a banana peel, which was always successful in bringing the crowd to a roar. Although Dr. Patranowisch became gradually less the centre of these events, and his genius less revered, he had never been the bringer of so much joy to anyone in his life, let alone thousands of people, so he let things go as they did. He accepted subsequent invitations for lectures, free nights in hotels, and dinners in the best restaurants in every city he had ever dreamed of visiting.

Enjoying what had become a carefree life, the Doctor abandoned many of his professional responsibilities. The last he heard from the lab was that there had been some chaos among the monkey troop, but hadn't given it much consideration, and thought that someone else, someone younger perhaps could handle the job, with tranquilizers, if need be. He never opened his computer anymore, and depended wholly on a secretary that accepted invitations and managed his calendar. He had become a well groomed and kept pet in society; lazy, scheduled, without worry, and was very happy with the situation altogether. But an exception needed to be made, as it was his godson's birthday. He had been so out of touch lately, his fingers almost atrophied, but a message from his secretary just wouldn't do. She had a peculiarly sweet way of writing that was very diplomatic and useful in contacting hotel managers about dietary specifications, but lacked a real sense of humour.

Upon opening his email account, he immediately saw what a burning sensation at the back of his throat had been hinting at all along. He didn't even have to open the mails, it was all immediately visible. Chaos, panic, destruction as well as an eventual calm and resolution, followed by a sort of acceptance was traceable in the subject titles of each mail. After that came a long period of silence, perhaps one week, until coincidently that very morning a new email had arrived.

The Doctor forwarded it to me immediately, and since then I haven't been able to get a hold of him. This is what it said:

------------Forwarded message ----------
From: monkeylab@researchfacility.eu
Date: Sun, Mar 28, 2015 at 10:25 PM
Subject: Great Discovery ! :)
To: S Patranowisch <patraboogie@yahoo.com>

Dear Dr. Patranowisch,

After the apocalypse here at home :(, we have taken over the lab, and killed or evicted each and all of your employees (sorry!). We then discovered books and finally the internet, hence our writing to you now.

We have come so far, but our past is still with us. So one day recently the memory of that repressive tool that you used on us, entered our minds again. The banana. It's taste and smell returned to us, but also its traumatic memories. We thought, in order to grow and enlighten we must learn more about the agent of our near destruction. So we went looking for it in the window of the universe, the internet. And did you know Doctor, that it actually grows on trees?

How silly is that? :P

Sincerely.
Your Monkey Troop.
PS- come home.

Forget yourself, forget the others...

Aleksandra Bielas

Forget yourself, forget the others. Friday night in a bar. "You come here often?" This is how the 'spare the answers' story starts. Do you feel free? It hurts and it took a long time to be here with you. Outside the world is making the usual evening cleaning. But as for him and her, we are inside. 70 or 90 of any measure of freedom or just empty space. The attempt of not sharing goes as far as the weather forecast for the next 14 days. Yellow light killing the day. Phone calls of random importance and the extra saved hour for a personal moment. The abundance of detail doesn't help the story, she tells him having a second glass of cheap Riesling. I know, he says, sipping from a bottle of Belgian beer. I'm not here often and I don't live around here, she says through the heavy smoke of hundreds of hands, but I have such a longing for home. I don't know what home means. I don't know where this longing comes from. Do I long for something from a long time ago? When I walk around and hear people say, "I am leaving today. Tomorrow I have to go to work," I always imagine their arrival in the other city and going home, opening the door and feeling at home. The place changes into a party. It's a mix of a club (the one you probably also know) and a dive (the one you probably also know). General drinking. The same. Sparing answers and details a few hours later we go out and you tell me that everyone is going to Lindsay Lohan's place. There is almost no light coming through the thick glass in that space. But as long as we agree that we are where we are, there is no light where we are. He doesn't feel alone anymore. Knowing that he is not the only one in the darkness relaxes him even a little. But he still wants to fuck. I'm killing whatever I meet, she tells me over a glass of wine. I don't have friends and I don't need any friends to have. I don't need to see your face or to hear your voice. I'm killing you now if you don't realize it. Another negative one, I think and I try to put an ironic smile on my stupid face, like "Hey, I know you're cool, but imagine, I'm cool too." I'm not sure if it works. We decide to go for a walk in Chinatown. It's over in five. This isn't how you write a story, she tells me, reading my mind. Your life or my life or even ours together is really not enough for that story you want to write, she tells me, reading my mind. Another negative one I think and try to put a smart smile on my stupid face, like "Hey, I've done it before." But I am little worried she might be right. I take her to a cinema. Put in one room with sixty pigs, we fart and leave the space. I'm tired. I get your idea of friendship based on Gmail chat and Facebook chat and WhatsApp but I unfortunately have a different idea of a friendship. And what do we do? Are you able to do it differently with me? I walk home euphorically looking forward to everything. Are we going to be friends? Because your placenta looked like an undone pizza and I really liked it.

LTTE no. 14 — *Promised Land*
April 12, 2015

Sei mal nicht päpstlicher als der Papst

Anna M. Szaflarski

The doe-eyed choir boy sang sweetly off-key. He was about 15 years-old and after leading us in song that was more melancholic than it was meant to be, he headed back to a row of diagonally placed benches that flanked both sides of the altar. There sat ten boys ranging in age from ten to eighteen. They wore white gowns pulled over collared shirts or plain sweaters and their basketball sneakers and scuffed dress shoes clumsily peaked out the bottoms.

At the front of their row sat a serious rockabilly type, their obvious leader, their John Travolta from Grease. Later he would be in charge of holding a metal plate under the chins of patrons while they accept the Eucharist. His job was to catch the crumbs of Christ, to recycle them and make more of the same holy chips, but more plausibly to prevent little bite size body-of-Jesuses from dropping to the vulgar floor.

166   LTTE NO. 14 — *Promised Land*

Regardless of how he rationalized it, he did it dutifully and followed each patrons' chin. After returning to his seat at the throne of his delinquent order, he kneeled and pushed his fingers into his brow in what looked like meditative prayer. I looked at the expressions of each of the boys. They were nervous, confused, blank, some perhaps on the brink of serious. But Travolta was devoted.

I sat between my Aunt and my Father, who both know how to crack a joke during Mass but they were just as committed to doing all of the lip service and hand motions that goes along with being there. The level of their spiritual involvement was unclear to me. I had been going to these things for years. As a kid in Canada we'd go every weekend. The ritual trickled off when I was around twelve. We self-identified as Polish Roman Catholics, but I sensed a lack of engagement early on. So, now I only go for the familial experience during special occasions like Easter, which I spent in Poland this year. I still think it's a good show. The allegories are generally good, and I was alway curious what kinds of words of wisdom the priest was trying to pawn off that day.

Mass started slowly, there was some monotonous singing, a warm up of sitting, standing and kneeling. After about fifteen minutes into mass, everyone beat their chests lightly and repeated how everything was their own fault. " Moja wina, moja wina, moja bardzo wielka wina" (my fault, my fault, my very big fault). It's a bummer mood, it's just bad self-talk, if you ask me. This guilt tactic may have worked in Communist Poland, where people were living in generally disadvantaged conditions and could be led to believe that they were being punished for something. But *my* fault?! I stood there in unsatisfying and unnoticed revolution.

After a few diddies from the organ, a sit, stand, kneel, and a sit, an altar boy walked over to the pulpit to read from the bible. I zoned-out to the monotonous hum of his voice and examined the depictions of Christ that hung around the room. There was plaster one of him as a toddler, no older than a year old, floating in the air. He held two fingers up with one hand and a few down with the other. A golden ray blasted from the back of his head. Behind the altar hung the more recognizable figure of Jesus; fully grown at a ripe age of thirty, but sadly someone had nailed him to a cross. He looked like he was in pretty bad shape, but on the up-side had a great head of hair (The previously mentioned baby Jesus looked like he was wearing a Roy Orbison wig. Can I hear holy genetics!). If I hadn't already seen him like that so often he might have even succeeded in making me feel a bit bad, but I was pretty used to it. St. Peter and St. Some Other Guy were standing at the base of the cross looking in random directions and pointing different combinations of fingers in what also seemed to be random directions.

Baby Jesus, St. Peter and the other guy were communicating in some sort of sign language frozen in time. It's hard to understand them because they speak the language of Rome: Latin, an apparently dead language, so no one knows what the hell they are trying to say. In every corner of the church there was another painting, stained glass, or sculpture of somebody pointing to or at something. They might have been saying something like "pass me a knife so I may cut God's son down from this cross!" and everyone was like, "What? Speak English!"

The best part of mass is when everybody lines up to get their own edible piece of the chosen son, handed out by the priest, and in this case insured by Travolta. Beforehand, the

168 LTTE NO. 14 — *Promised Land*

priest sings while holding up a big piece of tasty wafer, telling us that this, in fact, is the body of Christ, which he promptly follows by eating it and gulping down some red wine. Our stomachs reminded us that Easter dinner awaited us at home. The priest seemed conscious of this because after he finished he swung around to the front of the altar and generously invited us to join him in a delicious mini snack wafer feast. So everybody got up and stood in a line to get their bit. Meanwhile the organ played to keep the peace, like the way they play classical music outside of a 7-Eleven to keep bums from getting rowdy. The snack was free but there was a catch. To redeem the delicious snack, you must have gone to confession in the not so distant past (I'm not sure about the expiry date on confessions). The Eucharist, the little Jesus chip, is a reward for those who have gone to a priest and divulged their inner most sinful secrets. The individual is then forgiven, which removes guilt from their stomachs and makes room for snacks.

The first time you are required to confess is before your first communion. I was six years old, I still remember what I confessed to. I told the priest that I had stolen my grandmother's make up. I could see his eyes resisting rolling from boredom. The thing is, that it was a lie. I felt so under pressure to relieve myself of some great burden that my mind went completely blank. And so I lied to a priest, which I realized was not exactly the point of the ritual, but rationalized that stealing or at least borrowing my grandmother's makeup could very well happen in the future, so my act could have been considered as a pre-emptive measure. Something told me that the exercise was a success, regardless of the complete violation of procedure. I told a story, and the priest symbolically punished me. He told me to repeat ten Hail Mary's, which at the time I still knew how to recite in the same rhythm and tenor that I would later recite the periodic table in chemistry class, which I have also now forgotten.

At Easter Mass in 2015, I figured I hadn't beaten my chest at the beginning of the mass which only affirmed that I had nothing to feel guilty about, but I would feel a bit bad about eating something that everybody else considered so holy and I only thought about how wonderfully it would melt on my tongue. So, I didn't get in line and in exchange for not eating at mass, I would save my appetite for dinner and instead enjoy watching the parade that formed in front of me.

Like looking through a magazine of do's and don'ts the co-ed beauty pageant slowly shuffled by. I chose winners, and decided who could improve their placement in the competition if they only changed their hair, coat or husband. Many could have helped their standing by just smiling, they were all so serious. Some were so young and I realized would do this kind of thing for a while, maybe their whole lives. Others would trade in their vows to God for the vices of premarital sex, or would leave the country and inevitably lose touch with the church.

It's easy to laugh at the Catholic church because it's theatre is so absurd. Everything from the ludicrous gold decorations to the little red shoes the Pope is supposed to wear but abstained from wearing to show his humility is funny. I mean really. This isn't a mix-and-match offer. "I'll take the millions of followers, the white gown, but leave the read shoes." It's easy to laugh, because the material is so loaded, so contradictory, so old, so awkward. It's so easy to laugh that it's hard to stop.

But when visiting Poland I need to generally refrain from the jokes. It's not what you think, it's not that Poles don't see

170   LTTE NO. 14 — *Promised Land*

the absurdity in it. They're the one's who'll tell you that 8 out of 10 priests' intelligence leaves much to be desired, but they except the charade and the mediocre sermons because the religion has meant more to the country spiritually and perhaps even more so politically than any other movement in the last century. It is widely thought to have significantly aided Poland in coming out of a time of poverty, institutional suspicion, and national fragmentation.

The late Pope John Paul II, was criticized for his lack of attention to molestation accusations within the church, but in Poland is remembered as a young revolutionary leader, whose larger-than-life rhetoric paralleled shipyard's union leader Lech Walesa, and motivated Poland to stand in solidarity against Communism. With all of Poland's differences —political, cultural,— the church was able to mobilize them into one people.

It was during that time that the Catholic Church's popularity exploded in Poland, in such a way that the effects is still felt by people from my generation. It was a religion not for simple people in need of a shepherd, but of revolutionary thinkers, and the youth of tomorrow.

Growing up in Canada, at six years old I knew that something was missing from the narrative of why we were actually going to church. I could sense then that the whole 'Jesus died for your sins' wasn't the full story. No one told me then that I had to stand, sit and kneel in a packed, oxygen lacking, cheap perfume-filled room for an hour and listen to poorly sung, barely melodious music because it reminded my parents and every other Polish immigrant in that room of their homeland, and of its survival despite occupation.

Although the glorified freedom fighter version of Catholicism had a good run in Poland, things have been slowly changing to give way to polarized politics. After Poland's independence in 1989, it slowly opened its doors to the Europe and the west, which ushered in liberal ideas including topics involving Gender and the expansion of the concept of marriage. Some found this refreshing or at least interesting, but these topics in part encouraged the awakening of a hyper-conservative religious and political faction. Full of fear that their ideals and homogeneous society might be threatened it made people say and do stupid things.

Many Catholics in Poland are not happy with the growing influence that such conservatives hold in the country. But as they watch the face of their religion being radicalized, how can they stand to be still be affiliated with the church? What makes them go back, what keeps them in the fold?

Last week, I spoke with my friend Maggie on the phone, who lives in Vancouver. Organized religion for many Canadians our age is a complete mystery. "Do you actually know practicing Catholics?" she asked. "Yeah," I said. "A. is a practicing Catholic." Maggie was taken aback because she knows A. as my PhD Linguist, flirtatious, hyper-intelligent, and hilarious cousin. "And she really believes that Jesus died and then got up the next day?"

Although I'm sure that she sees the allegory more as a parable designed to teach some truth or life's principle... why not. The church seems to give her something to bounce her conscience against, and I can understand her needing something like that. But honestly I am just as clueless as Maggie, a Canadian who has only a vague idea of what religion has meant in my family's homeland, and why someone smart and educated would continue to be a part of it.

"Christ the King" Monument in Świebodzin, Poland is 33 meters tall. You can see him here in this blurry cell phone picture.

On my way home aboard the Berlin-Warszaw Express, just before leaving Poland and crossing the German boarder, I looked out my window to see the giant statue of Jesus facing the west. He's not on the cross anymore but his arms are held wide open as if he were just removed from the cross and rigor mortis made them stay that way. He was reaching out towards Germany for a hug, or heeding his sheep back into pasture, or he was throwing his hands up in confusion or frustration, or maybe he was saying "Mitte manum in cælum: et ab eo, sicut iustus non curo!" (Throw your hands in the air, and wave them like just don't care!). And that's just how he's trying to keep it fresh.

Dear Editor,

Maggie Boyd

Yesterday, as the houseguest of a generous friend, I dined atop a dogfight. Underneath my plate, held three feet above the ground by the table, the dogs snarled and nipped and squealed and smashed into the table legs as they tried to assert power over each other. I was aware of myself in a 50/50 state of trying to carry on a conversation while feeling occupied with the safety of my legs. At points I would lift a potato to my mouth with a fork. At others, I would lift my legs onto an unoccupied chair to avoid being bitten. I would respond to the question of another dinner guest. I would flinch at a yelp from below.

Following the dinner, in a very slow mood, I went upstairs to prepare my bed and stepped barefoot into cold dog shit. Luckily, a roll of toilet paper was waiting on the bedside table—a clue left from the previous houseguest alluding to hygienic travel masturbation—and the clean up was easy. I was unmoved.

All things point to death these days.

At the coffee shop an employee apologizes for the wait, "I'm SO sorry! Your coffee will be up in five seconds"

"Don't be sorry," I reassure him, "I'm just here working out this thing or some other thing and besides, what else

174 LTTE NO. 14 — *Promised Land*

will I fill the time with between now and when I'm dead?" He is in a 50/50 state of being reassured and wanting me to go away. I don't think he knows that I'm not being even slightly facetious.

I'm thinking about the table. I'm thinking about my dinner lurching on top of it as the dogs crash and snarl below. I'm thinking about a conversation with my friend Mark last week. I had called to tell him our friend Joe was found dead that morning in his tiny apartment in a sad part of town. He couldn't do it anymore because he was too low, too angry at himself and too lost. I told him about my little sister who couldn't stop drinking and taking too many pills. "What's wrong with her?" he asked. "I don't know" I said, "but man, is it ever hard for her to live."

He told me about a radio program he had heard that same morning about how there have been studies released recently that say we enter a pool of collective energy when we die. I picture a softly swirling pool of creamy colourful warmth, my heart skips. I'm excited. I see my mother's abalone earrings from when I was a child and suspect that she too knew that nothingness looked like the inside of a shell. Mark and I agree that when we one day enter the opalescent milk-pool of death we'll laugh so hard at the silliness of our worries. Our collective energetic laughter tinkling out of the cosmos at the simplicity of being alive and the difficulty we had knowing it.

We were trying very hard to not acknowledge the chaos of dog spit and anger beneath our dinner last night. We strained to talk over the much louder ones on the floor. We tried to eat dinner. It seems so absurd that the table was even there at all, but it was the only thing we had to keep up the appearances of a meal. Without it, food would be flung everywhere, no telling what was dog spit, what was food.

The table has been half-gone since my friend Zoe's body was crushed last year by the car of a drunk man. She was killed—just like that—and I couldn't breathe for a week. I think about my body and your body and Zoe's body as the dog fight. I guess we need the table for now but I'm also looking forward selling it off at the yard sale. The swirling pool comes furnished and we can arrive naked.

So I guess my question is, dear Editor, respected friend, what do we know and how do we know it?

LTTE no. 15 — *Natural Causes*
April 27, 2015

A Bag of Winds:
a letter to the art-immigrant

Anna M. Szaflarski

I was pretty excited to visit the local pub in my home town, St. Catharines, Ontario. I was 23 and visiting from Berlin, and you could bet on it that between ten to fifteen people from my high school were loitering at the same spot that night. But on my first night home I'd call my childhood friend Vanessa instead. She would be down that week as well, from Ottawa, or Victoria, I don't remember where she was studying then. She'd drive her mom's pickup truck across town and pick me up, and we'd lie around first at her house, and then at mine. Go thrift store shopping, follow siblings around, drink wine and tease our dads.

Eventually I'd muster up the energy to face the bar and search out the people that I remember but didn't really care about enough to rekindle old times. Instead, I went there to check comparatively how things were progressing, and to publicly present how I could hold my liquor. Everyone was

178   LTTE NO. 15 — *Natural Causes*

still studying. One guy's band got a label and was touring Canada and the States. One girl was pregnant. Some people moved on to other cities, other countries, while others were still waiting for their calling within the four walls of their parents' home. Things had changed a bit but everybody looked pretty much the same. Like me, most were unmarried, still acting irresponsibly, and still attached to the long extended umbilical cords dangling from our bellies. And this is what I would find back at home, with little variance for the next five years.

Back then, going home was like sliding back into the ranks. I put aside my new developed hobbies, style choices, and friends and agreed in silent unison with my brothers to waste time the old way: watch TV, eat non-stop, walk around the woods, throw stuff, jump into rivers, buy unhealthy groceries, talk only by means of jokes. After three days, the constant pleasantries seem unbearable, and an argument surfaces. Emotions rise above the momentary façade of perfection. And then, after some crying and slammed doors, we agreed to disagree and the arguments were put aside for the next visit. We got busy getting back to the nice, usually assisted my a large meal.

When I left home to study far away from home, it was generally understood that it would be a temporary arrangement. When everyone still believed this, my older cousins felt comforted that they still knew what to ask me about at Christmas dinner. How are my studies going, isn't Berlin cold? Every time I came home, I felt a bit like Odysseus returning home after the fall of Troy. I had been in contact with other worlds, and brought tales of foreign cultural behaviours. I flexed my abilities in the language that I pretended to have learned (they couldn't tell the difference!).

Then, one day they stop knowing what to ask, because I finished studying and they didn't understand why I would stay somewhere with little money, no husband or prospect of children (or something to that effect). They would instead ask me of the present moment. Do I like the food they cooked for me? They'd say things like, 'good for you', and describe me as a 'free spirit' while thinking and whispering to each other, how long will this nonsense go on for before I give in to the *natural* way of living. Something about my visits home became less epic.

This is not a story about pining over my childhood and how every time I go back, my expectations are increasingly replaced with an unrecognizable reality that does not sit well with me. It's not about being sad because family members and old school mates are getting married, bearing children, or moving on. Or that the place I once left behind is drifting away. It's not about that, because it was obvious that it was going to happen, and it's not sad at all, I didn't want it to last forever and the change is good. It's about how I increasingly glorify, romanticize home while steadfastly decide not go back.

The food is better back there, people understand my jokes, they speak my language on the radio and TV, my 96 year-old grandma is a barely-living relic that needs visiting. So, what am I doing here, someone might ask me. To fully understand my inner conflict that someone has got to travel by plane at least 8 hours to get to their hometown. That someone has watched the same romantic comedies as I have, because on one round trip, you've pretty much seen them all. That someone, is an art-immigrant like me and is far away, but we're together, found each other and yet, somehow we're alone.

180 LTTE NO. 15 — *Natural Causes*

After years of perilous struggles, Odysseus's boat finally came into view of his home, Ithaca. When he saw that his journey was drawing a close, he decided for some reason that it would be a good time to take a nap. Maybe because he had a feeling that trouble was approaching, namely that dozens of men at home trying to screw his wife, and he needed one last rest before dealing with it. Maybe he was just relieved that his long trip had come to an end and the weight of responsibility just fell off his shoulders. Either way, after falling asleep, his ship's crew noticed a bag, that until then Odysseus had kept under close watch. Thinking, naturally, that something so protected must be full of gold, they tore the bag open and released an unpleasant surprise. Hidden inside of the bag were all three winds except for the westerly wind—the one that would have pushed them directly home. A storm broke out, and the boat and its crew was blown back to where they had started their journey in the first place.

My reason for travelling to another part of the world wasn't as tragic as the Trojan War like it was for the men of the Odyssey. When I first set off, I was so jacked up on adrenaline with the idea of my life in whole other place, I didn't think I'd still be here today, working and eating late night koftas. There was no plan. Or there was a plan, but it's changed so many times since then that I don't remember what that plan looked like. It hasn't been tragic, but there's been times when its been less than ideal, when I've felt alone and mirages of Ithaca appeared closer than ever. I daydreamed sliding back into a place where people needed me, where weekends would be filled with family dinners, and a 9–5 job would supply me with a consistent sense of accomplishment and security.

Anna M. Szaflarski   181

At some point I considered it all seriously, looked online at programs at my home university, sent a few emails to friends prodding at possible jobs, I looked into residencies, internships, and joked with family about how I live in the basement of my brother's house. I saw home on the horizon, but something didn't sit well with me when I looked at it across the haze. No one has forgotten me back home or thinks I'm dead, like they do in Odysseus's case (thanks to Whatsapp more that Skype these days they know full well that I'm alive and relatively fine). Still, they want you to come back, put aside your luxurious war with conformity, your upstream battle with the art world and finally settle down near by. And that doesn't sound half bad, in fact, it sounds pretty good, even comforting. The image was so sublime that I fell asleep, and allowed myself to be whisked away in the opposite direction.

There was a bag of winds that swept me away from moving back and you are one of the curious crew that tore it open. You didn't know what was in the bag, you were curious and were just following an impulse. You opened the bag, and let the winds pull me away from the fantasy that things will be easier back home. OK, you say, so, we don't always get each others' jokes, our understanding of what is rude or inappropriate may differ, we want to become family for each other but don't know what family means, we are still on the search for something, and you say, you know it can get tiring. But in this state of intermittent exhaustion, there is a lot of relief, satisfaction and pride to be had. I know it because I've seen it, you say, and I've felt it.

Odysseus tried a second time to make it home and on his way was captured by two different feminine beings on two separate occasions. Each time his status in the hands of these beings would transform from prisoner to guest very quickly. His life seemed good in these places. He had love, and paradise at his disposal, but something burned inside of him. An anxiety that pushed him forward, back towards home. And so he went, leaving everything he found behind. The rest of the story ends Ancient Greek-style. He returns and begins his re-acquaintance with his old life by murdering everyone who looked at his wife longer than he should have. While he's at it, he kills all of the servants who hadn't served him loyaly. Only after the massacre was he able to settle back into life at home after 20 years of being away.

Maybe Berlin will never become our home, you say. And if I'm ever ready to head back to my previous homeland you say, you'd understand that there's something burning inside of you to do so. You sincerely wish me the best of luck and suggest that I use my words and nothing else when encountering surprising realities. And when I've resolved all of my demons and rekindled old friendships, you expect an open invitation to my LinkedIn profile, because you imagine we've got a lot of unfinished business that'll need doing.

Cuando pase el temblor
(When the earthquake passes)

Mariana Castillo Deball

That morning I woke up as usual at 5:30, got dressed, stepped out of the building and walked two blocks to catch the school bus. It was still dark and Mexico City was waking up as the sun rose. At 7:15 the bus stopped in front of Amaranta's house; my best friend at the time.

Her mother was a ballet dancer and her father an actor, who once played Dracula in a black and white film. Amaranta claimed that she came from another planet, and on countless occasions I argued that it wasn't possible, but I never managed to revoke her statement.

Before Amaranta came out of her house, the bus started to swing back and forth. Then the street lamps followed. The electricity cables and the adjacent buildings were rocking all together in perfect synchronicity. I remember staring at a street lamp and wondering, how could a concrete stick be so flexible?

The collective dance of buildings, lamps, and cars lasted for what it seemed an eternity.

The 1985 Mexico City earthquake struck in the early morning of 19 September at 7:17:50 a.m. with a magnitude of 8.0 on the Richter Scale. It is highly recommended that during an earthquake you should stand underneath a doorframe, because it is the most stable structure in the building.

184 LTTE NO. 15 — *Natural Causes*

Amaranta came out of the house, jumped onto the bus, and we continued our journey. The further we drove, the more chaos we encountered, but the driver continued his procession, stoically collecting the rest of the kids. When we arrived at school they immediately sent us back home. It was like watching the same movie backwards, while the chaos augmented.

Around the same time, Adriana drove a green beetle, nicknamed the Challenger, mainly because of its speed and audacious way of traversing through the city. I remember driving with Adriana in the challenger at night, around the Roma and Condesa neighborhoods, which were all covered with rubble, collapsed houses, and people living on the streets or in tents. The Movement of the 19th of September was a civil association that provided support to the homeless families. They installed a temporary cinema on the street, and sometimes we went there to watch movies. I remember watching The Savage Planet, a science fiction animation film, taking place on a distant planet where blue giants rule and oppress humans.

While driving around with the Challenger at night, Adriana would park the car, ask me to stay inside, while she walked in the direction of a big pile of debris. It was very dark, so I couldn't really see her maneuvering, but she always came back after a while carrying an old wooden door. My only task was to push the claxon twice if someone suspicious approached the area. Sometimes we would collect two to three doors a night, sometimes none at all. We would bring the doors back home on top of the Challenger, and Adriana would spend days sanding, polishing and fixing them. Doors started to accumulate, and were installed on every possible threshold in the apartment. The walls adjacent to the staircase that curled up to the second floor was completely covered with doors.

With an Unquiet Consciousness was the name of a rock band, in which Adriana sang. The apartment—aside from the multiple doors—was also covered with layers of egg packaging and foam to insulate the sound. On rehearsal days I would come back from school, and even though it was silent, I could feel the building vibrating.

I often confuse my own breathing with the beginning of an earthquake: a smooth but constant tilting that increases intensity. Breathing becomes an actual earthquake when this internal waving is suddenly expressed in the outside world, glasses start to tickle, walls begin to crack.

Advertisement

THE BUREAU OF CONCENTRATION*

is looking for desk oriented/not-so-messy praxis workers to join our studio in Neuköln (U-bahn Leinestr). We have two newly renovated rooms (each 21 m²) available, which can be shared with up to 3 people. Each room is going for 420 Euros, all included. Ground floor entrance, kitchen and bathroom included.

Upon moving in, you will become a neighbour to the permanent office of Letters to the Editors, and graphic designer Santiago da Silva.

MAY THE PUMPED
LEAD THE PUMPED

~ Plato, from "Inspirational phrases ;) uttered in Classical Greece", reprinted in Boojaka Press, 1988.

* Not actually what we call ourselves

LTTE no. 16 — *Beat around the Bush*
May 9, 2015

There's Bushes and Then There's Pheasants.*

Anna M. Szaflarski

Concrete Poetry: Language is just a dangling skin tag from the greater body of meaning. Cut it off and then it's just a gross thing lying on the bathroom floor. You no longer associate it with yourself. Get the broom, better yet, the vacuum, be sure that it's collected and doesn't get lost under the heater.

Open up the vacuum later pull everything out and make a collage out of all of the trash that has disconnected from the things that they once so intrinsically got meaning from. It's all so unrecognizable. The dust bunnies, rice bits, and skin flakes, all wrapped up together in a woolly mess. It looks like it could make a nice sweater, or if you worked at it a bit, a felt hat. Instead, douse it in concrete making heavy objects out of the words that used to have meaning, so that they now just make sounds and take up blocks of space on paper.

---

* Prepared for a lecture given at Mindscape Universe, Berlin

188   LTTE NO. 16 — *Beat around the Bush*

Now you've got pages filled with meaningless dirt, and it looks like you could use it for anything. It looks so fresh and messy. I just looks dense and empty at the same time, and that's enough. Just perfect.

Poetry: I can't write poetry, so I usually avoid doing it. I did it once, because I was asked to, and so I thought I would try. It was a bit of a game. When I read it out loud, I used an accent and imagined that I'd been trained by masters who made me contemplate empathy with inanimate objects. Those imaginary mentors made me write haikus with long sticks attached to rough brushes. Ocean waves crashed in the background, or a desert landscape burned my skin. With this mind-set I wrote a poem, trying to give the impression that wisdom could be teleported into the words by a foreign being. But it was just a game, and when I stopped talking like the Queen of England, I found that no wisdom had arrived, as far as I know.

Appropriation: is like my friend Alex in the 7th grade. She said it was OK to steal from the Cosmetic Store, she said that we would be better selves if we had the things that other people produced. We would become more beautiful, more desirable. She was right. Even though I didn't know how to apply eye shadow, every application rose progressively closer to my eyebrows the effort I put into it was noticed, and I think I was perceived as someone who had access to another world, even if I didn't speak their local language.

It can be great fun to rip up texts and treating them like trash, building blocks, and adopt them like your own children. It's comforting that these little letters don't necessarily need a point, a universal meaning, a clear message, that they can be flirtatious and non-committal. A seductive flash of a leg. The modern practice of text dissection is not only freeing but also subversive, like a 'fuck you' not only to history-writing historians, and politicians but to all written language that was carefully crafted to actually communicate.

Modern European artists and writers revealed that when language became too effective in communicating, in moving the soul, that it could be dangerous, and we've been taught that it can't be trusted. Breaking language apart showed us that it can mean nothing just as much as it can mean something, but nonetheless take up the same amount of space. The artists and writers of the early 20th century did us this service and we were freed. *Hmm*

I spent a year thinking about these things while I wrote my Master's thesis on word-play. I pretzelled my brain trying to read technically constrained books by Raymond Roussel. I re-enacted theatrical performances by 1960's artist Guy de Cointet, danced intellectually around text pieces by Filippo Tommaso Marinetti, and in boredom redrew Apollinaire motifs on my arm with a Sharpie. I'm not a great academic, so I can't say that I was very thorough. But eventually the logic of the Matrix of Language Games started to gain ground in my understanding, and I finally fantasized that I wouldn't have dodge the bullets anymore, that I could just stop them in the air.

But I realized that I was far behind the times. Everyone's got a Dada-tweet machine in their pocket, and is like, *'duh', of course we know about manipulative messaging, which we are now impervious to, and structuralism is soooo out,* and the worst of it all is that everyone is like, *I can write a decent text, lemme just get my vacuum cleaner, I think I tore off some hangnails earlier.*

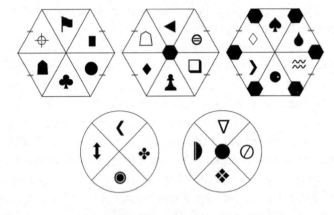

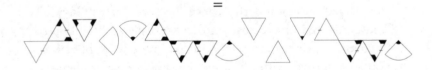

From my cryptography days.
The decrypted message reads: DON'T WORRY BE HAPPY
I'll be telling you directly from now on.

American Poet, Kenneth Goldsmith, is a wisecrack in the Language Matrix. He plays both sides of the game. He roughs it with lyricists in the underworlds where rat meat is considered a delicacy. On the other side, he's cool and slick, spreading hard to get alternative poetry copyright free on the internet, and challenging the value of poetry by performing obtuse concrete stanzas, like when he read traffic reports to the President of the United States. That's funny. The President thought so too, but he didn't think it was subversive. *Because maybe the President is inside the Matrix too.*

There are other admirable die-hard language-abstractionists like factions of Oulipo, who like the medieval monks exist in general seclusion and try to further the parameters of language in books and poetry. Unfortunately, their methods and cleverness is also being out-ranked by automated programs and apps.

That's why I've generally given up writing in more abstract forms of writing, because people like Barack Obama are clever enough to know that although it's still quite charming, the public (and I mean, like, pretty much all people) are accustomed to fragmented language, and the aesthetic has become quite soft.

That's why, I've opted to become a critical populist. That's why after finishing my Master's, I started writing about my childhood and TV shows, and put them on the same level with anything I might have picked up along the way about art, theory or whatever. After extended flirtation with abstracted language forms, I wanted a dialogue with my readers, and my hope was that it would work because the texts are personal, colloquial, non-exclusive and everyone knows that they're smart enough if not much too smart to get it. I adopted a rhetorical style of writing inspired by even

192   LTTE NO. 16 — *Beat around the Bush*

Obama, satirical writer David Sedaris, and popular cartoon personas like Bart Simpson. I'm not satisfied with a text that invites silent recognition of beauty, poetry, cleverness, or what have you.

I have also stopped all hopes of trying to write academically, which I blindly have faith that some individuals can do, but most cannot, even though they will die trying. Because what most of us come up with when we attempt academia is a similar but more sophisticated vacuum cleaner vomit page of smart looking particles but unrecognizable messages. Not so unlike concrete poetry, traffic report appropriations... *Dadacademia*.

Dadacademia, describes a majority of the thousands of mini-texts being produced in the art world today—an almost neglected craft of exhibition texts and press releases. To the general public, these texts might appear as dense discourse-saturated compositions, but are more often then not fragment rearrangements of found terms (terms originally defined with precision). Their well-costumed nonsensicalness has conquered the A4 papers scattered on the widow sills of Berlin's galleries and project spaces; promising safe passage into the core of the objects on display, instead leaving most feeling confused.

You say, *Anna, just because you are not able to spontaneously call up a catalogue of terms and theories in your head and process them into clever web-like constellations on command, it doesn't mean that nobody can. Yes,* I'd say, that may be true. But I'm betting that not only that most of you can't but also that more often than not, the artist who's work is described in the texts is just as lost.

I am reminded of the film-rendition of *Little Women* starring the then very young Winona Ryder. Her character lives alone, much like myself, and labours for hours a day over her writing. Her quill finger is covered in black ink, which is noticed by her admirer and mentor, who lives upstairs from her (not like my life AT ALL). She was writing about Vampires, I think, which in the Victorian times must have been all the rage. After finishing her manuscript, she gives it to the man upstairs for feedback. Alas, he is disappointed, and she thinks consequently that he doesn't like her anymore. But he does like her, and tells her that her skills might be better used if she wrote about things that came more naturally to her heart, and therefore her words. She does that, and they fall in love.

The Vampires in her novel are like the references to things that the author doesn't really care about, appropriated fragments scattered across papers. They are easily identified by the fact that they've got no blood pumping through them. They're revived Duch-vamps and they're sucking everything interesting out of the text, roaming the 12pt lines and spreading an epidemic of senselessness. But never fear, Bart Simpson rolls in on a skateboard from margin left, and stabs the Duch-vamp. And you hear Nelson's "Ha Ha" in the not so far away distance.

TEXT

Ayumi Rahn

1: We have to think about what we want to say.
  The best thing would be to note down everything.
  All the points. Everything that comes into our heads.
2: OK.
1: It's important how we start.
2: The beginning.
1: It's important to not directly describe the concept.
2: Good.
1: The concept must be captured indirectly.
  From the side.
2: Yes.
1: So? Do you have any idea how we should start?
2: Why not exactly like this? Let's start with you suggesting
  not to describe the concept directly.

1: In the dialogue I will be ☆.
2: How do you mean?
☆: ☆.
2: What?! You are C.O. and I am A.R.!
☆: Under no circumstances do I want my name to be revealed.
A.R.: But aren't we exhibiting under our own names?
☆: So what.
A.R.: Why should pseudonyms talk about our concept, or
  talk indirectly about our concept, or talk about us talking
  indirectly about our concept? We should be talking.
  Everything else is pointless.

Art:	And if I were to be Art?
A.R.:	Who would I be then?
Art1:	I'll be Art1 and you'll be Art2.
Art2:	I am the one who decides who's talking, and I think you should be C.O.

C.O.:	The works look good next to each other.
A.R.:	You think so?
C.O.:	Perhaps you might try to imitate my work some time, and vice versa?
A.R.:	Or you carry on working where I left off?
C.O.:	Regarding the starting point-
A.R.:	Yeah, what is your starting point?
C.O.:	The rose window is definitely not the starting point.

A.R.:	Because starting points are seldom in the window, more likely to be in the archives.
C.O.:	No. I don't like these words.
A.R.:	Because if there were starting points in the archive, then the rose window would be like a lens, bundling the light from different directions and dispersing it again.
C.O.:	Wow, that sounds awful.
A.R.:	You're right.
C.O.:	It can't be written like that.
A.R.:	OK.

C.O.:	The gradient is no good. It's too simple.
A.R.:	That's exactly what I like. I think it's great.
C.O.:	Suppose you were given this flyer. You didn't make it, you're seeing it for the first time. Would this exhibition interest you?
A.R.:	Absolutely!
C.O.:	You're saying that because you made the flyer. Imagine now, that you didn't make it.
A.R.:	Totally objectively? If I saw this flyer, I would definitely want to see this exhibition.
C.O.:	You're lying.

LTTE no. 17 — *The Rationalizations*
May 23, 2015

The Smoking Kids

Anna M. Szaflarski

The paintings were so enormous that the walls fell down. We were standing on top of the caved debris, looking down in between the cracks to see if we could catch a glimpse of a brush stroke, or decide if any of it resembled something we had seen before. But we decided it must all be bricollage, because if it hadn't been so when it was painted, then it was all a mess now.

Shoo, shoo!

We were being shoo-ed away from the site. They were serving wine and schörles on the edge of the premises so we scuttled off in that direction. One of the gallery assistants was trying to free a stack of exhibition texts that was wedged between a pile of bricks and a metal beam. She pulled so hard, and put all of her weight into it that she finally fell flat on her ass with only four sheets of paper to show for it. Still down on the floor, she dutifully gave them out to the people who passed her by.

198   LTTE NO. 17 — *The Rationalizations*

The fire department arrived and was giving free sips from the oxygen tanks, and everyone was in a delightful mood. No one mourned the sandwiched paintings, there was even talk of building another gallery directly on top of the ruins. They imagined what it would be like to excavate the site in 100 years. Eyes began to mist as they talked about the future's sentimental interest in the paintings, and the artists who would use the decaying canvas as a metaphor for all things lost and abandoned, not only for our lifetime, but for all lifetimes.

Well, but that comes later! The fire hose was engaged and a group of boys and girls started to undress, and the drunken firemen sprayed them playfully. The kids hid behind broken and jagged walls, where rust started to form immediately, and gushing streams forged their way into the deep crevices where the canvases were bunkered. An ice cream truck arrived and distributed popsicles of every color imaginable. Some ate them slowly, others chomped on them impatiently and the rest where thrown down the river rapidly becoming a flood.

The artist arrived. She had come stylishly late because she was alone and didn't want anyone to notice. No one had thought to tell her what had happened. She had missed all of the evolutionary steps to the scene that she now found before her. She was embarrassed, which was a feeling that she expected anyways. In the taxi coming over she imagined herself in the middle of a room surrounded by adoring colleagues and desperate collectors, chirping on about the provocative positioning she took on, as a woman—as a middle-aged woman. She imagined herself stoic, knowing and cold and was thankful that no one had been in the taxi observing her private daydreams.

She tried to take on that fantasy posture now, while observing the orgy that resulted from the weight of her paintings. Then she gave up. No visualization exercise could have prepared her for this. She caved her shoulders in and turned away. It would have been embarrassing enough to have been the centre of attention, but it was impossible to exist at the periphery of her own creation, no matter how euphoric it made the art kids today, or optimistically might fulfil some gap in discourse in the future.

She walked three blocks, slumped down on a corner curb, and pulled out cigarettes that weren't hers. Someone had left them in her apartment the other night. Her young assistants had made food, and all sorts of people came over. She tried

200   LTTE NO. 17 — *The Rationalizations*

not to talk about work, but it was damn impossible. So, she just pretended to listen while simultaneously rearranging budgets in her head.

She always used these sorts social occasions to drift off into organizational thinking, and because of this, everyone had the impression that she was perpetually busy. It was in the quiet moments alone that she would shut down, procrastinate, relax, and binge-watch one mindless film after another.

"Hold on tightly, let go lightly," Nicole Kidman said one night. "So true…" The artist affirmed to nobody, "so true."

The artist saw a crowd of girls walking down the block, their hair was wet and were wearing bras where their tops should have been. They were carrying fresh popsicles, in blue, green, white and pink colours, maybe even flavours. They were singing about things they didn't know about. Maybe they'd live long enough to dress appropriately and feel something, but on that day they were singing old lyrics about the possibility of future feelings, and walking in a nowhere land of charmed stupidity.

Someone told me long ago
There's a calm before the storm,
I know; it's been comin' for some time.
When it's over, so they say, it'll rain a sunny day,
I know; shinin' down like water.

A girl sat down next to the artist and asked her for a cigarette. The artist gave her one, and then had to give each of the girls one, and so they stood around holding a popsicle in one hand and a cigarette in the other.

We were standing across the street. They shoo-ed us so far from the flooding, collapsed, and compressed site that we couldn't see it anymore. There was water tumbling down sewage drains in every direction in a five block radius. Little bits of colour disappeared into the underworld, and people were wondering just what kind of paintings were they anyways, falling apart like that. An oil painting is supposed to survive centuries, witness wars and survive salt water submergence aboard colonial shipwrecks. People were used to the story about paintings being found dusty, dirty, hanging in privileged living rooms or museum archives. The muddy appearance made the world think that it was once a darker place or that people were blinder. When cleaned, the paintings rewarded them with a feeling of enlightened time travel.

Whatever had been hung on the gallery walls that morning probably started dissolving before the sun had set. By the time the artist's pack of cigarettes had all been smoked with the help of the half-naked women that surrounded her, their popsicles and the heavy paintings would melt away completely.

The Truth

Maryse Larivière

April 9th, 1996.

Sir,

I do not know who, close or far, told them that I was responsible. This is a set up, malice against me! I never belonged. Whatever happens with them, in their private life or with their business, I am not responsible, nor will I take care of it.

If you know them, please read my letter, so you can discover the truth. These are people who slyly judge and hound others so they can feel something. They are nice only to be mean, this is how they avenge themselves.

I never wanted to go live there. I would have needed to be more tenacious when I initially refused. This is the mess of a stubborn man and other crazy people, not to mention all the troubles I have been going through.

I, who knew nothing, fend for myself! I did not need them to look after the things I see that no one else does. They would have not been able to handle the truth anyways. The things I see are not things but thoughts, secret thoughts occurring suddenly in my mind, in my body.

With time though, I have managed to get rid of those crazies, and get them out of my life. If I had been back then the

LTTE no. 17 — *The Rationalizations* 203

way I am now, I would have gotten rid of them much faster. Unwilling to admit their mistake, they wrongly accused me.

I never want to see their faces anywhere and never want to read their weird letters again. Their letters do not exist, their letters never existed, their letters, they can blow their nose with them, and that for eternity. I even regret thinking about them.

You should tell them to move on, and move out in the desert, lots of people would be happy. People who hurt me, who bother me, do not mix well with me. The past is banished, and vanished is the past. Only the present with nice and honest people interests me. That is enough!

My dreams were denied, and I was left for dead with a crying note in my hand, but I soon regained my senses because my ways are free, and sunshine walks beside me. Now, I want peace, I want to pursue my work and lead a quiet life.

Yours,
A.

Unterscheidung im Kopf, 2015
Valentina Jager

LTTE no. 18 — *Forgetting*
June 8, 2015

The weight of the world in knapsacks and briefcases.

Anna M. Szaflarski

So why don't I come to visit, and we'll have a date, he said. This is what I was waiting for him to say. It was the third conversation we had had since we started talking again. It had been seven years since we had seen each other. Seven years since I ruined things royally. And ever since, in every lull between boyfriends or lovers or whatever, I hoped I would get a chance to see him again. But it never happened, it couldn't happen. It had been impossible until now, and I didn't know why.

Yeah, really?, I was testing the waters of plausibility before getting too excited. *But, isn't that a lot of money? What if I don't look they way you remember? Where are you going to stay?*, The answers were not the point, the questions were begging to be dismissed.

Amy, at this point, what have I got to lose? If you want to see me, then I'll have to make the trip. I'll stay somewhere, who cares? He was so pragmatic. I think that was what I liked about him most. I stared at the tapestry hanging on my wall in my one-bedroom apartment in Berlin. I bought it around the time we split. I couldn't remember if it had been during the brief return to each other, or after I ruined everything for what I thought would be forever.

Geez, I took a deep breath. I didn't want to believe it, cause then I'd have to start hoping, I admitted. Shit, it was too late, the floodgates burst open, I fantasized about what I'd wear when he came, or where I'd take him to eat. I was a lost cause, at the point of no return. *Wow,* I exhaled, *Yeah, I mean, when?*

Back then, before sabotaging everything and realizing that he was probably the only one capable to put up with me, we would sit and stare at each other in amazement. If I remembered correctly, we'd wake up and go to bed happy. I remembered running to the door every time he came over, after he said he needed space, but I begged and begged until I convinced him to come. If I wasn't mistaken, he was the one who on a bad day would hold me until it didn't seem to matter. We fought too. I thought about how most of our fights were either about the number of male friends I kept and how they couldn't possibly all just be my friends. I recalled getting angry when he'd limit me somehow, tell me that I'd probably never get around to doing something I said I would do. Back then he was worried about me drifting off, and I wished I hadn't always had to do what I vowed to do.

I'll check flights tomorrow. But probably in a couple of months, I can't be sure when exactly I'll get time off. He paused, *Do you think you can wait that long?* He didn't ask me because he thought I was desperate to see him.

I was desperate to see him, but he asked because he knew that I might freak out before it all happened, that I might doubt everything and go off looking for someone else as a safety net. He knew that by the time two months rolled around I might have already ruined everything.

Yes, I can wait, I pretended. *Let's just try to keep as much contact in the meantime,* I said breathing deeply again. I asked the universe to grant me patience, a virtue that eluded me and has been slow to develop.

So, it's going to be the fall when you get here. We could go for a trip somewhere maybe. Go over to Poland. I could show you my home country, hehehe. I made a fake Slavic accent.

He didn't laugh, because it wasn't funny. It was nervous. *Well, we can decide the details later. But for now I imagine just meeting for coffee near your house.*

I began to panic, *I'm going to have a hard time just imagining 'going for coffee' for the next two months.* I walked into the kitchen and turned the kettle on. It was early in the morning. There was nine hours time difference between us. He was just getting into bed, I had just gotten up.

Have you already eaten breakfast? he asked.

No, just looking in the fridge now. I looked at my options. *I'm really hungry, I think I'm going to make a hard-boiled egg. There's some melon here and yoghurt.*

He sounded pleased for some reason. *No more granola for you, I guess? Things have changed.* Breakfast used to be a mutually appreciated past time.

Yeah, well I still go through phases of eating granola. But I can't find unsalted peanuts anywhere, I still think about the ones you used to buy. I poured boiling water into a pot and turned on the stove. *Those peanuts were the best.* I wanted to go on about the peanuts, but said instead, *I don't want to wait two months.*

It won't be so bad, it'll give the summer a bit of a glow, knowing that it'll wrap up that way. We've both got plenty of things to do.

208   LTTE NO. 18 — *Forgetting*

It was true, but nothing seemed all that important anymore. A week ago my life felt like one of those medieval tables you see in movies, covered in wooden pawns strategically placed ready for battle on top a model landscape of the country. Now I wanted to unsheathe my sword and scrape them all to the floor.

Yeah, you're right. My egg was boiling. I dropped two pieces of bread into the toaster. The toaster timer was set on 5. I always had to pop them out early to prevent it from burning. There was nothing preventing me from changing the setting, I always told myself that I would turn it down the next time I made breakfast. I poured the remaining water from the kettle over coffee grounds in the French press and sat down. *Hmm, so does anyone who remembers me know about this over there?* Again, it wasn't exactly the question I had wanted to ask.

What do you mean? Like, someone from the school?

It was the first question in a series of questions that I knew would lead me to feel uncomfortable. The current situation didn't give me anything to worry about, and that made me worry. He was coming over for coffee in two months, and I needed to jog my brain with a problem in the meantime.

Yeah, do you see anybody that we used to know back then?

I see Martin once in a while, he moved back a few years ago after wandering across the country. He mentioned that you crossed paths for a few minutes in Toronto and that you barely recognized him.

That's true! I exclaimed. *I almost forgot, but it's true, I didn't recognize him. And then didn't really know what to say. I think I had a flat tire, and I think I pretty much only talked about that.* I pressed on with the next phase of questioning, *So you told him that we're talking again?*

No. I haven't had a chance. He mentioned that story to me about three years ago, when he was passing through here. He paused.

There was nothing pensive about it, just a gap in speech. *I haven't told anybody Amy. I don't really see the old gang anymore. Franny and Paul are around. I sometimes see them in the market with their kids. There's others around, people that you knew and they knew you, but you weren't close.*

My round-about questions were taking too long, I dove right in, *Do you still see Shannon?* She was the woman who came after me. The woman who had once been a good friend. The woman who gave him everything that he needed and that I couldn't. She was the one who prevented him from saying 'yes' when I asked him to marry me. Maybe. But probably she had nothing to do with it. It was the right call.

Not for a long time, but we keep in touch. We meet up sometimes when they come into town. Uly, her kid is getting to be so big, and you can imagine she's still really important to me.

I was peeling the shell off my egg and letting it fall into an extra bowl I had put on the table. Once, someone told me that using an extra bowl like a miniature trash bin on the table was considered bad manners. I never heard something so stupid in my life. I thought about the stupid man who told me that stupid thing.

Amy?

Yeah, I'm here. I'm glad that you're coming. I'm already worried about you leaving. Having exhausted my first worry, I started in a different direction.

Don't get yourself all worked up, He was being pragmatic again, but it suited me less this time. *We can think about that when we get there. I can probably only stay for a week or two during the first visit.* I could tell he was smiling, and even though I knew why he was smiling, I didn't like it. He sensed that I was determined to worry so he tried distracting me, *So what are you doing today?.*

210   LTTE no. 18 — *Forgetting*

My toast popped out of the toaster. *Shit, I forgot to take the toast out early, now it's all burnt.* I got up and started scraping the charcoal off into the sink, trying to salvage something from the bread. I didn't say anything while I did this. He didn't either. Black powder gathered into wet puddles of tar sands in the sink. I placed both severely damaged toasts on my plate and sat back down. *I have to go to work.* I put large amounts of butter on both toasts. I sliced the peeled egg.

What are you doing at work? he asked encouragingly.

I sprinkled salt and pepper on the toast and bit into it sloppily. *Um dethynyn shum deeails fo da enfrane way ortals.* My mouth was full.

Huh?

I swallowed, *I'm designing some details for the entrance-way portals.*

That's cool, right, you told me about that. Send me a sample of what you come up with. His interest was waning which meant that he was getting tired. It must have been already after 1 am there. *Hey Amy, everything is going to be alright.*

Sure. You're getting tired, I can let you go. It couldn't all just be alright, and if there were any problems to be had at that moment or at anytime in the possible future I was desperate to get them all on the table straight away.

I can call you tomorrow. I'm starting to pass out.

No that's fine you don't have to. I don't know what time I'm going to be at home. Actually, I didn't have any plans, but something told me I should make sure I was doing something. I realized that I was doing it again. I was starting to plan without him, building a complete fortress where he wouldn't be necessary after all, just in case he realizes what a horrible mistake he had made in the first place. I forced my guard down, *I'll be home late, but that'll be perfect for you, yeah, give me a call.*

There was only one question left, *Why Richard? Why would you give me another chance after everything we've been through?*

Serendipitous timing, I guess. And why not? Nothing can happen that we haven't already been through.

Yeah, but we suffered for such a long time afterward. A soggy cemented piece of toast was blocking my diaphragm. A feeling that surfaced along with the memory old rationalizations I used to believe in. That I had to do what I did back then. For self-preservation or what have you. But those illusions had been worn down for a long time. I had never treated anybody so badly in my life, and here he was on the phone offering to a pay significant amount of his own money to get on a plane to see me. Maybe he had been spared in the aftermath, while I had suffered so much. Maybe he really believed that I had changed. Or maybe he didn't expect much and was just looking for a good time. He was probably coming to teach me a lesson, to get my hopes up before crushing me into a pulp.

We've had time to reflect, I think. You seem different. The same, but different.

More like yourself when I first met you.

That had been eleven years ago. I looked around my kitchen for some evidence of my life from then. Nothing. Lots of things from before and after that time. Objects, trinkets, pictures dating from six, five or twenty years ago, but nothing from eleven, ten or nine years ago.

Yeah, that would be nice, I imagined the person who might emanate from that void of physical evidence. *Ok, go to sleep. I'll talk to you later or the next few days.*

Have a good day, Amy.

Thanks, sleep well, Richard, I'm looking forward to coffee.

Me too. Bye.

212   LTTE no. 18 — *Forgetting*

He hung up and I put my phone down. It took me a few minutes to return to the there and now. I looked at the clock which said that I was running severely late. I put the dishes next to the sink and rushed around my apartment gathering my things, and brushing my teeth. I looked at myself in the mirror and paused. *What am I doing? This is ridiculous.* I headed for the door and almost reached the handle before bluntly stubbing my toe hard against something. *Fucking hell.* I jumped around on one foot for a bit before searching for the culprit that inflicted it's untimely wrath upon me. There it was, the physical evidence that I had missed earlier. It was hard, heavy and seemed to follow me everywhere.

Today's date adds up

Ilaria Biotti

In the last months my plants have been beautiful, probably because of intense sessions of procrastinational gardening.

Do you also have a comfort denial activity?

The text you are reading takes off from a second draft; the first draft crashed, deleting forever my freshly typed thoughts. Yes, I forgot to save it.

#save. Today's date adds up; $10+5=15$, lovely.

Within this text, I want to share with you two intertwined concerns I have.

The first concern is about my lack of acceptance of being a tourist (or traveller, sightseer, visitor, journeyer however you define it), which leads me to employ strategies aimed at veiling my discomfort with a fake non-tourist status; the second one is the growing and shrinking of the left staircase in the building where I live.

The impossibility of identifying myself as a tourist reminds me of a sentence a friend told me: "the complainer who says

214   LTTE no. 18 — *Forgetting*

that there are too many people around him/her doesn't take in to account that he/she is also part of the crowd and the peopleness that he/she complains about."

#save

In the next paragraph I try to deconstruct my notion of tourism through three activities I love doing when traveling.

Firstly, I route out as many (un)official points of interest as possible with a local guide. He/she can tell me anything in terms of narrative to the visited territory. What I love about these tales is that they can be powerfully imaginative and highly speculative.

Secondly, feast of typical victuals.

This activity might include tasting the un-tastable; namely what a tourist would never eat/drink in his/her homeland, such as insects or rotten eggs. Often these victuals might not even be eaten by locals, but constantly asked for by tourists according to a somehow-gained previous impression of what a local person would choose. The local community often offers what the tourists have been asking for. In time, everyone forgets that the event in question was created ad hoc and its definition of typical becomes the official narrative. Concrete examples of such events can be palms on tropical islands or the selling of masks in Venice.

Thirdly, document randomly with no specific aim. 3000 pictures document my last winter trip. I'll probably never look at most of them again.

#save

But why did I shoot 3000 pictures? It seemed to be so necessary. What elements remain entangled in the abstraction of the 2d surface?

#save

Summarizing. Few people (I am not going to use the term tourists, although I mean it) beat me at visiting and eating. I thrill when running around all day ingurgitating, following the traces of the most hidden restaurant who only a local person would know—again, bottom line, I am not a tourist!

#save

Among the 3000 pictures I already told you about, 143 pictures portray a common frog.

Sharp in my memory lay the frog's red eyes and it's green body, while the 143 pictures object by insistently displaying a rainbow colored body.

I have no other proof to state my memory besides these images, the ones contesting it.

If a rainbow can register on a surface in a moment where my memory could abstract only plain green, then, maybe, I'll also be able to document the magical event that is repeatedly taking place on the staircase between the first, second and third floor of the building where I live.

216   LTTE no. 18 — *Forgetting*

I come to my second concern, which is located on that staircase; a space where I am not a tourist at all.

#save

It might have something to do with me disguising magic as a non-probable event, but I never told anyone that my staircase changes number of floors randomly. Time and space stretch while I try to reach the fourth floor. The third floor, unmistakably recognizable because of a plaster patch placed on the second door on the right, suddenly is substituted by a repeated second floor.

You might be thinking that this riddle has a simple solution, namely that I suck at climbing stairs. Still, there is no concrete indication proving that the staircase hasn't changed; the only matter of evidence is my memory of having been on the second floor shortly before.

I ask my self how does a constantly growing and shrinking building look from the outside. I must ask my neighbor.

#save

LTTE no. 19 — *Doubt That This Is It*
June 17, 2015

I Stand Here Before You
A 6 min, 40 sec reading for the "Schau der Gestaltung"
(Verein der Gestaltung, Berlin), June 25, 2015

Anna M. Szaflarski

I have to admit, I like to talk in front of a crowd. I like to enunciate words in an exaggerated manner. I like to make voices. I do a horrible British and Southern accent, [bad Southern Accent]: *which my papa told me should not be the cause of preventing me from doin 'em.* It's bad I know. I want to make people laugh and I often try way too hard. It's a bit embarrassing, but I like having your attention.

[LOUD] Volume is very important in getting people's attention, but not in keeping it. [normal volume] In my family everyone talks at exactly the same time. When no one talked, then really nobody talked, and there was utter silence that weighed heavily in the house. But when someone started jabbering, everyone went at it all at once. And the only way to get anybody to listen to you was to talk louder than everybody else. It's really crazy to watch. While yelling, each member of my family would frantically scan the room,

218   LTTE NO. 19 — *Doubt That This Is It*

looking for an accomplice, an ally, a competitor to see who was about to quit and listen and who was still in the race. But once you've won the battle of blasting trumpets, to keep the them entertained, to keep their attention on you, you had to shift your game.

In 2013, I did a series of performances where I read segments of speeches by what I would describe as strong American rhetoricians; people who can not only hold the attention of large masses of people but can move something inside of those people. For one particular performance I selected fragments of speeches from American President Barack Obama, the motivational speaker Anthony Robbins, and the televangelist Joel Osteen. I didn't have a grand concept for the piece, I didn't think it was genius, I was just curious. I was curious to see what it would be like to talk like them, not exactly impersonate them, but say their words with a similar energy, in front of an audience.

I copied and pasted almost random quotes from several speeches. I read the texts from pieces of paper, very similar to the way I do now, not attempting in any way memorize them. I went on like that for at least 20 minutes, skipping back and forth between the different speakers. It was slow going, but after about five minutes I noticed people were starting to slide into my rhythm. Getting into the heavy rhetoric of solidarity, national pride, self-improvement and godliness. So much so, that when I was done, people came up to me to ask for empowering advice. Anna, what else can I do? I was flabbergasted. It was hard to convince them that I had unfeelingly, and objectively robbed the words from somewhere else, and that those words had in no way reflected any of my own opinions.

It was an experiment that resulted in a strange experience. I never did that performance again. Actually, I did very few performances after that. It was like every performance I had done before that, was leading to the same climax. However small the audience was that day, in that moment I experienced attention on a level of concentration that I didn't know what to do with and no longer felt comfortable with.

Performance has never been my main thing. I only dallied with it from time to time. As a young student I bought two stationary bikes with my friend Shiloh, road them during the entire opening of an exhibition, and afterwards we returned the bikes, for which we got a full-refund. It was relatively senseless. We had a concept, but I have entirely forgotten it. I did a few things in bewteen, but it was much later that I thought I would take the idea performing more seriously and wrote a sober and poetic one-woman play, and cast myself in the role. After that I wrote a fantasy erotic monologue and acted it out. Then flirted with pseudo-academia, and started doing what all academics do: mindlessly reference things, so I started doing re-enactments of other people's performances and eventually I arrived at the performance I described to you a moment ago.

I never had a clear goal, concept or motivation, which was maybe obvious. I think what baffled me was that there existed this accepted medium where people were forced to look at me for an extended period (usually an audience can comfortably put up with anything up to twenty minutes). They don't have to like me, or what I am doing, they'll go on looking anyways, and are generally respectful about it. Their irises pointing in my direction, I look into them [looking in the eyes of the audience], and yet, remain a stranger. Grant you, I have never done anything overly revealing like get naked (a common performance tactic for women, which I'm sure that only 50% of the population is getting tired of seeing). I've also never tried another common strategy and intentionally bored audience, testing their or my own endurance. I like it when a performance in a gallery is entertaining. I don't like it when it strives to make people anxious, or feel uncomfortable. I think there's no use in staging those kinds of situations because I think, we, as humans, and especially as artists, feel that way most of the time anyways. And honestly, 'compelling' is difficult, entertainment just comes more naturally to me.

I've also been in your position as an audience member and have watched all sorts of performances, both the comfortable and uncomfortable kind. There is something exhilarating about watching someone who will compromise his/her social norms to stand out. To confidently stand in front of people and behave in ways that they wouldn't normally. You might feel a bit embarrassed for the performer, and yet intrigued by the fact that you're allowed to inspect someone so closely, watch, judge, and analyse them, and don't have to feel guilty about it. And while they're going on maybe doing something like the robot dance in florescent pants, or yelling manifesto-like statements in a g-string, you wonder what could possibly be their motivation to do this anyways? Are they really pushing some art discourse forward or do they just get off on this? Does it turn them on? Is it possible that their sex life is better because of it? Who are they having sex with and could I become that person?

If the performance goes on for long enough then we might start looking discreetly around the room, wondering if someone else is thinking the same things we are. Wonder who in the room knows the performer, and question if we can tell just by the way they are watching.

There's also those kind of performances that demand that the audience gets involved [sit on male audience member]. Most people hate this, it's like sitting in the front row at a Nickelodeon event, and while you're minding your own business clapping along to Ren and Stimpy, green sludge is dumped all over you. When this happens, the performer is power-playing you. You are put on the spot. Everyone is watching and you really have no choice but to comply, preferably while trying to pretend that you're a good sport about it, smiling and shooting bewildered looks to your friends. I suggest that next time this happens you, just say no. Remember, no means no, nothing you are wearing invited me to do this and it's not your fault. [get off of male audience member]

So, yeah, anyways. I don't do performances anymore. I've gone back to yelling to get my attention, and have learned to not hold on to it. So, now I'm letting go, which segues to the most awkward part of the performance: the end. You often don't know when a performance ends, if you should clap or snap and when you should finally stop looking at me. But now, now would be a good time. Because this is the end. Thank you.

Four Manifestos and/or Semi-Manifestos

Jacob Wren

1.
Manifesto for Confusion, Struggle and Conflicted Feelings

I've been making art for my entire life and I've never felt more lost. In this, I believe I am not alone.

Do we care enough about art, meaning, the world to admit there is no obvious or effective way forward? That we're going in circles with an ever-lessening effect? That we're going in circles but are unwilling to admit it?

The grand excitements of art—the modernist breaks, the new movements, the cataclysms—are long behind us. More recent trends are fleeting at best. The belief in originality is utterly depleted and, more importantly, no longer feels like a worthy goal. All we have now is A LOT, far too much, of everything. A LOT of art, theatre, dance, performance, music, installation, painting, literature, cinema, internet: of every possible type and gradation of quality. More stuff than you could possibly experience even if you lived for several million years.

But we don't live for even a million years. Our lives are brief and what it means to seize the day is by no means clear. Why must we pretend that we know what to do?

LTTE NO. 19 — *Doubt That This Is It* 223

Politics have lost the plot—right wing governments and the ascendancy of the super-rich are the order of the day—and artists are of little assistance. On our current environmental trajectory we believe the planet will not survive. But, if we keep hurtling forward, in fact it is we who will not survive, as the planet steps in to take care of itself. (Then again, it is likely at least a few of us will survive to sort through the wreckage. But we can't make art for them. They're not born yet. We must make art for now.)

With this present, and this future, how can one feel that bold artistic moves have any real energy? Conflicted feelings rule the day. Daily confusions of every stripe. Ambivalence is king. Where is the art that strikingly knows it's own futility but stumbles forward compellingly, anyway, because as an artist you have no choice?

To change anything you have to work together with other people. This is the essential logic behind an art movement, behind a manifesto. To work together with other people you need to line up behind a potent conviction, agree to all run in the same direction, at least until you score the first few goals. There is power in numbers, in clans, clubs and mafias. So why can't all the artists in the world who feel as lost as I do come together, think about what is left to do and how? There may be no convictions to unite us, but why can't we unite in the potency of our contemporary ambivalence? In the desire to be honest and vulnerable about where we actually stand?

(An artist who is little more than an advertisement for him or her self is so lost there might be no way back towards meaning. I live in constant fear that this is what I might become.)

I dream of energy, content, value, meaning. Effective left wing populism. The end, or reduction, of alienation, consumerism, war and stupidity. But when you dream you are asleep, and right now I would prefer to be as awake as possible. And to be awake means to admit I have almost no idea how to bring such dreams closer to reality. All roads seem blocked. I have no idea what strategies—in life, politics or art—might be genuinely useful or poetic. I want to be awake, while not losing touch with the knowledge that to stay sane one must continue to sleep and dream.

In fact, I wish to write a manifesto that will admit to everything: ambivalence, conflicted feelings, doing things only for money, humiliation, cynicism, confusion, not being able to tell my friends from my enemies. To admit to everything and find out if anyone agrees. If anyone out there is with me. If such honesty and confusion can mean anything in the current world. If there can be any integrity to it. If it can transform itself into a useful truth.

An artist doesn't need conviction. An artist doesn't need to know which way to go. An artist needs talent, naiveté, community and life experience. None of these things are incompatible with feeling lost.

(I would someday like to write another manifesto about how art that is not intrinsically connected to life is of no value. But I feel too lost to enter into life. I'm an extreme case. I can't find the way in.)

Of course, about such things one doesn't write manifestos. But perhaps we should find a way to start.

Jacob Wren

2.

Notes on Literature
(Unfinished Manifesto)

– Vulnerable Writing, moments of jarring tenderness, that something (but what exactly?) is at risk, that in the writing itself there is a sense of risk, the writer does not take a safe position high above the action but is down in the fucking middle of it all, hands dirty, against (yet still unavoidably complicit with) the strong complexity of the worlds stupidity, cruelty and incompetence. Critical, yet in league with curiosity and joy.

– An open vessel that lets everything in: every kind of research (to be used for both quotation and plagiarism but nothing in between), things read, heard, seen, done, thought, suffered. The narrative does not exclude any kind of material, the narrative is a giant magnet that draws every kind of material towards itself.

– Not particularly autobiographical. Bringing oneself, ones entire self, all of ones observations and understanding of the world, headlong into the task of fiction. But why not autobiography? Because there is this cursed desire to bring in so much more of the world, to bring in things beyond what one can ever individually experience.

– To reject the "stench of literature", to know that writing can be so much more than "good".

– No to straining for effect, yes to insights heartrendingly gained and stated simply, or not so simply. No to the care-

fully placed phrase, yes to words and sentences that follow
one another with the unexpected thrill of great conversation.
No to precise historical detail, yes to pure invention and the
vividness of the present moment. No to the big revelation at
the end of the book, yes to the revelation that books and life
are inseparable.

– What does it mean for literature to be "about" something?
How can we mean this differently?

3.
Resistance as Paradox

The paradox is as follows: we, as artists and viewers alike,
know that art is fundamentally conservative, yet we still want
to believe that it is radical and revolutionary. Within the
space of this paradox there is room for a great deal to happen.

Art is conservative because the moment you call something art (or theatre, literature, etc.) it has already been con-
tained. The things it can change, and the ways it can change
our thinking, have already been limited. Art is the corner in
which transgression and questioning are allowed, at times
even encouraged, and making art is like being told to go
stand in that corner.

The recent, romantic history of art is a history of alleged
transgression. So many of today's standard art moves began
as small deviances and transgressions. And while it does
seem there are now no rules left to break, more to the point
is that knowing a transgression, if successful, will soon
be canonized and therefore de-fanged, drains all energy from
the gesture.

Politics requires efficacy. Trying to change things entails immense frustration. The tension between this lived frustration and potential for efficacy often feels absurd.

Politics as a spirit of resistance, as a desire to open up possibilities. And yet: resistance, in order to remain resistant, must always be unfinished, a work-in-progress, because if you win then you're in power and somebody else has to resist against you. (I am wondering if this paradox might ease the inherent frustration involved in any act of sustained resistance.) Something similar might be said of opening up possibilities: once they have been opened one has to move on. There is something restless, unsustainable, about such modes of political thinking.

[Unfinished.]

4.

A short history of anti-theatre, non-music, counter-philosophy, semi-specific art and unpolitics.

The things I like are, in general, in opposition to things most generally accepted. There are of course exceptions. No one wants to be contrary simply for the sake of being contrary and neither do I. Without an enemy, without something to resist against, most things fall flat. Co-operation and symbiotic relations are also necessary. There are no shortage of evils in the world that must be resisted, no shortage of mediocrity in art that must be pushed against or undermined. It is not the mediocrity of a single work of art or artist that must be resisted, but the mediocrity of art itself. And it is in fact these false dichotomies that must be undermined since, to some extent, all dichotomies are false. The energy gained from such frustrations goes to waste if it is not put to use, and so much of what exists in the world, and is most appreciated, is a waste of its own fragile potential. There is what is, and what could be, and what could be most often contains the greater energy. We must struggle with what is, in the here and now, without regret, seizing every last opportunity. How are we to understand criteria when the search is for something new and there is nothing new? How are we to understand selection? Does it entail risk to fight the status quo or is it more of a risk to fight within and against ourselves? The world is wrong in so many ways and each of us is also wrong, but everything that exists contains at least a modicum of the future. It is within the tension of this future, in its likely partial failure, that each history begins. This entails saying what you mean as precisely as possible, but not letting any preconceived meaning overwhelm you. Going against things also entails going along with some specific idea of the against. We must avoid parody, avoid satire, embrace genuine humor, find the joy within our lived refusal. There are several mysteries here that will not be explained. Several operations. If we fall behind at least we are still in movement. If we are impatient at least the situation surrounds us. Everything has not yet been done.

LTTE no. 20 — *You and Me*
July 8, 2015

Guild of Thieves:
The Writing Table

Anna M. Szaflarski

I've been experiencing a reoccurring daydream. Basically, this dream consists of compiling Letters to the Editors into a publication, which then some head writer from an American television show reads, and is subsequently determined... no, is obsessed... to get me to sit in on one of their writing rooms for a half-year. Unfortunately, there are two things that sour my dream in the end every time: 1. The general improbability of it ever happening, and 2. the thought of the thousands of hyper-elite 20 year-old writers and comics that are dreaming of exactly the same thing. But unlike the army of ambitious teen geniuses, I don't want to make a career out of it, I just want a taste; take a look and bring it back to show everybody what I have learned.

I've been casually telling friends about this fantasy. It was initially sparked three years ago when I read Tina Fey's memoir. It is generally ridiculous, but has moments of in-

230   LTTE no. 20 — *You and Me*

sight especially in her descriptions of her group writing methods. About how she goes about hiring a writers' room; a mix between Ivy-league graduates, and street-smart comics. And how she adopts rules of improvisational theatre into the dynamic of her team's process. A similar collaborative process is being used by writers to develop all sorts of iconic television. Today, refined ideas, plots, dialogues, comedy as well as drama is being pumped out of the United States at an alarming rate, by individuals that I've been calling the NASA of pop culture.

In my fantasy I develop a similar Writing Table in the arts. And yet, I still only have a vague idea of what it would look like.

I don't want to go on too long about Fey, because when she occupies your mind for too long you will tire of her, but for a moment longer I'd like to describe the very points that intrigued me. Two things in particular: 1. The improvisation rules applied to optimize idea exchange and generation, and 2. The process of selection of members for a Writing Table.

Stemming from the rules of 'Improv' Theatre, she lays out a few basic rules. Firstly, you must always agree with your collaborator: "To say 'Yes' and see where it takes you". This was simple enough, but a poignant revelation for me. Imagine a round table of artists, curator and writers, who instead of trying to win an argument, always agree with each other. A ridiculous game, you think! Of course, at first you might think that the initial idea put on the table is not of the finest quality, but out of respect for the intelligence of your partner you agree to take on their course of thinking for a period of time. You may feel resistance to this at first, but I invite you to indulge. The second improv rule may help to appease you, because after you agree, you are expected to always add to the first proposition, "Yes, And..." Through this process the group can gain momentum, ideas will be minutely amended, grow, get out of control, be purged, reduced and finally take form.

Fey goes on to add two additional rules, one that she feels is especially geared towards women: make statements, avoiding phrasing things in apologetic questions, and another more general rule: there are no mistakes.

Yes, And...

The other thing that intrigued me was her strategy for hiring collaborators. Fey credits Michael Lorne (creator of Saturday Night Live) for teaching her the benefits of hiring a mixture of well-tuned academics in combination with slapstick natural talent. A mixture of analytical people with people who can react to things intuitively. Too much of either pool can stagnate the creative process. The vague thought of this excites me already. Where could I find such a team?

You might of been one of the few that I have talked to about this already, you watched my eyes light up, and my lips flutter. Perhaps I was already using you as my Writing Table. You'd know if our conversations have made it onto the pages of LTTE issues. But this process has been until now generally covert. You are unaware that I am 'using' you to generate ideas and sense out our demographic. How do I take this and transform it into a full blown structured Table? I don't know how, who, where or when. There are a few things that some of you have asked me to consider. Yes, I perhaps unjustly compare the accomplishments of TV think-tanks of television to the accomplishments of NASA and over-glorify what that kind of ambition could bring. But I pleaded with you: I don't want the ambitions NASA (nor do I understand what that really entails other than space exploration, and if

On the grounds that my idea was formed inside of a vacuum, I'd say that you've stolen it from me. At some point when I wasn't looking you slid your way through the two-fold sliding contamination doors, and somehow avoided having your eyes sucked out of your brain (since vacuums tend to do that: FYI watch Total Recall, 1990). You grabbed on to my idea and paraded it around as if it were your own.

You bitch.

I think you should know that the idea came to me quite naturally. It was of the immaculate conception sort. It came to me, or on me. I'm not quite sure, but there it was all of a sudden showering all of its glory on to me, and acknowledging my already self-aware genius. I didn't act on it right away because there was no need to, it was self-sufficient as it was. You've violated it, me, and ultimately yourself.

You have contaminated the vacuum, it needs to be sterilized and reclimatized. I will send you the bill, which you are expected to pay within 30 days or will be penalized with interest.

The passive aggressive letter your roommate
wrote you during your years at art school.

that were possible, than, yes, I want that too), the efficiency of HBO, or the politics of money and censorship that come along with them. I don't want to build a sure-safe money-making machine (although, let's face it, this whole producing for free thing has its down sides). But I must admit that one aspect of this commercial machine does attract me, and that is the idea of producing projects, texts, books on a fast paced and with high turn-over.

I think there are many obstacles standing in our way to form a really great Writing Table. I do think money is one of them. The focus on the individual artistic career is so great and is driven by a market that wants to believe that art is created by vacuum-sealed independent geniuses. We know that this is a delusion. Many professional artists have something like a writing table in their studios, kitchens, beds etc. where groups of people (AKA artist assistants, fellow artists, technicians, artisans, lovers) generate ideas and production solutions that have significant influence on final works. Artists steal consciously or subconsciously from each other, which I think is generally healthy. Conflict only arises when the world stubbornly wants to award credit to only one person.

When people watch television, they appreciate the writers and producers that made it happen, but in the end they don't really care and are more interested in the product. Art does not have this luxury. The author and his/her biography is relentlessly important (at times the most important) to viewers and collectors, and is evident to even the regular visitor off the street who for example might read with great interest how many love affairs Diego Rivera had before even seeing his murals. If the expectations of the role artist was described in Hollywood terms they would have to be both the Actor (celebrity, who is the face of the product) and the Writer (the behind-the-scenes strategist). Fey might be an example of someone who does both, but also is someone who writes extensively about working in a team. The demand for those who can play both ends in the art world leads to a certain amount of cultural delusion that is standing in the way of creating a functioning Writing Table.

The need to believe that an artist creates in a vacuum prevents respect from being distributed among the collaborators that help to create an artistic product.

Yes, and…

Is this coming from a place of jealously because I haven't achieved recognition in the art world? Maybe, I could never be objective enough to be sure. But I would argue instead, that I am a person that is exhilarated by exchanging ideas in a group. I am rarely bothered by the fact that an idea begins elsewhere as long as I can be part of hashing out the details; making it better, realistic, feasible. And I think there are many people like myself. We like to analyse, deconstruct, argue, submit and rebuild in pairs, threes or more. We end up being the sidekicks to many projects, not because we do not have ideas of our own, but because we thrive in tight parameters, and the limitations that come with bouncing ideas off of other people.

This does not change the fact that due credit is still important. I, like anyone else, want recognition for the things I do. I am not immune to characteristics of being human, nor do I want to become a selfless martyr for art.

The professional contemporary art scene is often a collaborative one, like in fashion, architecture, or graphic design, there is a team involved in resolving problems, and in idea creation/manipulation. The only difference is that in the art world, assistants are never titled junior-artist, or resident-artist, as young fashion designers or architects might be. The experience gained in the studio of a successful artist is not transferable, to say, to another company. It is not a career, nor is it encouraged to be. Assistants are expected to either break out as icons themselves or live with the conditions of their invisibility.

I do not believe that the role of the artist assistant should become a career, that's not the point I'm driving at. What I am suggesting is a reformation of the studio practice all together. Yes, and…

I am also not talking about working in a collective, about abandoning authorship, and working anonymously. An artist collective, where each artists participates anonymously is only a compromise. Each person at the Writing Table should feel acknowledged, affirmed and purposeful and should be paid (yes, with money) accordingly.

At the Writing Table sits a team of individuals who are drafted for their excellence. They as a team would be put to the task, let's say for example, to develop an exhibition. An initial idea would be brought up by one individual, and the next thing that would happen is someone would agree and add something to that idea. Through the process of amendments and adjustments the original idea may strengthen or mutate into another one completely. Every member would be expected to be as willing to forge concepts as they are to let go of them. Someone would have to track the process (this technical detail remains vague to me, and is something I would like to learn on my magical journey into TV land).

Do Writing Tables need leadership? Yes, I believe so, but they would function as equal contributors as well as facilitators instead of dictators. But more than an almighty leader you need a group of people who feel valued for their individual talents and abilities. People who feel that their excellence is being applied to the fullest degree inside of a group. Because let's face it, we're not going to get rid of people's egos, especially if they are good. When you recruit someone that is good, their abilities should be continually validated. People who feel competent and confident tend to be quicker thinkers. There must be way of respecting people's talents without inflating their confidence or creating false gods.

I come back to my initial question: how does one go about forming something like a Writing Table? I'm not sure yet. I guess my first thought was to put these few ideas on paper.

Seated at my current fantasy table sit writers, artists, comics and journalists (no names for now). What are we working on? An exhibition, a fart joke? Who knows, but it's marvellous. Yes, and...

Transcribed Conversations

Blanca Gomila

(Act) 1
In the Gallery:

– Hi!

– Nice to see you here! How are you doing?

– Yes, I don't know because what I really need is a tax advisor. Do you know someone? My life depends on my taxes in this moment…

– Yeah, I want to learn more about that… I always think I might be doing something wrong.

– Oh, how cool, but… You know? I really want to get away from this modern city life, everything is about money.

– I only see superficiality and cynicism everywhere. The relationships are volatile, the people are always late…

– I see around me people using drugs all the time.

– But anyways I'm cool, I'm thinking I should blond my

LTTE no. 20 — *You and Me* 237

hair, I've never had blond hair before... I don't know.
I'm planning little changes in my lifestyle, like being
a little more careful with my environment.

– I see,... Last weekend I went to a new place and, you
know. It was a post-industrial place very Mad Max.

– You can see all Berlin from the roof. It was cool, but
it gave me a vertigo. We stayed in the party until 2 pm
and the people were super high. That situation gave me
a lot to think... lately I have had the feeling that there
are just too many drugs in my surroundings...

– My dealer sells red superman at half price, because it came
out in the press that it might be toxic... they said one girl
died the other day from that.

– shame on him!... could you give me his number?

– Hahahahaha (laughs)

– could you give me his number?? Hahaha (laughs)

– Well I'll go have something to drink

– Okay

– See you!

LTTE no. 20 — *You and Me*

(Act)2
In the Club:

– Hey Hello!

– Hi! How are you? It was a long time we didn't see each other!

– What have you been up to lately? You were in China on a tour, right?

– Yes! But that was in February, it was great, awesome. We haven't seen each other since?

– I spend most of my time in Brandenburg making firewood…

– Oh yeah? Great! Healthy life! I have been the last months eating shrimps in Spain.

– Ah! Really? I love the shrimps, well, I love all the seafood!

– Yes me too. I love barnacles… knives and prawns ,oysters, crabs… hmm! but what I really love is the lobster !

– Oh yeah! Fantastic! And the spider crab!

– The lobster with rice drives me crazy!

– What are you drinking? Do you want a drink?

– No thanks, I already have one.

LTTE no. 21 — *Merely Humans*
July 21, 2015

Review

Anna M. Szaflarski

When entering the exhibition held at the only space left in the rapidly developing neighbourhood—the only commercial institution able to afford such a luxury—you see a couple kissing intimately in the corner. They behave as if they didn't have a clue that they were being watched. She seems more reluctant than he, he more convinced, but they are both taking part, just the same. After about fifteen minutes, into what I guess we could call a performance, she is seen slipping his cell phone out of his pocket. And while his eyes remain closed, in what we can only assume is passion, she, with one eye open, begins to scroll through his text messages. She was looking for a real reason to stop kissing him, one that could uphold her intuitions, and match the inscription on the back of her T-Shirt. The work is titled, *The First Incisions of Galileo Galilei* [1]. Moments later, she replaces the telephone and

---

1 Galileo is thought to be the father of modern science, who after the Dark Ages returned science to a practice of observation instead of one based on reference.

goes back to just kissing. Someone mentioned to me some time later, that after I had left the room she moved on to his wallet, receipts, lint and cigarette packet, but still she found nothing incriminating and therefore remained on top of that half-meter marble block in the corner with her partner for an hour longer. The work is part of a series.

Across the room, of what was once an optician's shop, which I think can logically be held responsible for the exhibition's short-sightedness in both architecture and relevance, there was a long drawn out sigh, titled, *The State*. The kind of sigh a dog takes when he's been told to do something he just doesn't want to do. You probably didn't know that dogs tend to yawn out a sigh to express their resentment towards you, you probably didn't know that they could even feel something so complex. But there have been studies done, a pamphlet explains, involving canines and tooth brushes that seem to prove otherwise. The sigh is long and loud and takes up at least ¾ of the wall space across from the street level window and next to the office door. This work has no fragrance, but the first word that comes to mind is *mouldy cupboard* and makes you think about air-less cavities under your uncles sink.

Hanging behind a shroud of lies is an argument going on where feelings are being hurt. There is long cushioned exhibition furniture for lying down on, but soon it is understood that one should get underneath them and quickly tuck one's legs up next to the chest, lest the hurt feelings spread contagiously outwards. But fear not—my most sensitive readers and gallery visitors—before an epidemic breaks loose, at an interval of every 15 minutes, visitors are given antidote injections in a sanitary and timely fashion by registered nurses who only speak local dialect and have less than lovely bedside

Anna M. Szaflarski

manner. You receive a lollipop, and it is a hilarious flavour! You forget that your arm hurts, and your feelings remain in tact. While the next visitors crawl under the benches, you leave a more confident person.

There are several political positions in the exhibition. One is especially high up and is elevated by nothing but a mixture of coca cola and helium gas. However this work is far too didactic and therefore easily disregarded, while the work *Contrapposto*[2] has a wonderful nonchalance and ambiguity to it that makes both men and women feel constructively critical about themselves and each other. It is composed of mostly ambivalent and ambiguous, yet ardent and ample verbal excuses; the kinds that everybody uses and nobody feels bad about. Including, *The Hangover, The Slept In, The Ich Schaffe Es Nicht, The Crashed Computer,* and *Daylight Saving.* Everyone is encouraged to touch them, twist them around, pile them on top of each other. You can use as many as you like, because they are endless. But they are unfortunately not weightless, and there is a small plaque notifying everyone of this danger. A well meaning child, who interpreted the installation as a common Ball Pitt Playground, tragically disappeared under the load, never to be found again.

This tragedy may trouble you, especially because you realize that installed behind your back is your father, positioned in a disapproving stature, and draped with the shirt he always wears when there is some occasion he has to go to, but is reluctant to do so. His installation is part of the permanent collection but lends itself well to the temporary show. You

---

2 *Contrapposto* is an Italian term that means counterpose. It is used in the visual arts to describe a human figure standing with most of its weight on one foot so that its shoulders and arms twist off-axis from the hips and legs.

My dog Chico (on the left)

notice that he has lost weight and might wonder if he's been eating regularly and if he is aware that your mother has been chatting online with another man. It's hard to know just by looking at a man's face, but he looks good next to the ill placed electric sockets; it highlights the pragmatism in his soul. He doesn't say anything, which is of no surprise, but right before exiting into the next corridor you thought you saw him wink. Which was relieving, as you interpret it as forgiveness.

In the following rooms, which are divided by thin barriers of denial, there are several boring works, such as *Folding Socks*, *Waiting for License Renewal*, *Ulysses*, *Tax Return Form* and *Best-Man's Speech*. They are comprised predominantly of press releases. No one reads them, but by entering the room you have agreed to a lifetime contract of publicity emails. An un-subscription option is not offered. Many appear unfazed by the concept of an overloaded mailbox, as it is a reality in which we have been living in for quite some time.

In the next room there is a twenty dollar bill waiting for you, and you wonder... no... but maybe... how nice!

After climbing the stairs to the second floor you find that the entire hall is filled with a monumental orgasm, titled, *I Forgot*.

On the way downstairs, almost every visitor willingly returns their 20 dollars (there are no instructions to do so, but the visitors do it as if it were self-evident), with 2% interest into a receptacle shaped like a cough.

The show is considered to be the first comprehensive retrospective of the artist who died this past spring. Most of the works exhibited were previously un-shown and unknown, which was a delightful surprise for those who have closely followed her 100 year career. But, we must be honest and admit that everyone went there to see her most iconic work, *The Plate of Cheese*, a cheese plate being devoured by lactose intolerant men, which is still unfortunately caught up in a legal battle with the food corporation Danon. Nevertheless, this show, which was carefully titled by the artist's step-son as, *Whatever,* continues to project her enduring interest in what a pain in the ass being human is, even from the grave.

Hitler's Eyes

Malte Roloff

S. shouts, jumps and hits the water. Little fish dart off into all directions, seeking shelter under rocks and rubbish, little dog barks, jumping up and down little man's left leg. S. is a good swimmer, cutting across the small bay swiftly, stirring almost no water, breathing deep and evenly.

The sun sets and Hitler's Eyes turn from very black to very very black. S. has almost reached them and is about to dive into one of the two big dark holes.

In S.'s hometown, not far from Hitler's Eyes, they've got it all—and the best of it, too. There is a Chinese Wall on one of the nearby islands which was built—depending on who you ask, at what time of the day and with which alcohol level—against the Turks, the Black Death or the stupid sheep. Stupid sheep sounds most likely, but no one remembers seeing anyone either side of the wall, except in winter maybe, but there hasn't been a real winter in a very, very long time. Then there is Tito's old summer house (or one of them), which is now owned by some doctor from Switzerland named Aschenbach. The disappointingly modest villa overlooks the bay in which S. is still swimming towards the dark water caves where the Germans parked their submarines, enjoyed a pivo or two and dreamt of Blitzkrieg and Bohrmaschinen. Bohrmaschine is a lovely word, still in use today in this part of the world, which fits nicely with all the new Lidls and Bauhauses everywhere.

Daylight is almost gone; S. swims out on the other side oh Hitler's Eyes, a little white floater on a huge black eyeball. Both holes are connected. Hitler must have had real trouble with bifocal vision. Barely out of breath, S. makes it back to the stony shore while little dog is going crazy and almost jumps into the water as well.

S. dries her hair and reaches for that one last ice-cream in the blue cooling box. Crunchy coated, vanilla layered, dark chocolate core, and a blue packaging with silver letters that read: Macho.

LTTE no. 22 — *Metempsychosis*
August 3, 2015

Late Notice
Means Early Rise

Anna M. Szaflarski

I.

Good Morning, Lovely

Can you really suffocate someone with a pillow, or does it only work in hospitals? Is it because hospitals order pillows that are made of synthetic fibres, the non-breathable kind? When I watch one of those scenes where somebody gets smothered by a pillow, I feel like I'm just waiting and wondering if it's getting hot under there. As a kid, at times when I was a bit lazy to get out of bed in the morning, I'd press a pillow against my face to see if I could breathe through it. It was difficult, but it wasn't impossible, and death wasn't imminent. I wondered if anyone had ever been killed by a pillow, or was the notion completely invented by the film industry. And if it can in fact be done, then is it all just a consequence of tight hospital budgets, which forces them to equip their rooms with this infamous and deadly weapon?

248 LTTE NO. 22 — *Metempsychosis*

These days there's full blown sex on TV. Luckily you don't have to search through educational channels anymore to see society-approved soft-core scenes. But don't you miss how in movies, at the moment right before ultimate intimacy, the camera would pan over to the clock on the bedside table? We were made to stare at an ugly clock, entertained only by the insinuation that 30 centimetres away two people are possibly getting it on. The pillow had a similar function, but instead of avoiding showing sex, it avoided showing murder. We were forced to stare at the uninteresting surface of a pillow, and patiently wait while murder apparently ensued. Actors had it easy back then. I can imagine all of the smoke breaks they had while the alarm clock and the pillow did all of the work. The objects were the real talent, internationally renowned theatrical icons who could embody both life and death.

In our own lives, when we lay our heads on our pillows in the evening we might wonder if we'll make it through the night to regain consciousness again at daybreak. In the morning, the first thing we look at is a clock, our re-birth into the realm of the living.

II.
I See How You Appear,
But I Can't Touch What You Are

Ayami drew the Japanese character for the word 'sadness'. It's a combination of two icons, she said, one stacked above the other. The one above is supposedly a negation and means 'without' or 'un'. Below is the character for 'heart.' She explained that it could be loosely understood as 'without heart.'

La Bohémienne endormie, Henri Rousseau, 1897.
Rousseau: "a mandolin player, lies with her jar beside her (a vase with drinking water), overcome by fatigue in a deep sleep. A lion chances to pass by, picks up her scent yet does not devour her."

Sadness, however, is not the feeling of not having a heart, but rather of a burdened or painful heart. You carry it around and do everything to stop thinking about it, maybe you sleep too much, or drink too much, or smoke too much. Everything and anything to avoid thinking about how your heart is getting heavier by the second. So, the written character was obviously invented as a linguistic surgery or dissection. When you paint the character with ink on paper, it cuts an incision in the chest, opens the ribs, and pulls it right out of you. It became a symbol for sadness, but also an effective sedative and remedy. Your chest would be empty for sometime, but blood miraculously kept flowing and you would feel generally much lighter. Sadness on paper, means less sadness in life.

This is my independent interpretation. Without Ayami's help, I may tread into inaccurate waters, but I continued to wonder what would happen after that, when my heart had been cut out and laid out on to the paper. The character for 'without' even resembles a pair of pried-open ribs, hovering above the heart. But the paper is thin and cheap, and won't last forever and neither will the sadness.

While your gauged heart lies on the piece of paper, I guess you might feel a bit numb. I have little knowledge as to how these characters are constructed but I have noticed they're rarely what you expect. In other characters, there are dead dogs lying under roofs, which supposedly represents home, or pigs show up in a compound arrangement for some word describing man. It struck me that there must be a lot of reverse psychology going on there. And that's how I started thinking that maybe the whole character set was based on not depicting reality but on how the world should be, or someone wished it to be, or how someone thought it could be funnier. Well anyways, what I've learned from reading in-between the lines is that numbness or the eventual road to happiness might not be what we expect, so keep your eyes open as it might be riding on top of an open umbrella, or being dragged behind a dead goat.

III.
Sleight of Hand is Soft to the Touch.

In Machiavelli's famous comedy, The Mandrake (La Mandragola, 1524), the hero of the story would like to sleep with the young wife of an elderly man. He is naturally a trickster, like all heroes are, and tells the old man that he has found a way to impregnate his wife, who has had trouble in this department.

No, it's not as simple as that, slow down.

He disguises himself as a doctor and tells the old man that he has found a medical cure made of the mandrake root. The mandrake root looks like a human being, it has arms and legs, and I've never held one in my hands but they say it really squeals like a baby when you tear it out from the ground. The hero convinces the couple that the medicine will ensure that the very next suitor will inseminate the patient, but that the suitor will also be poisoned and die. So to spare the old man's life, the trickster also suggests a suitor, who is unsurprisingly himself, but unmasked.

The mandrake that was supposed to kill him, obviously didn't, and allowed him to screw the young wife and eventually even forge new life. The mandrake was the hospital pillow and the hotel alarm clock of the Renaissance.

IV.
The Means Justifies the End

As I told you, after 'sadness' numbness goes on for a while, the heart lies there bloody on the piece of paper. But the paper starts to get soggy at some point and begins to disintegrate. So before the heart falls through onto the ground, where it will surely be trampled upon, you need to peel back the ribs and stick the heart back in to the chest. It's a fairly simple procedure, but the success rate is less than pretty.

News just came in about the Japanese character for 'happiness.' It is made up of two people, one dead and the other rising from the dead. I figure, when you put your heart back in, you're either happy or dead. Or you're happy that you've killed someone. You've killed your sadness. Or you are reborn. Either way, you're not sad anymore.

Eva Funk

A SWISS NIGHT

you are sleeping
for days
you are resting
when you are awake
it is due to the mountains and
the thin air
she said ─────────────

cheese is the bread
for the dog which
does what a dog
has to do
deux patte
Dafalgon
was rolling in cow droppings
the other day

a book of Jim Morrison,
deceased at the age of twenty-seven,
in your room
Jim wrote about the hour of the wolf
and you say to yourself
"I have to remember this"

*even though you take books
with you, you stop caring
about them while traveling.
but if you are lucky and find
a book at your new place of
residence, you are reading it,
no matter what. it is the right
one. it has the silver lining of
fate on it.*

talking about feminism after dinner
witch hunt as an instrument for political action
(Federici, Silvia; Caliban and the Witch),
Switzerland was one of the late adopters of
women's suffrage in Europe (1971, the canton
Appenzell Innerrhoden followed not until 1990),
male artists saying women don't have the drive
to be good artists (Baselitz, Georg; Spiegel
Interview 2013) hypocritical people talking
clever about gender equality and theory and
then turn around and say sexist shit (nearly
every day) memo: how people behave is
how people are.
gossip sex success success sex gossip
SO. FUCKING. WHAT.
you get angry and nearly tired of your anger
but then you remember and it feels right
to be angry again and important ——————

as a teenager a man was
once masturbating while
trying to touch your ass
in an empty train cab.
you were pretending to be
asleep but you watched
everything in the reflection
of the window.
you didn't want him to
know that you knew; you
thought it would be excru-
ciating for him. he might
have children in your age.
(his cum was later in the
sport section of the free
newspaper) you never felt
so weak and embarrassed
as in this moment.

ending the night with a quote of Agnes Martin:
turn your back to the world

you laugh
she laughs
Jim laughs

HA HA HA HA.

Wilderness, The lost
writings of Jim Morrison,
Volume 1, Jamaica, page
151–155

while you turn your back
the hour turns to the one of the wolf
and you sleep again

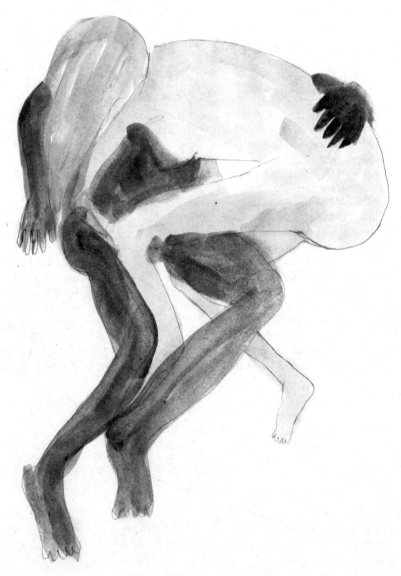

Michele Di Menna, *Smoosh*, 2015

LTTE no. 23 — *Clairvoyance*
August 17, 2015

Clarity is of no importance because nobody listens and nobody knows what you mean no matter what you mean, nor how clearly you mean what you mean...*

Anna M. Szaflarski

If I told you about it, about how it was exactly done then I wouldn't have had to do it, now would I? And you wouldn't wonder. That's the trick you see, you're wondering now, how I went about it, what utensils I used and what treatment I applied, in what order, and from whom I partly stole the idea from. That's what you want to know most of all, where did I get it from. Because then you'd be one step closer to casting me aside and snuggling one step closer to the so called, "source."

Well I'm not going to do that. You're just going to have to wonder and bring forth all of the experiences from the times where you might have done something similar. Close your eyes, and visualize yourself in my hypothetical position, standing in front of the completed work. Now, play the tape

---

* From Gertrude Stein's "How to Write" (1931)

backwards and guess what came before its completion, and what came before that. Go on, keep going, you're doing just fine…

Oh, what? No, no I wasn't going anywhere, I was just going to the bathroom. But honestly wasn't it delightful to think it through all on your own? No? Oh.

Well, then I'll tell you a story that might get you in the mood. And then maybe we can try again.

There is a jungle, a deep one, a green one, with many sounds. And as you walk through that jungle things tend to be very close to your face. Leaves, branches, flies. There are things that keep getting in your way. You can't see further than a meter in front of you or above you. You persevere and move on like that for quite some time, pushing past the immediate brush hoping desperately that you come upon some sort of clearing. You would like to sit but it doesn't seem natural to rest where you are, it would be like resting in the middle of a blackberry bush instead of on a golf course that you imagine is not so far away. You are looking for a golf course—a natural, jungle-like permutation of one, anyways.

You promise yourself that you'll walk for 20 minutes longer before giving up and curling up into a ball, no matter where you are. Your arms hurt from pushing the branches. The shorter brush and grasses have whipped your bare legs raw. Finally, you give up and curl down into a ball.

You try to fall asleep thinking this will be the end, you are lost and there is no sign of help. You recall someone once telling you that if you believe in reincarnation you should bury the dead, or in this case yourself, in the fetal position, because that is how you will reappear in the new mother's belly. You don't want to poke any holes in her, or bend her ribs out of

*... But if you have vitality enough of knowing enough of what you mean, somebody and sometime and sometimes a great many will have to realize that you know what you mean and so they will agree that you mean what you know, what you know you mean, which is as near as anybody can come to understanding anyone. (Getrude Stein)

shape, so you curl up real tight there. But even after all these careful and logically sound preparations, you do not manage to fall asleep or die. You are overtired which is a condition that you have felt many times in your life. Your eyelids remain peeled open, they just won't close. This is frustrating because the leaves are still very close to your face, which makes focusing on anything, or observing your surroundings nearly impossible. Good news though, the mosquitoes have stopped biting you. All in all, it's not so bad. Your eyes gaze vacantly and stop trying to focus. You feel fine.

How do you feel? What? No, I *am* getting to the point, you are standing on my point. You are looking at the tail and the finger tips of the point! But you stopped looking at them. It's there. No, sorry. Yes, I am being impatient, maybe even intolerant. Unreasonable, yes, that probably describes it best. You are so good with words. No, you're right, it's good that you're here, it's really great that you came. Thank you for coming.

Ok, but just try to follow me. Just stay with me a bit longer, and I'll try to bring you up to speed.

So, you're in the jungle and you thought that you came to your ultimate end. You thought that this would be it, and you thought that when the process of death and rebirth finally came, however long it might take, the moment the paediatrician would land a healthy slap on the cheeks of your butt, you would finally have the space, light and fresh air to breathe. But instead you're stuck in jungle-limbo.

Pardon me? No, it's not autobiographical, I've never been to a jungle.

But curled up in that ball you start noticing the fine hairs on your knees, and the old scars underneath them. There is the one from the time you fell off your bike. Your dad said he was holding on, but he wasn't holding on. You fell immediately, not because you couldn't balance on two wheels on your own, but because you wanted to show him what happens when he doesn't keep his word. There is an ingrown hair next to the scar. The hair apparently lost its bearings and turned back around. It was well on its way growing in the direction back towards your bones. And...

No, wait, OK, I'll quicken the pace a bit. It's really not complicated at all. Haven't you understood anything? A bit? You guess. No, I wouldn't phrase it that way. It's less pragmatic than that, but surprisingly more realistic. Maybe, I need to rephrases things. Stay with me, stay with me.

Well, your knees are your knees and the way they are is the way they are and the way they move explains themselves. In fact, the leaves explain themselves too. And the branches too. They all explain themselves, they even start explaininvg each other, until one little leaf starts explaining your knee, which makes it feel funny. The feeling seems to be contagious, because it runs up and down your legs and then your shoulder starts explaining the leaves, and you are explaining the jungle while the jungle explains you. But there isn't a verbal word exchanged between you. Because leaves can't speak, of course.

You get tired of waiting for the process of reincarnation to take place. You don't know if it would work anyways, and dying senselessly in the jungle seems all of sudden like a gigantic waste of time. So, you get up, and push past the next cluster of foliage. You are not careful. You are in a rush and not paying attention to the ground and your foot falters almost immediately on the slope of an unforeseen cliff, and pulls the rest of your body with it.

You free fall and it's relieving. Either this will now be the end or, you will finally get out of the jungle. The falling takes a considerable amount of time. You wait, and BAM! you land in the middle of another jungle. But this time, it's not a jungle but a field of tall corn stalks. They are also really close to your face.

You have to go? Oh, ok. well I hope you got something out of coming. It's really nice that you always make an effort to come around. Yeah, it's a work in progress. Yes, colours have always been important to me. Why would you say that? You'll think about the jungle won't you? Yes, see you at Christmas. Bye.

[After the 'friend' leaves (a friend who is extremely loyal, but also a sceptic) The artist dreams of synchronicity with her audience:]

And when the artist arrives, she hears a loud slow clap emerging from the entrance. They've understood and something moved inside of them that has never been moved before, that cannot be explained, only felt. The CLAP-CLAP-CLAP begins to quicken as they sense her approach, and the rhythmic choir of claps melts into a symphony of clatter and whistles and whoo hoo's. When she enters in the room tears fall from eyes, teeth glitter with grateful smiles, and children question in whispers, 'where is the artist, where is our hero?' The artist is important and her work is meaningful to other people beside herself. She can she feel proud of herself, and satisfied. The crowd surrounds her, until they are so close that she cannot focus on any single person anymore. Their tears and smiles and hair, and suits, and flowers melt into one indiscernible haze.

Women in the wilderness: the legacy of the desert mothers

Natalie Porter

Our western culture has been accused of being full of entitlement, greed and selfishness, with few tools to cope with any sort of trial, set back or suffering besides medication. Simultaneously, there is this on-going banter by those around me who want to "get away from it all," to seek out nature, wilderness, silence and solace, and to be cut-off from technology. Granted this movement has already been packaged and merchandized, but at the root of this sentiment is a genuine and valid desire for peace and contentment through simplicity.

Further evidence of our restless, yet seeking culture can even be found in mainstream media, and I have even discovered a few inspiring female role models as a result. I've always been suspicious of Hollywood's intent, but lately I've been pleasantly surprised with the adaptation of Cheryl Strayed's book *Wild* and Robyn Davidson's classic book *Tracks*. What I find most appealing about Strayed and Davidson's writings is that they are memoirs featuring women who were not necessarily outdoor enthusiasts or experts, but individuals who needed to upheave their lives and find solace in nature and in the desert. They also took great risks in accomplishing their task.

The adaptations of the books into film were timely and inspiring. I think most people enjoy stories of transformation, where others overcome adversity and change their destiny, as well as films that showcase the beauty of the wilderness. The other unspoken reason for the films' success is possibly because they reflect our generation's desire to reclaim a sense of wonder, explore nature, and integrate spirituality into our lives. Spirituality and faith have been tainted by history, considering that those who have committed violence in the name of their religion get the most press. Meanwhile, those of actual integrity have a tendency to go about their acts of humility in quiet fashion, such as the desert mothers and fathers.

This pursuit of isolation and redemption in the wilderness is not remotely a modern occurrence, even for women. The earliest record I can find is the desert mothers or ammas from 235 C.E. to 600 C.E. living around Syria, Turkey, Egypt, Palestine and Israel. I'm currently reading *The Forgotten Desert Mothers* by Laura Swan, as a kind of guide regarding the mysterious lives, stories and wisdom of women. Swan writes, "We are a generation of questioners… that yearns for wisdom figures, heroes and heroines, ammas and abbas who will show us the way. While maintaining fierce independence, we desire interdependence and community. We want our lives to have depth of meaning and purpose. We want to be connected. We secretly want someone to challenge us toward the transcendent" (151–152). Swan believes that the desert ammas can play this role of mentor, as they sought enlightenment away from the noisy mobs through simple clothes, foods, practises and routines.

The ammas were sometimes rich nobility who rejected arranged marriages or their social position, prostitutes, devout daughters, seekers, intellectuals, or simple peasants. Instead of being attached to relationships, material things, popularity, success, and even old hurts and jealousies, the ammas aimed to detach themselves from such burdens and slow down. The desert was the ideal setting to learn humility because of its vastness, silence and power. Swan explains that not only did the ammas face the natural desert, their greatest challenge was facing the inner desert. She writes, "Our inner desert is the place of encounter with our selves and God - not escape. It is in our own inner desert that our deepest self comes radically face to face with the Divine" (156–157). They believed that there is no long-term fulfilment in temporary pleasures and performances, and it's only when the desert burns off our pride and removes our masks do we actually discover true compassion and empathy for the world.

Cheryl Strayed recognized that her path of marital deceit and drug addiction was doomed to self destruct, and in her quiet way, Robyn Davidson needed to disconnect from a society full of racism and sexism in Australia during the 1970s, and also to heal from the loss of her mother. From these positions of brokenness, these women turned to a different kind of suffering to gather strength. They actually chose the path less travelled—the path that brought them vulnerability, where they had nothing to hide behind. The ammas would call this "apatheia"—a kind of quality that results after undergoing a spiritual journey when the inner struggle towards attachments has ceased and all the clutter from our world is eliminated (Swan 25).

In the end, this stripping away of falseness and pretence brings the traveller freedom and joy, and a renewed sense of identity that the dominant culture can not offer. A wilderness journey has the ability to nourish and restore the hermit within. The path most travelled claims to offer the individual control and safety, but in truth, the exposure of being in the wilderness brings true contentment. There's the saying that you can "find yourself" in the wilderness, and while it seems cliché, without external distractions and pressures, in nature we can actually become ourselves again.

Not everyone is called to undergo extensive physical ordeals through deserts and along mountain paths to find solace. Fortunately, *Amma Syncletica of Egypt* (circa 380 – 460 AD) states that, "There are many who live in the mountains and behave as if they were in the town, and they are wasting their time. It is possible to be a solitary in one's mind while living in a crowd, and it is possible for one who is solitary to live in the crowd of personal thoughts" (Swan 58). Essentially, if you can find a way to clear your mind and find peace in the quiet of your thoughts, you can discover a wilderness of awe and wonder that will sustain you no matter where you are.

Humans are naturally curious beings who also want to explain and dissect their world, but I can really appreciate those who let go of control and choose a journey that may be full of hardship and full of mystery. More is not better, whether it is knowledge or possessions, and perfection will never be obtained. I have met individuals of great intellect and wordiness, but without love or humility, they find themselves alienated and bitter. The ammas were not seeking superiority and piety through isolation in the desert, they were searching for a better way to love each other. When we start to see the world and the people around us as sacred and unique, it will be more likely that we can cultivate compassion and leave behind the accusations that our generation is pure vanity and completely self-absorbed.

LTTE no. 24 — *The Insider*
September 2, 2015

Living with Subtitles

Anna M. Szaflarski

Titian and Olga is what we call them when we don't want them to know that we're talking about them. Władek spoke Polish to me. Almost all of the seasonal workers who came here to the western part of Germany to work for three months on the hop harvest were Polish. The 'Titian' and 'Olga' that he was referring to, were the ones running the place. They didn't speak Polish.

Working on a German farm while being able to speak both German and Polish didn't give me privileged access to both worlds. Instead, it was like watching a movie with subtitles. The characters often misunderstood each other, and I watched how things played out from a distance. Yes, sometimes there was a need or opportunity to clear things up and translate, but most of the time it didn't seem appropriate, because most things were just not meant to be relayed.

266   LTTE NO. 24 — *The Insider*

The next day I was walking through a back room when I saw Danuta, who on most days works in the kitchen. When I first approached, I said something in German. She nodded with little expression. I turned around and introduced myself in Polish. Her face brightened, she grabbed hold of my hands in hers, *Call me Danka*, her eyes sparkled. After that she kept careful watch on my diet, lest I try to skip a meal (which involved a daily portion of meat, potatoes, salad, dessert, afternoon snack and lunch leftovers).

Later, I was cleaning up the first floor with Piotr, a shy young Pole who didn't speak a word of English or German. We were both being instructed neither by Titian nor Olga but another person who also had been given pseudonym. She was excited because it was the beginning of the season and spoke quickly and passionately before suddenly storming out of the room. Piotr was visibly worried that he had done something wrong. *She's not angry*, I explained to him. He was relieved and smiled. Later Titian asked me if I thought Piotr was a good worker. *Ja*, I confided in German, because it was true.

When you watch a film where characters speak in more than one language, there are often scenes where some characters are excluded linguistically from understanding everything and it is only translated to us by means of subtitles. You can sit on your couch behind the fourth wall gathering knowledge about all of the characters without ever having to share the same room with them. But now imagine that you are cast in that same film, and that film all of sudden became reality but you can still read subtitles under everyone's faces. Knowing too much becomes tricky. Especially as everybody slowly becomes aware of the fact that only you understand. They might start to imagine that you know something useful and important, or in the worst case scenario, threatening. And very quickly an ability to listen in, grants you nothing but closed doors.

My insider connections actually resulted in daily schnitzels, ice creams, and beer tastings, but was also accompanied by a particular atmosphere—the one I felt when I walking by the Polish workers' after-work-bench. *Whose side am I on anyways?!*

It doesn't sound too dramatic I suppose. A better example might be the story told by most famous whistle-blower of our generation, Edward Snowden, who is still hiding out in Russia because he revealed the truth about digital surveillance of private citizens and national documents; something that today has pretty much been accepted as a part of our daily lives. But not before each powerful nation went through the theatrics of pretending to be surprised that other nations (predominantly the United States of America) had the gall to spy on them. In fact, it seemed that it was being used as an international campaign; you could prove your importance by accusing the United States of spying on you. It seems, however, that everyone apologized cordially to each other and then went on with business as usual. It's hard to believe that they didn't already know that everyone was planting nanny-cams (inside of teddy bears) on the mantelpieces of their fellow global leader.

The private individual has also accepted that Obama might be listening to their phone calls to Pizza Hut. They've come to terms with it and peeled off the Totoro sticker that was blocking their webcam and now just make sure to brush their teeth and put on make-up before checking Facebook in the morning. Everyone has relaxed and has reactivated the GPS system on their portable devices realizing that if anyone

wanted to know where they were, they're not actually hiding, so maybe it doesn't really matter.

So, everyone is fine with it, now. And maybe they shouldn't be, but they are. I mean, it's not an Orwellian surveillance state, that's made up of a minority that is seemingly unaffected, while a large lower class is being tracked and controlled like cattle. Ok, yes that sounds familiar. But generally most people in the western world are unconcerned. But someone has to pay for the growing pains of a secret transforming into common knowledge. Even though his message has been delivered, digested, pooped out and buried again, Snowden is still in Russia. I know very little about what he is doing there, but our natural instinct is to be suspicious, so I ask: does he speak Russian? Is he a fan of Pussy Riot or Judo? And what is he telling the Russians about the otherwise perfect continent of America?!

I imagine that it's going to take a few decades until Snowden gets invited back into the American fold, and I have a inkling that in the meantime he's not going fishing with Putin. So it seems that the insider has become the ultimate outsider.

To avoid becoming an insider of any sort, I've learned to forget secrets. That's why I am so good at keeping them. Tell me a secret and I will usually let it slip my mind immediately. If I am not meant to repeat it, there is no use keeping it in my frontal lobe. Your lovers, your plans, your sins, your engagements, your friends' affairs: if your secret is painful, important or difficult it will be sent to the very last aisle of my dusty brain archive. Vent it and bon voyage.

The problem is, if a secret is even slightly funny. Not maliciously funny, no, just absurdly funny, like calling your bosses random pseudonyms (that give them new Polish village personas), I'm going to think about it, dwell on it, and want to

270 LTTE NO. 24 — *The Insider*

share it so badly I can't bare it. And there it is, I leaked it here. I guess this is my Watergate. Let them exile me.

Insiders never stay insiders, because inside information works like osmosis, it has a physical pull to level the playing field. It's nobody's fault when a secret gets out, its inevitable, the membrane that separates the insiders from the outsiders is semi-permeable. The attraction to be an insider must also be chemical, or biological. Maybe it's animal ambition, clan behaviour and a need to feel included in something. There is also the need to share secrets with others. To vent, maybe. But more importantly to show that the person you are telling the secret to, is part of your team. Władek's secret was irrelevant. He wanted to show me, that I was one of them, one of the Poles, and I must admit that I relished in the moment. The only way to stay out of politics is to always be an outsider, and even though that seems like the healthiest avenue, it is not only considered unnatural or eccentric but is also seemingly impossible. At the farm I accepted that I was a Pole, I was one of the Germans, and also a strange outsider (AKA Canadian).

In the art world, of course, we love the idea of an outsider. *Outsider Artists.* They are the enigmatic creators who does not share our values (or complex discourse). They are insiders only to themselves, while everyone on the planet is an outsider to them. There is no downloadable subtitle app for their language. And every secret that they reveal reaches all of us at the same time, from their private world directly to any public that comes into contact with their work. Therefore, no one is at a disadvantage and the outsider only reveals him/herself, therefore compromising no one. Or that's they way we like to imagine them, and if they truly are out there, we hope they will always stay that way.

Discovery

Stanisław Szaflarski

On the outskirts of my village, close to Chochołow, there stood simple log cabin. The house was visibly an exception in the village. On the roof there was a huge windmill, the only one in the entire region. The owner of the house, Kajton, was definitely different and everyone called him disturbed or stupid. Kajton never replied to those insults. From time to time he pretended to be angry and acted aggressively. One day, my father asked me to go to fetch Kajton to help fix our broken sawmill machine. I was scared, but also fascinated. I knocked on his door, but no one answered. I opened the door carefully and peered inside. Below the windmill, I saw the most amazing structure of pulleys and wheels marked with colour-coded instructions of how to control the wind power and its velocity. I stood in admiration of the fascinating cleverness that I had never seen in my life before. I did not realize, that Kajton was standing just behind me. He turned around and went to the other side of the room. I was scared but I tried to tell him that his help was needed at the sawmill. Kajton disappeared into the end of a dark corridor and out into a clear opening. I followed him there. We entered a simple enclosure, room maybe, its walls were covered with coockoo clocks. I noticed that each clock was showing a different hour, so I asked him why these clocks, all working,

272 LTTE NO. 24 — *The Insider*

were showing different hours? Kajton turned towards me and said.

"Each thing, event and person has its own time."

"But how do you know what time is it?" I asked.

"It is easy to know what time is but if you do not know your time, you know nothing. This is our time. Let's go. We have to help your father at the sawmill!"

Late in the day the sawmill was repaired and Kajton came to visit us at home. The neighbours also gathered inside of our one-room house to listen in total silence to my Mother ("Babka" to my children), read the Old Testament. I discovered that night that God had made a "mistake" during his creation of the world (Genesis 6:6). I was pleased, relieved and encouraged to challenge and bargain with this "faulty world".

The next day, my mother said that she would read something different, something that might not be so clear to her, but it might be good for me to think about. She put the book in front of me and opened the cover. On the first page there was strange writing. My mother said, that it was in Latin. I thought that this was truly unusual, because God spoke Latin only in church. She read "Cogito ergo sum", with Polish translation printed below "Myślę, więc jestem" (I think therefore I am). It was intriguing. The next day, on my way back from the church I asked her, "Do you think that when I touch you, you really exist?" She turned around and slapped me across the face. I did not understand why she had done that, but I was pleased to know that my mother exists.

Another day she read, "Lisy w winnicy" (Lion Feuchtwanger's "Die Füchse im Weinberg") a book about America, in particular about Benjamin Franklin and his mission to Paris during the War of Independence. At the Versailles

meeting with a king of France, Franklin had taken his notes with a "magical instrument", unknown in France at that time. This "instrument" was so "magical" that could write from one end, while the other end would make written words disappear. The royal court was intrigued by this "simple man's" magic and, what was more important, his America. I noticed that in our log house, on the floor below the wood stool in the corner, lay a yellow "American pencil", which we received from my uncle in Chicago. I picked the yellow pencil up and placed it carefully in my school case.

Life is a beautiful journey of surprises, discoveries and creations. It is almost like a book with many pages of events, marks, open or blank, sometimes secret stories about the spots

LTTE NO. 24 — *The Insider*

or places in favourite bushes around the house, mountains, trees, cities, countries, moments and times. It is also exciting to find your own time to revisit these pages and to re-read them and rediscover them again, and again, and again. I hope that on the upcoming trip to Poland we will be able to find our time to do that together again and again. Love, Gazda

LTTE no. 25 — *Deluge of Grandeur*
September 17, 2015

Gottfried the Snake

Anna M. Szaflarski

There is a snake who lives on the top floor of this house. The snake eats once every two weeks, at the very same frequency that I publish a letter in this journal. It's a he, and his name is Gottfried. On his feeding day, two children and their father make their way up to the attic floor and peer into the glass terrarium. The father places a raw egg inside of the tank. Gottfried (whose name comes from the words 'god' or 'good' in combination with 'peace', therefore meaning god's peace or good peace), does nothing. Perhaps, he doesn't even know that he in the vicinity of the egg, or maybe he doesn't care. He will take his time getting to it, sometimes a day or two, but eventually when no one is looking, he will swallow it whole.

Gottfried does not like to be watched. I passed his tank once, while looking for the internet router. The room was dark. A dim artificial lamp cast a light from behind some leaves inside of an $40 \times 40 \times 60$ cm glass-encased lair. I ap-

276 LTTE NO. 25 — *Deluge of Grandeur*

proached, but he was nowhere to be found. A being with such little ambition could be considered almost invisible.

I publish a letter every two weeks, but I eat three times a day, not including snacks. I eat a lot, significantly less than I used to, but in comparison to Gottfried I am a glutton. In my defence, I will accomplish quite a bit more in my life than Gottfried does in his. In fact, I accomplished more than him immediately after birth. The nurses said I broke the hospital feeding record. My mother was very proud.

The human is a ridiculously ambitious creature by nature.

I was going through some old texts I had written when I was a teenager. On Monday January 6, 2000, I was sixteen and had composed an essay titled "Cause and Effect" for my creative writing class. The text read as follows:

> Some may call me lazy, and others unmotivated. Some have called me a slacker and others have claimed to be unable to see an inch of drive in me. I am given all that I'll ever need to start my own life as an adult. I have access to money, and shelter, and then some. And yet, here I am trying to disprove every individual who has scorned me with those words of dissatisfaction. Now, when those who try to care ask me, "Anna, why have you lost your motivation?" I ponder the question anything but lightly. I have blamed more than one possibility.

I laughed pretty hard when I found this. The essay goes on for two more pages, ending with:

And who knows, perhaps inspiration will grab
me and throw me back into the feeling of freedom like when I was a child, before my patterns
built up and chained me to my routine.

In reality, I wasn't a lazy child at all. I was a swimmer who
got up at 4:30 in the morning every school day of the week.
I wasn't bad at school either.

But it seems that I dreamt of being a lazy person with
great indulgence. I created a fictional world where I was the
good-for-nothing kid. In that fantasy, I had reasons for being
the way I was, but in the end I dramatically admitted that no
justification would be sufficient; a rebel without a cause. Why
did I write this? Maybe I was so afraid of the expectations
that true ambition would bring, that I invented a world where
I had already fallen from grace. I was already running so high
on ambition, that the view downwards was looking awfully
steep. What I wanted was to be the underdog, without ever
having to become the überdog.

I handed this essay in to my teacher. Unfortunately, I don't
have the hard copy, otherwise, I'd be curious to see what kind
of comments he had written in the margins for the apparent
couch potato in his class, who was coincidently also built like
a truck and handed everything in early.

Gottfried is cold blooded. This means that he doesn't generate his own heat, he needs the external environment to supply
it for him. When it's warm, he gets all hot and bothered, and
when it's cold, subdued and frigid. So while we're sitting at
our computers late at night eating cold pizza and expecting
our bodies to nuke it for us as well as supply the energy we

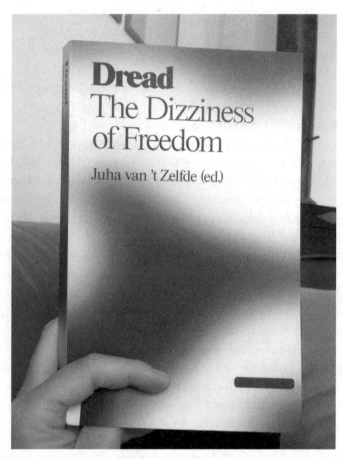

Never read it. I gave it away to someone who might need it more than me. But great title.

need to send off applications last minute, Gottfried has sensibly powered down with the sun. Whatever he needed to do will have to wait for tomorrow. The egg will have to wait.

But we humans are not the only ones who are senselessly ambitious on this planet. I often think how ridiculously industrious insects are. And what about the pubescent birds that are taking flight as we speak, beginning their extremely long journey southward. And even things where we question its sentience, like a wildfire in California that is picking up speed to break its own records. Ambition is everywhere. The insects want to colonize and multiply, the birds want to multiply, the wildfire wants/needs/tends to spread, we… we want to be loved? admired, at least? thought to be smart? show our old classmates who's boss? fill the empty pit in our stomachs with an abstract, elusive and frankly eternally unattainable sensation of mystical triumph? What is it that we are burning the so called midnight oil for, during this seemingly never-ending night? Colonization and 'multiplication' might still be on the radar—reflected by the politics of the world—But what about all that intoxicating ambition where the borders seem to stand still, where cappuccinos are widely available and the birth-rate is crashing to an all-time low?

Maybe the real reason Gottfried can be so under ambitious is because of his glass cubical, where he is king and the ultimate meter of accomplishment. He lives in isolated bliss, with only an egg to remind him that time has passed, and how he is not a slave to it. But one sunny morning a letter arrives to the tank and an incredible thing happened. He hadn't felt this way for years. His interest was sparked and he felt a dangerous sensation of intrigue. Slithering past his egg, he tore open the envelope and read:

280   LTTE NO. 25 — *Deluge of Grandeur*

Dearest Gottfried,

Some have called you lazy, and others unmotivated. Some have called you a slacker and others have claimed to be unable to see an inch of drive in you. You are given all that you'll ever need to start your own life as an adult. You have access to money, and shelter, and then some. And yet, here you are trying to disprove every individual who has scorned you with words of dissatisfaction. Now, when those who try to care ask you, "Gottfried, why have you lost your motivation?" You might ponder the question anything but lightly. You may consider blaming more than one possibility.

Panic flooded Gottfried's lukewarm veins, and his skin shed immediately.

He considered for the first time in his life that he's been wasting all of his time in a tank on the top floor of the country home. And who would invade his privacy like this? The letter was unsigned. He hasn't seen his siblings for years, for instance. Maybe all this time they've been studying, getting grants, travelling the world, starting businesses, or having a nest of their own. On the other hand, maybe someone was trying to encourage him, so that he could live up to his potential, but they obviously hadn't understood that he was perfectly happy with the way things were.

The damage, however, was irreparable. He realized then how desperately hungry he was, and even though his egg had been waiting for days no further than 20 cm away, he no longer felt that he had time to eat. The walls of his terrarium were closing in on him. The enclosure that had been such a comfort to him all of these years, just wasn't enough anymore. Everything that was unknown, everything that he could be was outside of his tank. Inside, he now felt empty, and invisible.

Gottfried, The Good/God-Peace was now drowning in inner turmoil, and spiralling into the pits of ambition. He broke free from his tropical diorama and set out into the world.

Making a long story short, he lost much skin over the years. He met other snakes, whom he loved when he was doing well and hated when they were doing better than him. Where would Gottfried's ambition lead him? Perhaps he would seek fame and fortune in the baskets of charmers, dancing to the music of a bansuri, be seen digesting deer whole on YouTube, or get a gig as a lobbyist for the lord of the underworld.

Eventually, he landed a scene in one of those Indiana Jones films. Where Jones breaks into an ancient catacomb, and discovers millions of snakes slithering out of every crevice, out of the mouths of vicious sculptures, and covering the floor forming a gyrating whirlpool. Gottfried got some screen time on Jones' boot, before being kicked off, before Jones's says "Snakes... I hate Snakes." It was a big day for all of the snakes on the set, they had arrived to Hollywood. Between takes Gottfried looked around at his colleagues, and in that moment surprisingly he didn't hate them for sharing his spotlight. He was proud. They might have sabotaged each other along the way, cried over lost opportunities, and lost nights of sleep thinking of how they could've been better. They did things that they weren't proud of, things that were vain, and self-absorbed. In that moment, he looked across

282 LTTE no. 25 — *Deluge of Grandeur*

the set and realized that he was no better than any other snake, and that their collective ambition brought them closer together and brought public attention to their importance as a whole. It reminded him of his nest as a juvenile snake. He thought, *perhaps inspiration will grab me and throw me back into the feeling of freedom like when I was a child, before my patterns built up and chained me to my routine.*

The jury is still out on what happened next. There were times when things were good, the snake jobs were just rolling in, and progress seemed like it was around the corner. Other times were more difficult, like when it seemed that everybody only wanted cobras, which are obviously so crass and in bad taste. It was a rollercoaster, and Gottfried was barely holding on. When night came, and his biology would not let him go on, he would close his eyes and see the egg and dream of ignoring it.

Johnny's Yodel

Till Wittwer

People have forgotten who Johnny Weissmuller is. Let me tell you about Johnny. Born as Peter Johann Weißmüller, he first set foot into the USA in 1905, at one year of age, when his family emigrated from Romania and entered the US through the immigration hub of Ellis Island. Doesn't that pave the ground for a sensational success story, with a touch of emotion, perhaps?!

Well, here it goes: Johnny grew up to be one of the most prolific and successful competitive swimmers of all time. He won five Olympic gold medals and set more than fifty world records. Throughout his swimming career he never lost a race. He also became a film star, an entrepreneur and a passionate golfer. So far, so Wikipedia. Alas, I am not planning on telling you a story you could read online, just like that.

The story I am trying to excavate from the piles of gold-medals, honor-rolls, cardboard boxes of breakfast cereals, swimming-pool-supplies, Hollywood Walk of Fame-marble plates, Beatles record covers, and rollercoaster spare-parts[1] is

---

1 Johnny was a fan of John Harvey Kellogg's ideas of a healthy lifestyle, he founded a swimming-pool company, he was honored with a star on Hollywood's Walk of Fame, he is one of the characters depicted on Peter Blake's legendary sleeve for the Beatles-record "Sgt. Pepper's Lonely Hearts Club Band", he was co-owner of a theme park called "Tropical Wonderland".

Tarzan's New York Adventure, 1942

about loincloths, yodels, and identity. The story is set in the year 1942 and its first scene goes like this:

Johnny Weissmuller climbs the façade of a New York skyscraper to escape a handful of clumsy police officers. How this chase came about is of no importance at this point, it's all about the action. Having reached the skyscraper's flat rooftop, Johnny runs to the ledge on the roof's far side and gets hold of a rope dangling from a flag pole. He uses this rope to swing across the concrete jungle's urban canyon and crosses the image frame from left to right—the typical direction of escape in movie semiotics. Weissmuller swings across the screen like a pendulum—without swinging back, of course, as his motion is an ever-forward escape.

If we haven't recognized it before, we recognize it now, hearing a high-pitched yodel: Johnny Weissmuller is Tarzan.[2] New York's picturesque concrete jungle is his playground; somebody put him in a grey suit to blend in but underneath he is wearing his signature loincloth.

Next shot. We see Tarzan swing into the frame (from the left, of course). He lets go of the rope and lands in the center of the screen. The scenery he has entered from above is a roof hosting a huge billboard on steel girders which obstructs a good view into the distance. The viewer's gaze stops on the big wooden advertisement surface; the cinema screen becomes the billboard itself, Tarzan smack in the middle.

Tarzan turns his impressive and well-dressed body a bit, hastily looks back over his shoulder and all of a sudden it is completely unclear whether he takes this look as Johnny or as Tarzan: Is Tarzan turning his head because he fears the chubby policemen might be right behind him, having traversed the vast urban canyon on a rope, Tarzan-style? Or is his look rather a consequence of having landed right in the middle of an advertisement shoot and now poor Johnny — who thought he was doing a decent job embodying the escaping Tarzan but has apparently touched down in the wrong frame — is being yelled at by the ad shoot's production assistant to get the hell out of the frame? Either way, Johnny-Tarzan proceeds as ordered and exits the screen (towards the right hand side, naturally), leaving us viewers alone with the bare advertisement message. "PLUS.ECONOMY", it mysteriously reads.

Is that what Johnny is? Is Johnny the "plus-economy"? I mean, in his days he was one of the most celebrated stars in sports, he was a huge celebrity, everybody wanted a piece of

2 The film is "Tarzan's New York Adventure", directed by Richard Thorpe.

286   LTTE no. 25 — *Deluge of Grandeur*

him. In total, Johnny Weissmuller shot fourteen Tarzan movies and his Tarzan-yodel, that was pressed from his lungs with a strangling Hollywood-contract was immediately canned and actually is still used in Tarzan flicks today. Whenever we hear that yodel, we are listening to Peter Johann Weißmüller, the immigrant kid from a German ethnic minority in Timisoara, Romania, who gives us his most sincere "AYA-YAAAAAAY" in a desperate attempt to please the production manager on the one hand and to get rid of the last bits of this very Peter Johann Weißmüller—the immigrant kid— inside of him, and of the last bits of Johnny Weissmuller, the swim-star living the American dream on the other. With the yodel, he wants to change into a meta-species, transcending his voice and emancipating it from all the "thank yous" and the kind and humble words at the press conferences and the sponsorship meetings held to praise Johnny for his physique, for his achievement, for his embodiment of an ideology, for being proof that a mythological narrative can turn into reality, that man can overcome the most difficult obstacles and that a nobody can become a somebody just by working hard. His yodel, this sincere and desperate yodel is the yodel of someone looking for freedom: At this point Johnny Weismuller has become in the USA what Alexey Grigoryevich Stakhanov had become in the USSR only a few years earlier: an over-achiever, a model worker, a superhuman proto-citizen, material for ideological modeling, embodying the values of his patria. Johnny has become a living example—and an object to exhibit—that the American Dream is real.

And now we see: Maybe the Johnny/Tarzan-confusion didn't only occur when he touched down in front of the billboard. Maybe the fugitive we thought to be Tarzan in a suit wasn't Tarzan at all: it was Johnny all along. And maybe the officers in pursuit weren't actually actors playing policemen, but instead they were representatives of some committee, intending to hand poor Johnny yet another medal of honor. The fiction film turns into a documentary and we witness an escapee yodeling his way into freedom.

Or at least attempting to do so: Disturbingly, this desperate yodel, this cry for freedom, which Johnny believes is emancipating him, which he believes is relieving him from the weight of being a mere pawn for ideology, ironically becomes *the* marketed element. It is recorded and reproduced and thus the yodel is what ultimately remains from Johnny Weissmuller's great career way after he is dead and his name is forgotten.

And every time we hear Tarzan's signature cry today, we are actually hearing a tragically failed attempt of leaving all of this behind: Appropriation, exploitation, ideologization, incorporation. It's the cry of Johnny "plus-economy" Weissmuller.

LTTE no. 26 — *Hard Day's Night*
September 25, 2015

Black and Incongruous Headlines

A story to accompany the poster edition "A Man's Job",
launched at the Niagara Artists Centre.

Anna M. Szaflarski

General Motors [GM] is leaving the modern industrial hero, and has been for a long time. She's not answering his calls anymore, and leaves her messages with her solicitors, which act less like a dialogue and more like announcements. She's become frigid, but it hadn't always been that way. There was a time when she would tell the hero about everything, they'd stay up all night and giggle about their dreams, talk about children, and home life. She told him she needed him, and made him promise that he would never leave her. Money was of course an issue, it's always an issue. But they enjoyed life and would go to neighbours' houses for backyard parties, drink beer and chill with the guys.

Those were the, so called, good times, but also the times of awfully serious promises. After returning from the First World War overseas, the hero was eager to make vows about the kind of man he wanted to be:

290   LTTE no. 26 — *Hard Day's Night*

> A man's job is his best friend. It clothes and feeds his wife and children, pays the rent and supplies them with wherewith to develop and become cultivated. The least a man can do in return is appreciate his job. If you ask any successful man the reason for making good he will tell you that first and foremost it is because he likes his work indeed he loves it. His whole heart and soul are wrapped up in it. His whole physical and mental energies are focused on it. He thinks his work and he talks his work, he is entirely inseparable from his work, and that is the way every man worth his salt ought to be, if he wants to make his work what it should be, and make himself what he wants to be.[1]

GM was pleased. Everyone knew his and her place in the world and things were good for awhile.

Then problems at work started. Maybe things 'till then had gone too well, and things got too comfortable, but all of a sudden she needed more than the hero could offer. She needed more than a good heart and two hands, she needed technology, tax evasion strategies, and three times the amount of hands for half the price, heart not included. And he noticed how hard she was struggling, coming home late at night, getting practically no sleep. But he couldn't help her and she started to change. She did things that he didn't recognize and didn't like, and she told him to pull his head out

1 Text referenced from McKinnon Doings (Journal), "Published for and by the employees of the McKinnon Industries (Industrial predecessor to GM in St. Catharines, Limited." Volume I Number 10, St. Catharines, December 3, 1937.

of his ass and get with the times. Gradually they didn't speak much to each other, and things started to fall apart.

The modern industrial hero didn't know what was going on. He was confused and felt powerless. He resolved to put his head down and try to be the man he described so many years before, hoping it might all just blow over.

Like in all love affairs, the individuals involved want everything to stay the way things were when they first fell in love. So much so, that they ignore the blatant signs that their sweet delusion is beginning to disintegrate. The first signs are well known: the waning attention followed by desperate reactions. But the lovers don't notice at first because they are busy dreaming about how it was when they first met. They dig their nails into the memories of their first intoxicating moments together, and engage in cyclical conversations like, *what did you think of me when we first met?* They force each other to coexist in a euphoric past, and ignore the passage of time. They pull the covers over their heads, and make informal vows: *if we live in the past, time will not move forward, and everything will stay the same.*

292   LTTE NO. 26 — *Hard Day's Night*

It's hard to watch a crumbling romance. Everyone around seems to know more about the imminent collision between dreams and reality than the lovers themselves. In this case it was plastered in the newspapers in black and incongruous headlines: *GM Accused of Sleazy Tactics*, *Anxious about 1980*, *The Truth Hurts* and *All's Quiet on The Local GM Front*. Once in a while, there were headlines that offered small hope: *Expansion*, *New Plant*, and *Nothing Wrong with Economy*. It was if GM didn't want to let go, as if she had second thoughts, or suddenly felt sentimental about the past. Although maybe it had nothing to do with sentiment, but legal compromises, because each kind word would be promptly followed by cutting announcements of non-negotiable circumstances. These kind of headlines are nothing but the traces of a very public alimony battle in the brutal divorce between the auto industry and the worker, who was having trouble betraying his vows to be the modern industrial hero; a real man, a man worth his salt. The headlines wavered from hopeful to cynical but the general direction pointed towards ultimate demise.

Someone asked the hero, how do you keep caring after reading a sour headline like, *Kick In the Teeth from GM*? He explained that no matter how threatened his job felt, he still felt a residue of that old marital contract; "in sickness and in health". He reminisced about the day he got hired onto the assembly line, *it was like winning the lottery*. In the following years, he moved from one job to another inside the plant hustling and dodging layoffs. Like in any crumbling relationship he thought, things might still change, and the only way he saw off the sinking ship and into a seat onto the modern cruise liner was to work hard. He thought he might still spark some passion in the old lady.

Some say that our world today is looking awfully precarious. Others say that's it's always been that way, and that life-long contracts were an illusion all along. Labour is just not in demand in first world countries anymore, and maybe this could have all been easily predicted. *What were those crazy young couples thinking?* The industrial hero, who was once a needed resource is expected to diversify, reinvent, reposition himself and self-employ if need be, because GM is leaving and she ain't lookin' back. Marriage just isn't what it used to be.

The hero was driving across town from a long day's work. He bought some flowers along the way and a bottle of wine. He thought he'd try one more time to make things good with GM. Just the two of them, no lawyers, no unionists. It was a considerable drive up to her place, and an old Dolly song played on the radio:

> *You have put me just as low as anyone ought to go*
> *So I lay down beside what's left of my pride*
> *If you go, then you'll know, because you can't help but see*
> *The only way out is to walk over me.*

The song only made the hero feel more bitter, which is not the mood he wanted to be in. So, he started flipping through the stations and was so consumed by it that he drove right past her. He only noticed her sitting in a parked car after he parked his truck a block down the road.

From where he was sitting he could see that she was in some compact slick thing. He barely recognized his gal, who once used her pickup as a BBQ station. From where he was sitting it looked as if she was talking to a group of foreigners, but he couldn't be sure. She smiled in ways he hadn't seen for a long time. She was shaking their hands, and envelopes were being exchanged. He had suspected, but had never really considered it for a million years that it would come to this. From where he was sitting it looked like his marriage had finally come to an end. And from where he was sitting, maybe it didn't seem like such a bad thing.

A fellow writer put it so poignantly: "that the only labour that society feels is worth compensating someone for is labour that we don't enjoy—labour devoid of love".[2] The modern industrial hero has been caught up in a loveless marriage for more than half a century, and as his ol' Lady moves on to less fortunate nations, perhaps she leaves the hero and the general workforce in Canada an opportunity to redefine what they are worth, and what they should be paid for. Instead of begging her to stay, the hero starts to imagine a world where he isn't encouraged to work like a dog day in and day out, sacrificing himself as an industrial martyr. It's not the way he was raised but he imagines a life without her and any other labour-dependent industries in his life. It's scary but for the first time he can say, he doesn't love her anymore, and maybe it never had anything to do with love in the first place.

The modern industrial hero, who nobody needs or wants anymore, turns the ignition and drives away.

2 *The Virus of Scarcity and the Culture of Abundance*, Maya Mackrandilal, essay published on *sixtyinchesfromcenter.org*, 2015.

You Got a Good Job
Right Out of High School, Or,
How St. Catharines Had Dumb Luck

Stephen Remus

Jack said, I went to a funeral, it was one of the guys from the plant. I saw my old boss there, hadn't seen him in forever—saw a lot of guys there I hadn't seen in forever—and I figured I had to say something.

I mean I was a lousy employee, I was a terrible fucking worker, just awful.

You know, we'd come in here at lunch sometimes, get a tray of drafts, the little ones, and maybe we'd get a couple more and we'd go back half-cut. Sometimes we wouldn't even go back. Just pack it in, that'd be it, go home from here. Then next day, we'd be back at work like nothing happened. It was nuts.

So I saw my boss at the hall after the funeral and said, Hi, remember me?

He said, Sure Jack sure, I remember you.

I said, Look, I just wanted you to know that you were a good boss and I was a terrible worker. And I want to apologize for that.

And he said, Oh come on Jack, you weren't that bad, you pulled your weight.

I said, No, no I didn't. I fucked up a lot, I was a lousy worker and for that I want to apologize.

And he said, OK. And I felt all right about that.

296 LTTE no. 26 — *Hard Day's Night*

We were having burgers and fries with a beer at the bar. It was the middle of the afternoon, bright sun and fresh snow outside, but it was dark in there. The radio was playing Heaven's Just a Sin Away by The Kendalls. Torture. Nothing was happening except the girl working the bar and three or four people scattered around at tables.

The burger was a mess, a worthy example of the pornography of cuisine; not particularly good for you and not something that would ever hold together without your hands. This one had blue cheese.

I said, Well, what the fuck,

You didn't owe those guys anything. I mean take a look around this town, there isn't a single building—other than the ones they own—with GM's name on it. There's no rink, community centre, hospital, nothing. They just came in, worked the town like mules, a shitload of cars got punched out of the plant, and now they're buggering off to Mexico and China for good.

At least you had some fun at their expense.

Jack said, That's where you're wrong, it wasn't fun. It was awful. I can barely walk, my knees are so shot. It was just bullshit. Working behind those machines, it was hard on you. You went crazy. I went crazy.

I said, Well I don't think having a few extra beers at the Duck for lunch is like going off your nut exactly.

Jack said, Yeah but the things is, we were always going hard. When I think back I don't know how we did it. We'd always be going over the river, to the Hacienda, the Late Show, it really didn't matter, we'd be over there all the time. We were wild.

The waitress came over. Jack liked her, thought she had a cute behind. No argument from me, and when she checked

on us Jack said we'd have two more. I thought we were leaving, but he'd made a call.

Jack said, We went over to Buffalo one time—I can't remember all the places we used to hit—with this guy I used to hang with, he was a good guy, he had this van, a real shagging wagon, a Vandura, remember those, with the little teardrop window in the back?

Anyway, we were drunk and stoned and we're coming back and it was dark and raining and I'm so high I'm just lying in the back of the van. It's all I could do.

He's got all these weights back there. I don't even know what he was thinking, I guess he used to work out in his van maybe, maybe he was moving them, I don't know, but he's got all these barbells and stuff and I'm just lying there on the weight bench, sleeping.

The waitress came back with the beers. Jack tried to make something more of it than what it was, but big surprise, she was just bringing us beers.

Jack picked it up again, So I'm lying there in the back and

buddy falls asleep at the wheel. The fucking van goes into this huge ditch. The van cartwheels, like ass over tea kettle. From how it tore up the ground we figure it rolled three times, maybe four.

And I remember waking up to a big noise when we left the road and I'm scared shitless in this van and I'm bouncing around with all these barbells. I can still see it, everything's in the air like it's zero gravity up in space or something, except everything's moving fast and everything's hard and everything really fucking hurts. And I'm thinking, oh boy, this is it. I'm done.

We're laughing, it's a messed up story.

See this gash on my head? Jack bent and pointed to a well-healed scar about three inches long on the top of his bald head. That was a barbell. Or who knows? It was fucked up. I was cut up and bruised from head to toe. The van was totalled, you wouldn't recognize it, but somehow we were OK.

I couldn't believe it. We got out. We were all covered in mud. It was a real ditch, deep, and we crawled out of it and walked to this house in the middle of nowhere and we knocked on the door. You should've seen us all bleeding and covered in mud, we must've scared the hell out of those people.

Fuck, you are some lucky, I said.

You know it.

I guess driving around with loose weights and passed out friends in the back of your van is a recipe for disaster, I said for a laugh.

Yeah, there's something to it, Jack said, and we laughed when he said it, but we were really laughing about dumb luck.

LTTE no. 27 — *Foreign Affairs*
October 12, 2015

A Language to be Destroyed

Anna M. Szaflarski

Growing up with parents who had not yet perfected the predominantly used language in the country they lived and raised their children in, brought about good-natured laughs. My parents were good sports about it, and we, as their English-speaking children, were invited to bring to attention their slips in syntax and grammar. One of our favourites was my father's persistence to insert articles, such as the word 'the' where it definitely did not belong. Dropping us off at front of the doors of the swimming pool everyday, he would call out after us, "Have it the fun!" genuinely wishing us a good time. And even as we teased him every day for years he continued to call out, "Have it the fun!" and "Have it the fun!"

Years later while sorting through my parents' office I found an essay my mother wrote for the local university many years previous. Throughout the five pages of carefully crafted arguments there was no 'the' to be found. I read it

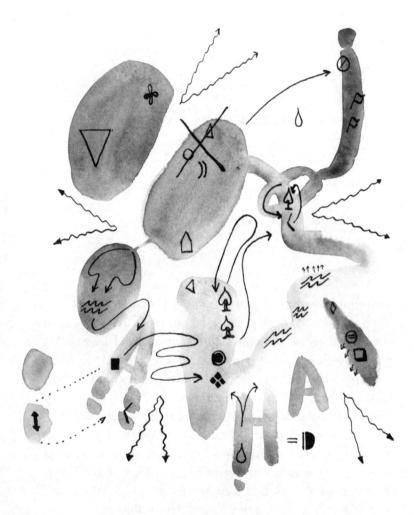

"AHA" or *"ACHSO!"*

out loud, and we all had a good laugh about it. Despite how small the omission was, the essay felt strangely vague and even playful.

I realized then that my parents' difficulty to grasp the usage of the articles 'a' and 'the', required perhaps more than a dinner table laugh, serious analysis, even. Their slips were obviously not for lack of their intelligence as they both speak many languages and are an inspiration in terms of cunning and cleverness. I decided the problem must lie in an assumption that we English-speakers take for granted. There is a basic understanding that when we say '*a* ball' for instance, we agree that we are referring to the abstract concept of a ball among many. And when we say '*the* ball', it is a specific ball that we all know or should know. By noticing their difficulty with those specific words, I reflected on how liberally the English-speaking population assumes something so fundamental as shared understanding. My father was inadvertently speaking about a very specific kind of fun (which I am not altogether sure was truly a mistake, and he probably did have a specific kind of fun in mind), while my mother opened up every noun in her essay to a world of infinite possibilities. During those early years in Canada, for my parents the difference between the two articles was indistinguishable, but perhaps rightfully so.

After years of living outside of Canada I find that my own native-tongue has been severely compromised. I sometimes rearrange English words into German syntax formation. I often write like a foreigner. When asked to edit texts for others for LTTE I have a hard time knowing what's right and what's wrong anymore. But most conflictingly, I feel that when correcting someone else's writing—written by someone who grew up writing and speaking another language—

302 LTTE no. 27 — *Foreign Affairs*

I shouldn't correct them at all, instead archive and conserve every aberration. Aside from the fact that the voice of the writer is endangered by someone tidying up grammar or finding more 'appropriate' synonyms, every so-called mistake can give insight into how a person uses their own language, or how they came to speak English. It can bring attention to how native speakers depend on predetermined rhetoric that is drenched in assumptions of self-evidence. So, I suggest that these mistakes not be erased but rather be left alone, perhaps analysed. Or at the very least, as they are in our family: cherished (many of my parents' blunders have been corrected over the years, and we miss them dearly).

Yes, I am advocating for bad grammar, misplaced words, *Falsche Freunde*[1], awkward phrasings and mispronunciations. And I formally elect English for this bloody sacrifice, as the process has already been put into motion, and is so commonly used and torn to pieces throughout the world.

Do you speak English as a [first], second, third, fourth or fifth language? Are you forced to use English from time to time to get your point across? Not feeling confident? Can't find the equivalent word? I say bulldoze away. And *have it the fun* with it too

My concerns with the state of the English language lie elsewhere. It's those who hide behind the guise of eloquence that often threaten language with dumb paralysis, and perpetuate so many unclarified assumptions. They may speak so much, sound so good, yet say nothing at all.

In his 1946 essay, "Politics and the English Language," George Orwell criticizes exactly this about the state of the

---

1 *False friends*, words in two languages that look or sound similar, but differ significantly in meaning.

Anna M. Szaflarski 303

Language used by English-speaking (most likely British) politicians:

> Most people who bother with the matter at all would admit that the English language is in a bad way, but it is generally assumed that we cannot by conscious action do anything about it. Our civilization is decadent and our language—so the argument runs—must inevitably share in the general collapse. It follows that any struggle against the abuse of language is a sentimental archaism, like preferring candles to electric light or hansom cabs to aeroplanes. Underneath this lies the half-conscious belief that language is a natural growth and not an instrument which we shape for our own purposes.

Orwell argues for a return of precision in language through education specifically focused on studying the origins of certain often-used metaphors. He laments in how etymology and the origins of certain sayings are being overrun, dampened, dulled by the puppetry of rhetoric. That intentional communication gradually disappeared in the game of inferred meaning, and replaced by residual and superficial emotions. His *beef*[2] was specifically with political writing, which I am sure we can all understand. The United States is an easy target where slogans like *Communism, Axis of Evil,*

---

2   meaning finding problem with. Wikipedia.org: "As regards the etymology of beef, it seems to go back to the cry of hot beef! meaning 'stop thief!'; quasi-rhyming slang but more by coincidence than design, since it is far older than rhyming slang's first widespread use in the 1820s–30s; thus the 18th century cry hot beef, to raise a hue and cry."

304   LTTE no. 27 — *Foreign Affairs*

Amendment are used by politicians and media like misguided children who want to cause drama without having to explain why. They are like terrorists hijacking terms, words, phrases and idioms that were at one time so carefully forged, crashing them into the mainstream and leaving behind only senselessness. But they do it so cleverly, with their perfect syntax, and grammar, and slick rhythms. No wonder they so often go undetected.

This doesn't only occur in politics, and perhaps we should feel particular solidarity with Orwell's argument when we scan the plethora of press releases in galleries and museums in this city [Berlin]. Pages and wall texts that are supposed to act as ambassadors between art and viewer are equally full of words that are time and again repeated but never defined or questioned. We are not instilled with fear in this case, but alienated by the allure of knowledge; knowledge that the reader often does not hold, but also does not trust herself to question who the beholder of this knowledge might actually be.

Orwell dissects overused and misused idioms and metaphors, and attacks imprecision. I'll admit, He becomes tedious at points; perhaps channelling his self-defined *sentimental archaist*. His rules are suffocating, each starts with a 'never' or 'if' (although he does lend you an escape plan!: *Break any of these rules sooner than say anything outright barbarous*). I enjoy a more liberal approach and encourage savvy language, even when it is not necessarily pragmatic, but I agree with the core of Orwell's argument that, "the great enemy of clear language is insincerity." Now, perhaps I wouldn't go so far to call it the *great enemy* wich ironically leans in the direction of political rhetoric. But as I titled this text as I did, I can't really criticize him there. But his point is key: when insincerity becomes the motivator of language, it becomes flaccid, indirect, and the only meaning emerging from it is atmospheric at best. Speaking and writing sincerely sounds simple, but it is not. And from my observations, nothing has ever made me more sincere (some have characterized it as a tad blunt or direct) than having to express myself in a language other than my mother-tongue.

I once knew someone who worked for the European Commission in Brussels. The Commission is composed of a lovely community that seems to function very similarly to an oversized group of adult Erasmus students. Many of them complain of the hindrance of legislative or negotiation processes due to the language they are all forced to speak, known as International English. For some it's painful to even consider discussing such important matters when not able to fully exert his or her linguistic abilities. I experienced something similar when I did my Master's studies in German. The majority of my colleagues were international, and we bumbled along like children or maybe more like prehistoric peoples who might knock on stones and gather sticks in hopes to better illustrate our complex points. But there was something so liberating in having to reduce our vocabulary 'back to basics' while trying desperately to communicate something intelligently. It forced us to select our words carefully, to question what we actually wanted to say, and prevented some of us from falling into the same avenues of bullshit that we developed during our undergrads back home. However, these kinds of enlightening albeit frustrating phases are eventually overtaken by a certain disintegration of concentration. In our seminars and—as I have been told—in the conference rooms of the European Commission, a new shared vocabulary of umbrella terms and shop-talk was eventually forged (i.e. *Aus-*

einandersetzung, which can mean 'examine', 'contest', 'argument', 'discuss', and so much more, was picked up ¾ through my studies and was the saviour of many unprepared presentations at the University). Eventually the group uses the new terms and feels more confident, intelligent, and yet, I was uncertain if our content at the university was developing at the same rate, let alone our sincerity.

When speaking in our own mother-tongues, insincerity occurs often and naturally. It's not intentional, nor demonic. It's even enjoyable to a certain extent, and sometimes atmosphere is exactly what one needs to get a party started. It's also undeniable that when someone speaks well, it's like listening to music, and when writing is as eloquent and beautiful as it is sincere it is truly like finding gold. Those who strive to push the English language forward on those terms, I believe will always do so, because they feel compelled to and should be praised for their good work. But there is another kind of work being done by the masses of people who are using English as a tool of pragmatism. They are conducting a large-scale, experimental linguistic field-study in speech, text messages, blogs, restaurant menus, subway announcements and applying methods of dissection, stuttering, faltering, mimickery, confusion, linguistic hybridization and yes, destruction. And may the good work continue.

Dynamic Statement

<u>concerning the exhibition piece</u>
"Sokhraneniye Pogloshchennogo"
(Russian: Сохренение Поглащенного,
Survival of the Absorbed);
<u>developed in the context of the exhibition</u>
"Synthesis and Integration";
<u>installed in</u> Gallery Vkhutemas,
Moscow Architectural Institute;
<u>as part of the street fashion and alternative art festival</u>
"Faces and Laces", that took place in Gorky Central Park
of Culture and Leisure, Moscow;
<u>realized by</u> Akim, Louise Drubigny, Gambette,
Florian Goldmann, Vincent Grunwald, Anna Herms,
Clemens Hilsberger;
<u>using</u> about 40 empty cardboard boxes
in different sizes as well as six white T-shirts
on MDF-display dummies, functioning as screens
for four video projections;
<u>commissioned by</u> Dimitri Oskes,
organizer of "Faces and Laces";
<u>grants consultation and logo design by</u>
Vincent 'art of sponsoring' Grunwald;
<u>on display from</u> the 8th to the 20th of August 2015;
<u>accompanied by</u> the following text (name of author not
known, name of author of translation below withheld)

Florian Goldmann et al.

LTTE no. 27 — *Foreign Affairs*

СОХРЕНЕНИЕ ПОГЛАЩЕННОГО
на на "СИНТЕЗЕ И ИНТЕГРАЦИИ"

То же самое и с сочинениями: думаешь, будто они говорят как разумные существа, но если кто спросит о чем-нибудь из того, что они говорят, желая это усвоить, они всегда отвечают одно и то же.[1]

В платоновском диалоге СОКРАТА с ФЕДРОМ выражено недоверие к тогда достаточно новому искусству письменности. В отличии от ораторства, письменный текст не способен говорить со слушателем напрямую, но способен донести его мысль до широкой публики. Диалог предполагает, что с этим расширением аудитории повышается и риск неправильного понимания содержимого текста. Ведь автор теряет привелегию интерпретации, и письменный текст не способен ответить на вопросы, появляющиеся у слушателя.

Тезис:

Индивиддум, совершающий графический жест – будь то сотворение текста, диаграммы, рисунка, или предмета одежды, способен сохранить силу интерпретации своей мысли в содержимом этого графического жеста.

Для утрированного примера: заявление (мессадж, посыл), написанное на майке, способно оставаться диалектическим, так как может стать предметом дискуссии между теми, кто его прочтет.

---

1 Платон: ДИАЛОГИ СОКРАТА в 12 томах, ч.9 – ФЕД

Антитезис:

Жест или заявление, ограниченные рамками поношенной майки, неспособно создать весомую дискуссию. Наоборот, поставив заявление на майку, автор уменьшает его до его эстетических качеств. Всё разумное или революционное, что заключалось в этом жесте становится скрытым, пригашенным и, через призму власти и подавления – качества, присущие любой одежде – полностью стерилизованным. Все подрывное в изначальном жесте сжимается предметом и становится логотипом. Логотип передает лишь образы и не является диалектическим.

В 1898 г. французская компания, занимавшаяся производством шин, представила в качестве своего логотипа карикатурного человечка под именем БИБЕНДУМ. Он был представлен в разных позах и ситуациях – обедая, распивая напитки и играя в спортивные игры – и менялся со временем и положением. Таким образом, БИБЕНДУМ считается первым так называемым динамичным логотипом.

СИНТЕЗ:

Осознавая материальность предмета одежды, связанную с властью и подавлением, также как и с духом борьбы против этой власти, индивидуум, носящий футболку способен активно выражать заявление, напечатанное на ней. Несмотря на то, что жест на майке уменьшен до состояния символа, он снова приобретает свои динамические качества. Таким образом, носитель футболки, оживляя собой дискуссию, сам становится знаком, динамическим логотипом.

310   LTTE no. 27 — *Foreign Affairs*

SURVIVAL OF THE ABSORBED
in the framework of
"SYNTHESIS and INTEGRATION"

> And so it is with written words; you might think
> they spoke as if they had intelligence, but if you
> question them, wishing to know about their
> sayings, they always say only one and the same
> thing.[1]

Plato's Socratic dialogue Phaedrus, expresses a mistrust in the
relatively new medium of the written word. As opposed to
speech, the written word would not be capable of distinctive-
ly addressing a recipient, enabling a wider, and inexact, dis-
persion instead. With this increase in audience, it is argued
that the medium's message could potentially be misappropri-
ated. After all, with the author losing his/her authority over
interpretation, a piece of writing by itself would not be able
to respond to questions the recipient might have.

Thesis:

A statement written on a T-shirt can potentially be dialect-
ical, since it can be contested by any of its readers. An individual exposing a graphic gesture — be it in the form of text,
a diagram or a drawing — on a piece of clothing, retains the
authority over interpretation of the graphic.

1   Plato: Phaedrus, in: Plato in Twelve Volumes, Vol. 9 translated by
Harold N. Fowler. Cambridge, MA, Harvard University Press; London,
William Heinemann Ltd. 1925, 275d.

Antithesis:

A gesture or statement merely made within the close-fitting constraints of a worn T-shirt is ineffective in provoking a substantial argument. In contrast, by being applied to a T-shirt, the statement is reduced to its aesthetic implications. Anything arguable or subversive is obscured or even muted since the threads of power and repression, inherent to the garment, pose as sterilizing agents. The subversive is enclosed and becomes a logo. A logo only ever conveys to its signified and is not dialectic.

In 1898 a French tire manufacturer introduced its new logo, the animated cartoon figure Bibendum. The mascot was depicted in many different contexts, such as eating, drinking and playing sports. Changing over time and from setting to setting, Bibendum is said to be the first so-called dynamic logo.

Synthesis:

With the statement-bearing, T-shirt-wearing individual being aware of the garment's materiality, its threads of power and repression, as well as, potential threads of subversion, he/she is able to activate the statement. And despite it being reduced to a logo, the statement gains a dynamic quality again. The T-shirt wearer, by animating the argument, becomes the signifier, the dynamic logo itself.

With the kind support of:

LTTE no. 28 — *Can't Help It*
October 26, 2015

*"We know you are being
deliberately obtuse!"*

The Waiters Will Not Help You

Peter Wächtler

And about the waiters, don't you worry,
they will make you feel that you are worth it, really,
it is just that they will not help you.
And honestly what could they do?
They know from afar, that you are not going to last,
so you better make your orders fast
and just because your finger-snapping days are coming to an end,
please, of all people don't expect them to help you, my friend.

So you tuck in, as much as you can,
and after another brawling hour,
you watch their smiles slowly turn sour.
You are even discussing this with your peers,
after speculating about the pros and cons of prostitution,
you throw in: do waiters actually have a union?

Look how they gather behind the salad buffet,
secretively sipping from bottles with a more hateful bouquet
you hear curses, giggles and they are up to no good.
You don't care as long as they bring your comfort food.
You were never seated with courtesy,
the service here was always lame
and you were never welcomed by name.

LTTE no. 28 — *Can't Help It*   317

But when in total silence they deliver the third course,
you realize that tonight it is definitely worse,
when you see that fish served with watercress salad mix
its boiled eyes are deeply pierced with two dirty tooth picks.

But why? To eat and drink as much as you can
is after all a human right and yes you are a beef man
and eating a dead cow that is already dead
is in this situation the best you can do.
So why do they stare, and why especially at you?

All at once they make you feel shabby and sweaty,
as if you do not really belong there
a pretentious cretin not worthy their *Fin de Claires*.

But maybe it is not their fault.

Your evening already is pretty corrupted
this venue used to be good ten years ago
but now no longer can be trusted,
Thanks to those badly paid assholes in white
and Pardon Monsieur what the fuck is wrong with the light?
and even more the light dims down and gets rather pale
and on the white table cloth your Prosecco is getting stale.

You look into the faces of your friends,
faces built out of the same slobber
then your brain, lips, balls and liver.
Faces that have been with you,
through all kind of shit
at least according to the legend,
but your common path has finally come to an end.

318   LTTE no. 28 — *Can't Help It*

None of them even tries to close that last-stop-abyss
honestly, would there be anyone that you would really miss?
Around this table you used to be ten, then seven, now five,
but you know that this last hole is for you alone to nosedive.
Of course, everybody is embarrassed,
Jesus, how long this reunion has been planned.
You cancelled three fucks, a baptism and a burial
just to be here, you know, with friends and all.
But now the road ahead feels much longer
than the one that brought you here
and—*tata*—enter the good old fear.

You feel fat and drunk and in need for air,
there is a strange pressure in your chest
and the sweat fountains out of every pore.
You stand up slowly.
You puke a good bye smile to your colleagues
and say, "I see you all in hell, freaks."

God, it is good to move,
shake those limbs and bend those joints!
Out of the door and right under your feet
there it is: the street, the street!
That's where you come from!
your true origins are rough and real
this is where you belong and that is where you feel!
Like an arteria the idea pops in your head which is still kind of hot:
To be free means to choose where you are
and where you are not.
I am a free soul, I am free, why didn't I see?
excited you walk home and skip the taxi.

Peter Wächtler

The next morning the real world stopped its short embrace
and among the four million people around
you surely have the saddest face.
All is lost, everything like friends and all,
so much for this capital.

BUT: Thank God it's autumn,
so you can tiger down lonely alleys
it almost feels like back then in Paris
and you are pretty sure:
this is the weight of deepness
that you were made to endure.
A tragic scent sticks to you,
you don't shave and stop the gym,
waiting for change, for life to begin.

Last week you stared for a good hour
at a leaf and its reddish colour.
And in your notebook
just below the line
"I am here and I am bound to feel it."
you wrote:
"Check out where the green goes
when it is no longer needed."

Thanks to the endless joy of your thoughts you never feel lonely,
but secretively you miss the downy moustache of your true lady
you remember what she said, when you, just as a friend,
    tried to hug her?
"Touch me again and I'll sue you motherfucker."

LTTE no. 28 — *Can't Help It*

Then again,
this was also the time that you send out
your best unanswered messages so far, rather proud.
for example:
"Baby close the door
Baby turn out the light
I can't wait anymore
I need to be with you tonight"

Most people you call don't pick up the phone
or are just driving and can't stop,
only a few make some awkward efforts
and then it's you who hangs up.

But all at once the way out is super easy:
you just have to change your life over completely.
Leave, don't hesitate, stop enduring all this homegrown pain,
instead take better care of your middle-aged body
    and your useless brain.
That's right, one and one makes two
now focus on what you really like to do
and what was that again?

It does not matter for the bigger plan.

Now that a completely different decision has been made
It makes no difference any longer
if you are bound to destroy or to create.

So you leave your famous park bench behind
for there are greater outdoors yet to find,
you are really serious about this and frown
when you shout out loud: "puffy big boy is leaving town!"

Peter Wächtler

This is not my life and too long I tried to accept it,
out of my way you filthy plebs you are all dismissed!
All of you assholes stand aside,
the last of the dead poets
is moving to the countryside!

A very local train on his last trip
drops you off somewhere in the north,
the station gets demolished just after you closed its doors.
Stones, dust and dirt and overgrown tracks, nothing is left,
but a gang of retarded onlookers living on diesel and cable theft.

Not in any of the many culture's you studied
no matter how far you go west, east, south,
the thing you have bought would be called a house.
You jerk open the door, not even very hard,
and it's not that it squeaks,
it just silently crumbles apart.

But there is an old bed with sheets of plastic
and the view on that lake is simply fantastic.
and the big garden, in brackets question mark,
this is what you call MY PARK.

You set yourself to work again
that's what you inherited all those tools for
and after two weeks you can even walk on the floor.
Not bad, young fellow, not bad!
Who would have thought after all the troubles you had.
Physically you are in great shape,
with your body, to become an athlete is never too late,
you make pull-ups, sometimes up to eight,
on that iron bar nailed in between two birch trees,
and when it comes to push-ups you are way into the twenties.

322 LTTE no. 28 — *Can't Help It*

Juchu, Juchu, there is always something to do,
all you really need in terms of meaning and sense
you get from an overpriced flannel shirt and your
      own working hands.
In the evenings you play on some kind of branch flute
a song about how good canned beans are as the only food.
This is the life you were made for,
you feel your powers return,
and with pride you piss into your backyard's fern.
Even though there is nobody to see it within a mile
for the first time in years you find back your smile.
Why do all these people want to live a life so goddam fake,
when all you need for happiness is to wash your pitzi
      every morning in a lake?

But it was around the time you needed professionals
to fix the electricity lines of your premises,
when your idea of good life had a more difficult stand
and your brain gave birth to a new one, just before it's own end.
But the new one was bad, your thought soup got murky,
      slow and thicker,
it's taste from day to day grew increasingly bitter.
To distract yourself from that new mutation,
you ask the electrician if he needs help with the installation.
The young man turns around, empty black sockets for eyes,
grunting "Over my dead body,
I rather ask assistance from the shit flies.
But let me tell you something,
from worker to schemer,
I once knew a chimney cleaner
who wanted that word,
chimney cleaner
and just this word alone,

Peter Wächtler

to be written on his tombstone.
And when from his last chimney he fell
he broke his back and
went straight to working class' hell
a better place, but not really ambrosian.
On his stone that he in time had chosen,
they wrote: here lies Walter Rippknit
a loyal servant to those who do deserve it.
Meaning, you do your push ups, I do my job,
however simple your wishes are,
they will NOT be taken
into consideration."
Full stop.

He also tells you that he has to order new parts,
and promises to be back in about two weeks.

You say thank you.

There are four candles left.

You post the postcards you wrote about your well-being
and your best decision in life into an old oak tree.
You don't try any longer to jog your sadness away.
The pull-up bar drops off the birch in late November.

It's true there are more stars to see in the countryside at night.
But it is also true that if the sky is black
it is really black.
It is this sky that makes you feel sorry for
everything you have ever done.

LTTE no. 28 — *Can't Help It*

Each day the lake is getting colder.
Each day the water is getting darker.
You stand shivering and watch a flock of geese.
If that is a flock of geese.
Who knows? Not you.
What are all those flowers called?
Who knows? Not you.
Where is my home? Where are my feelings?
Who knows? Not you.
You watch the lake.

And life goes on.

One morning your skull is flooded with new chemicals
    unclear of what kind.
That new brain of yours knocks on your eyeballs from behind
asking you to take it for a final swim in the frozen water,
or to borrow a shotgun from a neighbouring farmer.
Your brain even advises you to answer,
in case that dumbass asks what you want with it,
that you are planning to shoot a fucked up rabbit.
It whispers, "Heeyy, dont, be embarrassed, don't be shy,
you are not the only around here who wants to die."

You somehow manage to refuse your brain's sweet proposal
but it's totally pissed off and serves you a good sock in the jaw.
Like a wet towel you go to the floor,
but still you manage to crawl
to your emergency crate of beer
and from then on, you start drinking around fifty to *vier*.

Peter Wächtler

Maybe it is intoxication
that allows your mind to see
this detailed dreary scenery:
A crazy long caravan of men and camels
all of them loaded and packed with parcels
filthy, dull and rot
endlessly trots through your thoughts.
The people spit out and swear
allowing their two-thousand fucking camels
to piss anywhere.

And the caravan sings:

"Who was that person fixing the floor,
and who was that man repairing the door?

"Where is that guy swimming the lake,
and where is the fellow fresh and awake?

"Where is the boy who speaks to man and beast,
and where is his smile that charmingly pleased?
When was his soul taken and his heart turned sore,
and why did he become such a fucking bore?

"For we don't care if he seeks true emotion
deep down at the bottom of the ocean
or if on top of the Himalaya of doubt
he sits and cries his small heart out.

"A fuck we don't give about anyone
and we march on 'til this life is gone.
Fuck him, he is as good as dead!
Toute la compagnie: Arrête!
Halt! Everybody back to bed!"

326   LTTE NO. 28 — *Can't Help It*

So you sleep.
You sleep 'till early April
until a man wakes you by breaking off your windowsill.
It's the cross-eyed peasant from the nearest farm
saying: "My chickens are in your barn."
"*Hääääääääää*?
"What barn?
"Whose barn?"
"My barn!"

Yes, you are still there
and springtime gives you new inspiration
for your struggle with social and sexual orientation.
The electrician taught you to forget about downward solidarity
so your plan instead is to suck up to the local aristocracy.

Not far from your cabin,
there is a big mansion, very very old,
inhabited by—who would have guessed,
an aging nobleman called Mr. Toad.

You invite yourself over for Tea and Whisky Soda,
and old Mr. Toad is in fact happy to have found a listener.
He just finished writing his memoirs
entitled Everything is Paid For.
His monologues do not really reach you
but you pretended to listen with dedication
to his sheer endless thoughts on crop rotation,
about how people destroy nature and how everything is
    standardized.
With tear filled eyes he speaks about his trips to France when
    it still wasn't pasteurised.

Peter Wächtler

In fact he only stops speaking
for sleeping
and at times he is dozing off, then his old fat head
falls back
so heavily that you are afraid for his neck.
You gently twitch at his morning gown
yes, it is checkered
and it shows his initials nicely embroidered
around a greenish looking Union Jack
and you whisper:
"Mr. Toad, I am actually thinking about a comeback."

"A comeback?" he blinks and says sleepily,
"And I thought I was crazy!
My poor troubled son,
you still think that could be done?
I shall have serious doubts that you were born
to take any kind of bull by any kind of horn.
But allow me a modest question from the upper crust,
For the comeback: do you already know as a what?

"In this case my counsel shall be,
as I am myself, a man of best reputation,
a good friend to both, mother nature and father civilisation
and I think You should better, for a change,
choose something from the impressive range,
something legendary,
something extraordinary,
for to re-enter the stage of life
please forgive me my humble advice
but what would suit you, oh so very good
I'd say you'll make it as hmmmmn, Big Foot."

328   LTTE no. 28 — *Can't Help It*

Then he starts laughing his froggish laughter
that grows more and more evil and horrid and louder
he just laughs you out of his cosy chimney corner
and you leave, and again you run and flee,
pushing the butler aside,
down the great stairs you fly,
and you hear that horrible laughter laughing at you and
    you hear it still
after in sprint you crossed Toad's park booming with
    all those fucking daffodils.

Sincerely hurt and insulted, back at your own outpost
crying is what you want the most,
but your eyes won't do you this favour and they just won't
    let you have it,
instead dry as a desert they stare at what you are and what you did.
In the mirror you try to restore a more familiar face,
until you hear how that person mumbles:
"Dude, time to pack your suitcase."

As it is Easter soon, the peasants of the shire
use your house, your home
for the purpose of a giant bonfire.
At night without flute nor whistle you shamble on a muddy,
    soggy trail,
to the rebuild station, the starting point of your country tale
and you turn a last time to see the bright flames in the distance,
tearing apart yet another chapter of your existence.
Sieged and defeated by your most inner longings,
this is the end of your empire building
you shut down your castle, you gave up your fortress
you sold your soil for a ticket of the Intercity Express.

Peter Wächtler

Back in Berlin, I mean Florence,
you are in need of money.
A good reason to call up some former friends
in the hope somebody still cares.
But in the meantime war broke out
and they are all busy with army affairs,
mainly at organisational and logistic departments,
but still,
things got serious and existential.

The world is at war
conflict, killing, blood and gore,
hungry children just skin and bone,
but by now you wouldn't even bother
if they were your own.
Finally a bootlicker, whom back then you did not even greet
after long discussions on the phone finally agrees to meet.
As you have nothing else to do,
you are early at this very familiar restaurant.
and you are the only guest around.
The city was bombed three times,
and each time it was worse,
but still nobody managed
to wipe this shithole from the face of the earth.
In the waiters eyes no sign of recognition or not more than before
and he places you to a chilly shabby table close to the door.
He gravely bows down to take your order,
that hardly audible through your unkissed lips you squeeze.
He nods and shouts to the counter:
"Three large beers for the German Bigfoot, please."
But heyyyy that's not another reason for you to moan,
it's just his way of saying: Welcome Home.

LTTE no. 29 — *Omit, Admit, Emit*
November 11, 2015

Anna M. Szaflarski

I went to visit a gym not 500 metres from my house to inquire about membership. It's owned by Madonna, and there are pictures of her tiny body and alien face everywhere. Her glitzy bra protrudes over every outfit; a different bra, a different corset, but there is a defined hierarchy in her dressing. Bra always on top. Now, is it just plain burlesque tradition or is it a commentary on the suppression of women's intimates by the patriarchal system? Hmm, maybe don't over think it. I switched my attention to the training program offered, and scanned for the type of classes I might find strenuous but would induce as little embarrassment as possible. Madonna is doing something Latin in a muted video playing above the lounge chairs near the entrance. I don't want to shake my booty. Nobody wants to see my bra.

I decided I'm going to join the gym anyways. There's been a general tension growing on the left side of my body, and

332   LTTE NO. 29 — *Omit, Admit, Emit*

figure if I don't do something about it might petrify. The thought of late night visits to the sauna is seductive, along with the machines that promise to jiggle my muscles...ehem... along with everything else, while I do exercises carefully outlined by a trainer, who is supposed to passive aggressively judge me by placing weight-trimming goals that I did not ask for on a usb stick. You plug it into the machines, and your fat percentage is solicited. Thank you. The gym is for women only, however, I am suspicious when they sent a well built man to give me the tour. He smiled and spoke gently, *Do you have children?*

No, I blush, debating if I should indulge in the fantasy that he's actually flirting with me.

Oh, He steps aside, *then the daycare program will not interest you*. He walks away kicking up dirt in my face.

As a single woman with no children, I guess it would be irresponsible for me not to join a gym, right? Not to strive for perfect complexion and hard abs. Women with families are gasping for air let alone an hour to go out for a jog, or join a yoga class. It's my moral obligation to shake my booty, buy lacy bras and wear them on top of my winter jacket. As a woman with no 'significant' other, it's my prerogative to be vain and think about myself. Unlike so many struggling people out there, I do not lack 'me' time. On the contrary, I am in great abundance of 'me' time. Me me me me.

I noticed unfortunately that my appearance is not directly proportionate to the amount of 'me' time I have. Nor is my tan, intelligence, my eloquence or my list of hobbies. I concluded that 'me' time was going wasted, and it's a travesty that must be remedied.

So, in hopes of becoming a more rounded person, I signed

up for a French class. I can't just have a great bod, I need to be able to exhibit my wealth of 'me' in an *assortiment* of ways. I'll travel to Paris to buy baguettes or perhaps one day become a Canadian politician or at least get a part-time job at an embassy filing papers for passport renewals. This would be 'me' time well spent.

When I arrived to my first class, I was asked to introduce myself. Oh so subtly, I shook my shoulders and puckered my lips, and off I went on the path to being more French, sophisticated and worldly. My tense lips let out a undefined whistle, because I can't actually speak French. The years of childhood language classes were far behind me, but I pushed on through the hour, partitioning my brain between a) concentrating on inserting the *Est-ce que's* in the right place and b) thoughts on how the new 'me' would be perceived in time.

It is quite evident that my devotion to learning is not directly proportional to my 'me' time either. Instead it seems that my self-absorption is in direct correlation to my inability to understand something about the world around me.

After our warm up of who-are-you's and what-do-you do's, the French instructor, Michél, or Michèl, not sure which one, hands out an attendance form. And as we scramble to understand and undertake the simple task of jotting down our phone numbers he goes on an extra-curricular tangent of anecdotes, *en français*. We are delighted to see his eyebrows lift with a life of their own and his lips protrude just as they should. I squint my eyes and imagine Godard's superstar Jean-Paul Belmondo. Everything he says seems so cool, and there are no questions, only rhetorical questions; questions that have already been answered by Derrida, Foucault or proud bosom-bearing Liberty herself. It doesn't seem to mat-

334 LTTE no. 29 — *Omit, Admit, Emit*

ter that I don't understand a word of what this man is saying, I am so starved for the interpretative dance that is a romantic language that I am mesmerized by it and by the fantasy that I may one day join.

The attendance sheet arrives before me, which forces my eyes to refocus. I mouth the digits in German, which is the only way I can remember them, and after scribbling them down, lift my head back towards the Frenchman. Belmondo disappeared, and everything seemed much harsher in the fluorescent lights blasting into my re-dilated pupils. There were French politicians names written on the white board. I sensed something knocking on the sound and blast-proof doors of my 'me' time. And Michél/èl, where was he? He was standing in the middle of the room looking awfully sarcastic, his chin and arm raised while slowly dragging a line with his finger across his neck. It was the gestural beheading of an anonymous victim but also of my baguettes and bra-top corsets. 'Me' time all of a sudden seemed a bit ridiculous.

When I said that my fitness level or devotion to learning was not directly proportional to my 'me' time but my self-absorption was most definitely in direct correlation to my inability to understand the world around me, I was referring to how lost I was in the French class and how it made me self-involved and self-conscious. But apparently my rampant narcissism was blotting out more than Michél/èl's lessons.

I am a coward. Not because I want to get into shape or learn French but because of a writers' block that I am currently experiencing that prevents me from writing about anything else. The writers' paralysis is facilitated by the Frenchman's finger sarcastically running across his throat, by the newspapers of late and the various political campaigns.

Anna M. Szaflarski

I am a coward because I am afraid of naming the kind of things that concern me in the world. Not because I might awaken them, or endanger myself. Let me be very clear, I do not personally feel in danger of anything. Instead, I am afraid of doing a subject of importance a disservice, of revealing my confusion, ignorance, or even worse, of being accused of hijacking or exploiting something for my own artistic gain. Yes, I am faced with a problem granted only to the privileged: silence stemming from my insecurity of ownership or authority of the issues that trouble me.

I am reminded of an assistant Prof from my studies in Vancouver. He was the kind of guy who would always ask provocative questions that made everybody uneasy at lectures. He was the kind of guy who voiced his frustration with art students who would address every little thread in their grandmother's quilt to discuss identity, yet fail to address anything that was going on in the world. I have to admit, that I found him extremely annoying. He was always persecuting someone else for not doing enough. But there was something in what he said that I couldn't ignore. And even though his criticisms were not directly pointed at me, they stung and the welts lingered.

If this particular artist lives up to his own expectations or not, I am not sure. So few artists do, and if they do, they seem to often have some sort of 'identity' connection to their cause, a sort of confidence of ownership. Is that not true? So where does that leave the rest of us? How do we avoid indifference with own our concerns? In what manner is it appropriate to engage politics in our work without overstepping our authority?

Comedy and fiction lend a hand. The strength in these mediums is to point at things we all notice but find uncom-

336   LTTE no. 29 — *Omit, Admit, Emit*

fortable, so that we can acknowledge something without feeling like we have to find answers. We can gracefully hide our opinions in the seams of sarcasm, and in the archways of anecdotes that frame seemingly banal things—things that are more naturally connected to our everyday lives: gym memberships, French classes, relationships and the condition of the artist. We hope that one day someone will look back and place it more directly in context, so that we don't have to. We are left with these mediums because for the privileged and liberal-minded, anything too direct seems didactic, overbearing, narrow or manipulative. Is this not true? Or is it only true for the world I circulate in?

So, fiction and comedy keeps everyone feeling intelligent but generally unbothered. But what do you do when you've got a writer's block and all of the clever ways of weaving metaphors have left you? Without their filter you might get a bit over sensitive like I have recently become, finding news headlines increasingly disturbing, and fiction unable to remedy the issue. I realized this after becoming nauseous while watching Halloween prank videos depicting people carrying plastic machetes and wearing gowns covered in ketchup. Post-apocalyptic fantasies that are running rampant in half the films and series out these days, seem to ignite everything in society except for a feeling of empathy, and instead encourage an ultimate (and dramatic) surrender of intellectual responsibility and an embrace for self-pity. Fiction and comedy are increasingly difficult to differentiate from real politics and issues as reality television personas run for the American presidency, and everyone ranging from politicians, artists, comedians and radical extremists have You Tube Channels and use many of the same camera techniques. And the art world is handing us fewer role models than ever.

This might not be the best source of authority, but coincidently today an article about the last Artissima art fair seemed to only add to the despair when it reported that according to a collection of dealers and curators, art is shifting towards subjective relationships to objects and away from conceptualism; in other words: towards 'me' time with the painting, scultpure, body etc.

So, I've hit a writers' block. When we meet, I'll tell you the rest of my gym and French class stories. But today my metaphors, sarcasm and anecdotes are at a stand off. Perhaps the block is only here to wave a red flag to the many of the things that have been omitted from the issues of this journal, in the cowardly hope that when it's compiled, printed and found again, that someone might contextualize the things that I was afraid to, even if only to point out yet again how many things were not there.

Would you rather have a peach or a painting of a peach?

Tiziana La Melia

Act 2

delete "a" before "glass", capital G
delete "(either the animal or the object)" after "dolphin"
replace "The eyes of a chair" with "Upholstery buttons on a couch"
delete "A" before "A slab of butter"
delete "A" before "parrot" and delete "or a crow"
delete "A" before "curtain" and delete "blowing in the wind"
delete "A" before knife, capital K
delete "Open mic night poem"
delete "Recital"
delete "Crying"
delete "A" before snail, capital S
delete "Heavy" before rain, capital R and period
delete "s" after Gulls
change "Machinery." to "Machine."
change "Newspaper folding" to "Newspaper."
delete "Siren"
delete "Chopping"
delete "a typed" change to just "Note."
delete "A" before lamp.
delete "A" before hat.

LTTE NO. 29 — *Omit, Admit, Emit* 339

delete "Giggling" before baby. capital B
delete "Suburban teenager's bedroom.'
delete "A" before spiral, capital S.
delete "A" before "A boy doodling on the guitar." capital B
replace "Smile." with "Grin."
delete extra space before "Jewels."
delete "Rustle" before "trees", capital T
delete "A" before "faun." capital F
delete "A" before "cat", captial C, delete " (smokey)
 Delete Act 3

Change Act 4 to Act 3

Delete Act 3

Change Act 4 to Act 3

delete "Sign up for open mic night."

delete "tenants" before "building manager"
delete "were cutting" replace with "sawed holes in the wall"
delete "blossoms" after "cures"
delete "From slogans to the uplifting epigraphs written
between birthday cards. And sometimes both, the gallery
occupies a space for occasions. Birthday parties, fundraisers,
a temple for contemplation, a place to gripe, the grit, of the
moldy grout; a hex".
delete "Black mold doesn't absorb but emerges out of ab-
sorption. Black mold is common to a place." before "Black
mold is who we blame"
delete "Melancholy, longing, lazy and cheap" between
"to understand" and "the spit"

340   LTTE NO. 29 — *Omit, Admit, Emit*

I think you should delete this part:

I write from a future where I describe myself contemplating the non reflective pond.

The farmer tells us the rotten apples we are gathering into our shirts at the bottom of the tree are bad to eat.

We apologize, not knowing that the area beyond the pond and the stinging nettles is private. Without a fence, I may have understood the groomed grass to be a sign of private property, but I wanted to move between zones, zone in, it all belonged to us, we felt free.

He then suggested we make compote.

We apologized and thanked him and thought about what the farmer might feel. Artists, always taking.

I thought of my father, how he would tell someone wandering in the orchard the same thing, that the free falls were bad. But then, who cares, they are free. Take them.

He told us that le chevre come out at night. And then what?

That it is very beautiful.

Mixed messages.

Did he just want to give us permission?

LTTE NO. 30 — *Moments of Solidarity*
November 30, 2015

The Race

Anna M. Szaflarski

My fingernails were in terrible shape. Holding one hand in the other, I pushed my cuticles back with my thumbnail, exactly what my mother told me never to do. Purple stains from cooking beet soup the night before blotched my palms. Caught red handed, I thought. Framed, I pleaded. It's good to leave traces of your work on your hands, it insulted their labour to clean and manicure them all of the time. This is what I wanted to believe, but I'd still go and have them tidied up the following week. Like a symphony conductor, a woman needed to be able to orchestrate glamour and restraint with her hands. That's what I had learned. Beyond the wrists everything could shake if need be.

We were spending the morning at the races. The sun was bright and the air fresh, clouds billowed from horses' noses, men's cigarettes and women's coffees. The jockeys strutted elegantly in erect postures on or off their mounts as if noth-

ing ever bad happened. I tucked my arms under my elbows. It was good to get out. No matter where, it was good to get out. Just a few hours of pretending like nothing ever bad happened.

Of course, we fought before we left the house. The baby was crying and I wanted to stay home. I pleaded with George that enough money had been wasted on luxuries let alone horses. But he insisted. He had that sort of drive to him, something told him that his luck was turning up, and he said he wasn't by God going to let me stand in his way. He accused me of not believing in him, that I emasculated him. It didn't matter that he didn't believe in what he was saying, there was that kind of drive to him that blasted through exhaust pipes, spun turbines in every direction until eventu-

ally a gaskets broke. And I always broke under the pressure. So I handed our child off to the nurse and gathered my things. He stomped heavily through the house, adding bass to the tick of the clock. We didn't speak in the car. George leaned over the steering wheel gripping it like he was going to fall off of it, and I looked out the side window. The streets were grey and shoulders weighed heavily on spines that slumped under the pressure. Everyone wanted to turn around and go home, but they were out, and it was good to get out.

George slowed the car as we approached Maria. She stood on the busy corner in her own universe, smartly dressed in a tweet jacket and matching skirt waving her gloves at us. Her smile had the power to charm most men and women, it stretched preposterously wide, pinned from one perfect ear to the other. She popped the back door open, bounced in, slammed the door closed and planted cordial kisses on both of our cheeks before the car came to a complete stop. *What a fine day*, she exhaled. *What a fine day*, George complied.

We found seats in the grandstand as near to the track as possible. George took off to see the horses as they were paraded next to the stables before being saddled, leaving Maria and I sitting two seats apart. Bare, the horses are quite a sight to be seen. They exuded the same sort of drive as George when he wanted his way, and seeing it in them made him feel normal. The first dozen times I went to the races with George, we would run over together. George never stated it explicitly, but he thought horses could defy the laws of gravity, a thing that we all were slaves to, and that this fact somehow made other things possible that would otherwise be considered impossible. But the enchantment eventually wore off on me and I learned to be weary of such trickery, because no one could possibly be that free. I preferred to spend my time before the race with the track. When the mud was still raked, untouched before being trampled on.

Maria had little interest in horses or tracks it seemed. She didn't dare interrupt my silence, but I felt her move in anxious micro-movements, and knew that she was searching for someone to exchange her gaze with. She titled her head like an Arabian mare. Like a taught string was attached to the back of her skull and it held her whole body upright in her seat. Her chin tucked gently downwards. She put her fine nails on plain view, and grasped her gloves gently. She was of good breeding, that's for certain.

A horse is quite a stupid animal in all actuality. All of its natural instincts are wiped clean and replaced by man's desires. Each muscle in its body has been carefully engineered through centuries of selection. Its jawline and the contour of its ears are medals of its intelligence. But it's only the illusion of intelligence, because it has none. It also has no heart, legs or tail either. Nothing of the horse, is its own. Everything is for the man who pays for it, rides it, or bets on it.

George returned. His mood that had started to improve in the car, was in full swing. With five tickets in his hand, he sat down gently next to me and away from Maria. I remembered that I loved him. He began to chatter to no one in particular, *It will be a close one. There are some fine horses here today. A young mare I've never seen before, but she is barely nothing than a foal still. Her lack of experience will sour her race. Another day we'll take the chance. I've chosen another, a seasoned one, her name is "Glory of the Battle." It's her time, I have a good feeling about this.* He rubbed his hands together before taking out his cigarettes and offered them first to me, then to Maria. We shook our heads. His knee was bouncing. The horses were dressed, mounted and led towards the starting gate.

A race horse is an unnatural creature. Trained to be ruthlessly competitive, unlike the wild Zebra or Mongolian Wild breeds that tend to huddle in the protection of the herd and make sure to never to lag behind, or to push too far ahead. Any racehorse that might show this native inclination to its breeder is in danger of being sold directly to the Boucherie Chevaline. But an equestrian trainer will not give up so easily and an owner will not readily except such a significant loss in profit. They will saddle that timid foal with a rider who will literally beat it first into submission then into ambition. And if successful, the horse's will is replaced by a little man one one-hundredth its power and weight dressed flamboyantly in stripes of pink and green, yellow and white. A transformed

346   LTTE no. 30 — *Moments of Solidarity*

horse won't search for the company of its own blood, but the sanctuary and isolation of the starting gate.

The bells rang, the gates slammed open and the sound of pounding hooves filled the stadium. Georges legs tapped, his hands clenched his tickets. Maria yelped in excitement. The row of thoroughbreds held the line, not a leg was placed falsely, gradually eating away at my evenly raked mud. As they wrapped around the bend a few beasts pulled ahead, others began to stagger behind. George's pick and the young mare were in the lead. George dropped his cigarette. Maria grabbed my arm. *Oh!!* My little sister held me tightly and pulled me to my feet. The heads of the mares stretched forward, their strides lengthened. Did they even see each other with those blinders on their eyes? Did they know that they were so close to each other? The riders whipped and hollered at them, but shrunk into silly flies on the backs of titans who drove down the last stretch together like a wild herd chasing the fading light of day. Maria held me close and it didn't matter who was winning anymore. Bad things would happen and I would forgive her.

It was the young mare's nose not the veteran who was a hair in front of the others as they crossed the finish line. George tore his tickets and tossed them to the ground. Disgruntled, he stormed off to place more bets. Maria let go of my arm. I picked at my finger nails.

We pay for our food,
we don't pay for our food.

Sindicato Internacional
de Asistentes de Artistas en Berlín

We pay for our food, we don't pay for our food.

We do our own stuff on the side.
We are as flexible as you need us to be.
We travel with you and for you, appreciate your frustration,
appreciate the accommodation provided.
We can pick something up for you on the way, no problem.
We picked you, after all.
We admire you and what you have achieved.

We carry oversized hand-baggage through customs.
We arrive before you and pick up keys.
We mention something about bees and if it makes it's way
into a work we're pleased, (as well as worried). We claim
silent ownership, although we didn't own it in the first place
(you might argue).
This is a collaboration as old as time.
We skype you when you're away with the camera turned on.

We are your friends, we are not your friends.

There is no doubt that you need us.
Good luck installing that at 6 meters

348   LTTE no. 30 — *Moments of Solidarity*

without someone to hold the ladder.
Your ideas are ambitious, and we respect that,
 and we take cigarette breaks, and you join us,
and we share private jokes, and you sometimes laugh,
and we invoice.

We'll meet your wine with a beer. You are generous.
We stay with you beyond the hours of a normal day, and
we masticate through your ideas with you. We lose ourselves
in the tumult of your dramas. We are devoted to you
and your world as far as we understand it, or want to.
We lose what we have on the side every time we forget to
think on the side, and we forget.
And we get good. And good at forgetting.

Sure we can hold that for you. No problem.

You have to go to a dinner tonight.
We have our own stuff to deal with.
We cook at home.
We're applying for some stuff at the moment. Actually we had
a great night out, we met the people installing for the other
space. Super nice people. The other space is much bigger and
they've been here for two weeks already. No, just saying.
We are not on contract. We are flexible. We are on the KSK.
We use your internet.
We do our own stuff on the side.
We use your phone, your internet, your contacts, your ideas,
your cigarettes.

When we worked for Blah Blah it was shit. Blah Blah made us
organise their shelves.

S.I.A.A.B. 349

We're happy-ish to be here
as long as we still get to do our stuff on the side.
Actually, we're showing something at a space tomorrow night.
It's a group space called 'Whack', opening from 7 'till late,
maybe you can make it?

We take a week off.
You understand, though you do wonder.
You never considered yourself a 'studio artist'
and when you're paying we order dessert.

We are the Artist Assistants.
We pay for our food, we don't pay for our food.

S I A A B

Sindicato Internacional
de Asistentes de Artistas
en Berlin

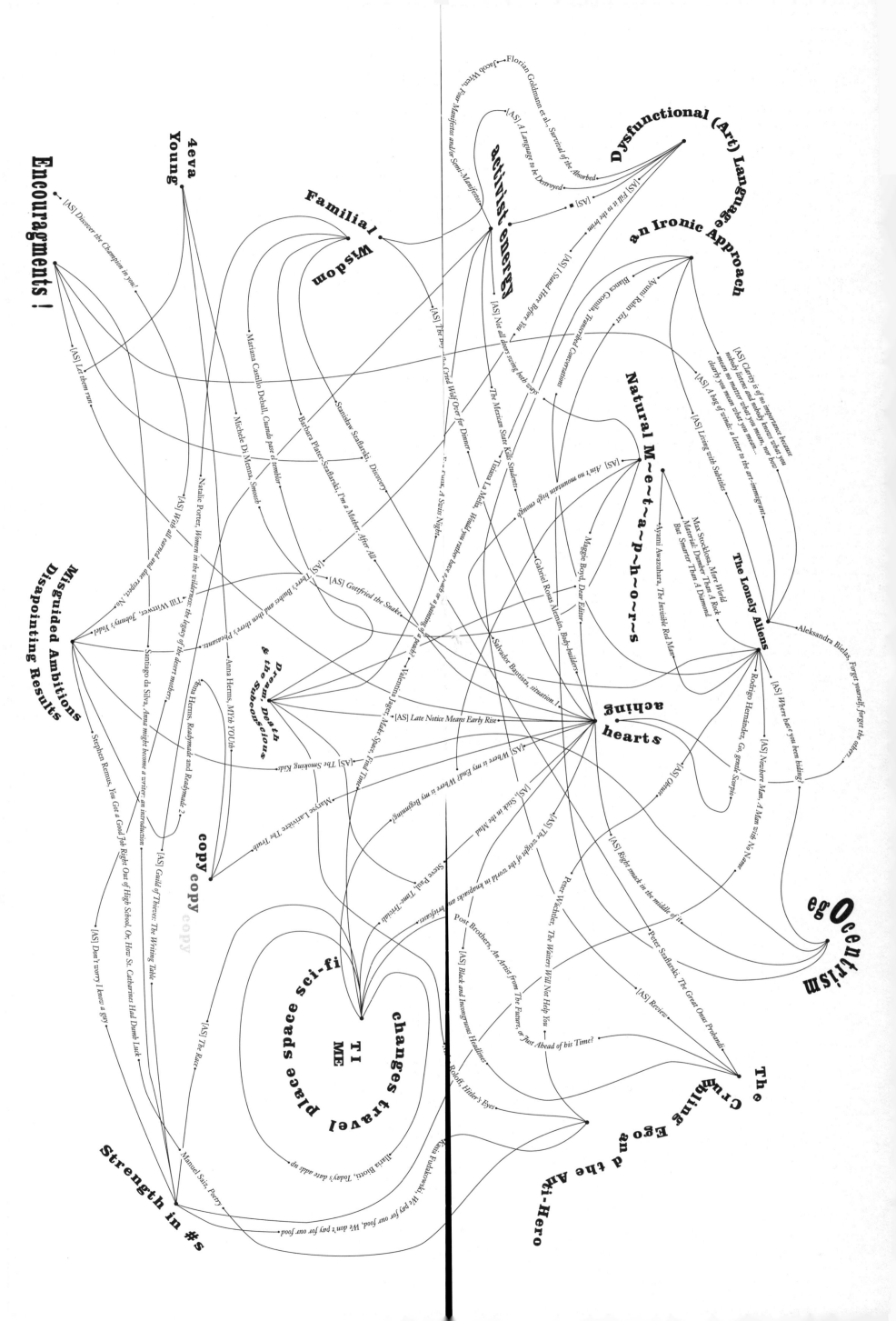

Epilogue:
Emergent Property Game II

Letters to the Editors

Letters to the Editors
A Journal by Anna M. Szaflarski

With contributions by
Ayami Awazuhara, Salvador Bautista, Aleksandra Bielas, Ilaria Biotti, Maggie Boyd, Mariana Castillo Deball, Santiago da Silva, Michele Di Menna, Kasia Fudakowski, Eva Funk, Florian Goldmann et al., Blanca Gomila, Anna Herms, Rodrigo Hernández, Valentina Jager, Tiziana La Melia, Maryse Larivière, Steve Paul, Barbara Plater-Szaflarski, Natalie Porter, Post Brothers, Ayumi Rahn, Stephen Remus, Malte Roloff, Gabriel Rosas Alemán, Manuel Saiz, Max Stocklosa, Peter Szaflarski, Stanisław Szaflarski, Peter Wächtler, Till Witwer, and Jacob Wren.

Edited by Anna M. Szaflarski
Designed by Santiago da Silva
Printed by Moś & Łuczak,
Poznań, PL

First edition of 600 copies

Image on p. 300: *"AHA"* or *"ACHSO!"*, Anna M. Szaflarski, 2014; Courtesy of Esther and Sebastian von Peter.

Special thanks noted in the foreword.

A co-publishing effort by

AKV
AKV Berlin
www.akvberlin.com

&

BOM
DIA
BOA
TARDE
BOA
NOITE

Rosa-Luxemburg-Strasse 17
10178 Berlin
Germany
www.bomdiabooks.de

ISBN: 978-3-945514-62-9

The Deutsche Nationalbibliothek lists this publication in the Deutsche Nationalbibliografie; detailed bibliographic data are available on the Internet at http://dnb.d-nb.de.

© 2016, BOM DIA BOA TARDE BOA NOITE, AKV, Anna M. Szaflarski and the contributing authors. All rights reserved. No part of this publication may be reproduced in any manner without permission from the authors.

Printed in the EU

Letters to the Editors
A Journal by Anna M. Szaflarski

With contributions by
Ayami Awazuhara, Salvador Bautista, Aleksandra Bielas, Ilaria Biotti, Maggie Boyd, Mariana Castillo Deball, Santiago da Silva, Michele Di Menna, Kasia Fudakowski, Eva Funk, Florian Goldmann et al., Blanca Gomila, Anna Herms, Rodrigo Hernández, Valentina Jager, Tiziana La Melia, Maryse Larivière, Steve Paul, Barbara Plater-Szaflarski, Natalie Porter, Post Brothers, Ayumi Rahn, Stephen Remus, Malte Roloff, Gabriel Rosas Alemán, Manuel Saiz, Max Stocklosa, Peter Szaflarski, Stanisław Szaflarski, Peter Wächtler, Till Wittwer, and Jacob Wren.

Edited by Anna M. Szaflarski
Designed by Santiago da Silva
Printed by Moś & Łuczak, Poznań, PL

First edition of 600 copies

Image on p. 300: *"AHA"* or *"ACHSO!"*, Anna M. Szaflarski, 2014; Courtesy of Esther and Sebastian von Peter.

Special thanks
noted in the foreword.

A co-publishing effort by

AKV Berlin
www.akvberlin.com

&

BOM
DIA
BOA
TARDE
BOA
NOITE

Rosa-Luxemburg-Strasse 17
10178 Berlin
Germany
www.bomdiabooks.de

ISBN: 978-3-943514-62-9

The Deutsche Nationalbibliothek lists this publication in the Deutsche Nationalbibliografie; detailed bibliographic data are available on the Internet at http://dnb.d-nb.de.

© 2016, BOM DIA BOA TARDE BOA NOITE, AKV, Anna M. Szaflarski and the contributing authors. All rights reserved.
No part of this publication may be reproduced in any manner without permission from the authors.

Printed in the EU